Illustrated **BUYER'S ★ GUI**

MERCEDES-BENZ

Frank Barrett

MBI Publishing Company

Dedication

This book is dedicated to the 30,000 members of the Mercedes-Benz Club of America, who are involved enough with their cars to understand why it needed to be written.

First published in 1998 by MBI Publishing Company, 729 Prospect Avenue, PO Box 1, Osceola, WI 54020-0001 USA

MBI Publishing Company books are also available at discounts in bulk quantity for industrial or sales-promotional use. For details write to Special Sales Manager at Motorbooks International Wholesalers & Distributors, 729 Prospect Avenue, Osceola, WI 54020-0001 USA.

Library of Congress Cataloging-in-Publication Data
Barrett, Frank.
  Illustrated buyer's guide. Mercedes Benz/Frank Barrett.—2nd ed.
      p. cm.—illustrated buyer's guide series)
  New ed. of: Illustrated Mercedes-Benz buyer's guide. 1994.
  Includes index.
  ISBN 0-7603-0451-3 (pbk.: alk. paper)
  1. Mercedes automobile—Purchasing. 2. Mercedes automobile—History. 3. Mercedes automobile—Collectors and collecting. I. Barrett, Frank. Illustrated Mercedes-Benz buyer's guide. II. Title. III. Series.
TL215.M4B37   1998
629.222'2—dc21   98-14353

On the front cover: The SLK is the first real Mercedes-Benz sports car since the demise of the 300SL. This beautiful 1997 SLK230 is owned by Mercedes-Benz AG. *Dennis Adler*

On the back cover: (Top) The 300SL is the most recognizable Mercedes-Benz collector car, whether in its Roadster form, as here, or as the famous Gullwing. *DBAG* (Bottom) In 1968, this four-cylinder 220D was the most popular diesel model. *MBNA*

Printed in the United States of America

Contents

Acknowledgments

Without the help of dozens of experts, this book would not exist. Alex Dearborn contributed mightily on the postwar 170 and 220 models and wrote most of the material on the 1950s 300s and the 200SL. Henry Magno wrote on prewar cars plus the 170 and the 200, while hearse-owner Bob Gunthorp and SL expert Will Samples sent useful information. Through previous contributions to *The Star*, the magazine of the Mercedes-Benz Club of America, others who contributed include Dennis Adler, Scott Grundfor, Frank King, Peter Lesler, Frank Mallory, George Murphy, Robert Nitske, Bob Platz, and the many readers who wrote in with questions and comments.

Many thanks to Tim Parker, Zack Miller, and everyone else at MBI Publishing Company for offering the opportunity to write two editions of this book and for their commitment to the project. Thanks to the members of the Mercedes-Benz Club of America, especially Technical Director Frank King, for offering the opportunity to assemble much of this experience and knowledge. Technicians (what we used to call mechanics) Stu Ritter and Mark Yoakum gave great advice, too. Not least, thanks to Daimler-Benz AG and Mercedes-Benz of North America—especially Max von Pein, Dieter Ritter, A. B. Shuman, Fred Heiler, Steve Rossi, and Maryalice Ritzmann—for photographs, information, and other valuable assistance.

Preface

Whether you're looking for a Mercedes-Benz to show or to drive to work, this book can help you to find one that will fit your needs, give you excellent value for your money, and be a joy to drive and own. This is a buyer's guide, not just a collector's guide.

Almost any Mercedes-Benz can be reliably enjoyed for both utilitarian and enthusiast pursuits. You can drive a postwar production Mercedes-Benz to work or on trips, then clean it up for a car show. The older the car, the less practical it is to drive daily, but every morning thousands of people climb into 25-year-old Mercedes-Benz cars and head for the office or the store. For that, you can thank the engineers and builders who endowed these cars with durability and reliability.

You can also thank Mercedes-Benz for keeping a strong parts inventory for older models. No other foreign maker remanufactures and stocks more mechanical parts for older cars than does Daimler-Benz. The firm keeps technical literature available longer, too. You can still buy owners manuals, parts books, and workshop manuals for most postwar models from any Mercedes-Benz dealer.

How you'll use the car affects your choice of models. A diesel sedan and a 280SL are both reliable and practical, but most people find the sedan more suitable as a daily driver, the convertible more enjoyable as a Sunday afternoon automobile. Surprisingly, both can make good show cars. Speaking of shows, don't let nit-pickers keep you away from them; most people appreciate an old Mercedes-Benz, whether or not it has the "correct" taillight lens gaskets.

Is a Mercedes-Benz a good investment? See your accountant. This is an automotive guide, not an investment guide. Price guides are often out of

touch with reality even before they're printed. Worse, they do not just report the market, they influence it. This book is written for enthusiasts, not investors. It will help you find a car that you'll enjoy, which is the whole point, isn't it? Rather than recite history best covered elsewhere, this book is designed to help you find the best car. For similar reasons, detailed technical specifications are not listed, and rather than splitting hairs, only the most significant options and production changes are mentioned. Because this book is intended as a general buyer's guide rather than a detailed list of technical specifications (enough to fill a book in themselves), the simplified figures in the tables are mainly for comparison purposes. More detailed numbers can be found elsewhere, as in the book *Mercedes-Benz Production Models, 1946–1995* by W. Robert Nitske. Although we concentrate on U.S. models, significant non-U.S. versions are mentioned where necessary.

We've concentrated on the most attainable cars, mainly postwar models of both the collectible and daily driver persuasions. In many cases, these are one and the same, as today's Mercedes-Benz is often tomorrow's collector car.

Unless noted otherwise, years listed are model years, not calendar years. Production for the next model year typically began in September and ran through the following August. Thus, a car built in September 1965 could be considered a 1966 model. Then, because of varying laws, the year on a title may differ from the model year indicated by a chassis number. In the question of model year, the chassis number governs.

We can't turn you loose in the used Mercedes-Benz market without a few words about safety, a subtle yet significant reason to invest in these fine but not inexpensive cars. Mercedes-Benz has led the world in automotive safety. That's one reason the cars cost what they do. When choosing a car that you or your family will drive, remember that ABS brakes, air bags, and computer-designed body structures offer tremendous advantages in avoiding and surviving accidents. If you or your family will log a lot of miles in this "new to you" Mercedes-Benz, pick one with the latest safety features.

Mercedes-Benz first installed ABS anti-lock brakes on a production car (the 450SEL 6.9) in 1978. By June 1983, ABS was available on all European models. Beginning with the 1985 model year in the United States, ABS was standard equipment on the 500SEC, 500SEL, 380SL, 380SE, and 300SD, and an option on the 190E 2.3 and 190D 2.2. By the 1989 model year, all Mercedes-Benz cars sold in the United States had ABS.

Other than to cleverly hand you the belt in a coupe, Mercedes-Benz has never used motorized seatbelts, preferring air bags and self-tensioning seat-belts, which appeared in the 1984 model year. By 1985, the Supplemental Restraint System was standard on the 500SEL and 500SEC and optional on the 380SL, 300SD, 380SE, and the 190s. By 1986, a driver's side air bag was standard on all models, and right-side air bags appeared in 1989. By 1990, all U.S. models had dual air bags.

Because so many Mercedes-Benz models have been created since 1886, the space available here to each one is limited, so we've focused on the most popular, most collectible, and most remarkable cars. This book is intended as a guide to purchase, not a complete list of all technical specifications. Other books give you the numbers; our goal is to give you the feel.

Finally, a word to the wise. When shopping for your first Mercedes-Benz, avoid the trap of expecting too much, then being disappointed when reality intrudes. No car, not even a Mercedes-Benz, is perfect. Gottlieb Daimler was wise enough to say, "The best or nothing," not "Perfection or nothing." If he'd held out for the latter, not a single car would have ever emerged from his factory.

Investment Ratings

While all Mercedes-Benz cars are good, various models have been designed and built to best satisfy different needs. Some models are faster or more economical or more sporting than others. Some are appreciating in value; others are depreciating. Some are more desirable or collectible than others.

Like other titles in this series, this buyer's guide uses a five-star rating system to help the newcomer to Mercedes-Benz to judge various models in general comparison with others:

★★★★★   High performance, elegant styling, museum-grade collector value, and/or very rare.

★★★★   Excellent performance, elegant styling, high collector interest, and/or low production.

★★★   Moderate performance and good styling, moderate collector interest, modest desirability, and/or not uncommon.

★★   Moderate performance, modest styling, depreciating, little collector interest, and/or readily found.

★   Modest performance, utilitarian styling, depressed value, almost no collector interest, and/or supply exceeds demand.

Like any other, this rating system is unable to represent the priorities of every buyer, but it will help you to spot those models generally thought to be most desirable. Of course, feel free to establish your own ratings; ultimately your individual judgment will guide you to the car that best suits your needs.

Mercedes-Benz cars are generally good investments. New models have low depreciation, and older models appreciate or at least hold their value. The biggest risk comes in buying a car that needs more work than the car is worth; not only do you lose money, you also lose the time and enjoyment of use and experience the frustrations of properly curing the car's problems. When looking for an easily found model, it usually pays to ignore cars needing serious work in favor of finding a better example, even if you must spend a bit more.

Chapter 1

Choosing and Finding the Right Mercedes-Benz

Why Mercedes-Benz?

The best of anything—art, clothing, food, wine, even company—rewards you beyond the ability of its ordinary equivalent. Daimler-Benz is the world's oldest and most experienced automobile company, and its Mercedes-Benz cars enjoy similar longevity. As other car builders drifted away, Daimler-Benz not only survived but led the world in engineering and often on the racetrack. Old or new, these cars project a distinct character, a unique feel that defies imitators and thrills you every time you drive them.

Which Mercedes-Benz?

Which of the hundreds of models do you want? Are you interested in style, economy, performance, safety, comfort, rarity, or practicality? Will your car be old or new? Who will maintain or restore it? Which can you afford?

Start by considering how you will use your Mercedes-Benz. Will it be a show car or your everyday driver? A sedan or a sports car? Will family members drive it, too? Can you afford to maintain a complex model, or should you shop for something more basic?

Can you afford to insure, and garage the car properly? Do you prefer a collector car appreciating in value, or can you forgo that for the practicality of a daily driver? If you plan to keep the car only a few years, how easy will it be to sell?

Antiques

Pre-World War II cars demand special financial commitments to buy and to maintain. Their usefulness is limited, and you'll need a tow vehicle

For some, a factory-built Mercedes-Benz is just a place to start. This is a Koenig-modified special.

and a trailer to move them. Your thrill from these cars will come in preserving and demonstrating automotive history to others.

Postwar Coupes, Convertibles, and Sedans

Postwar cars can be enjoyed more, and prices are generally lower. Your choice is between sedans, convertibles (and coupes), and sports cars. Invariably, the price rises when the top drops. For a bargain, buy the similar sedan version of a convertible. If you want a rare convertible with plenty of available spare parts, choose one with a sedan equivalent.

SLs

The 1950s and 1960s SL models will always be collectors' favorites. They are among the easiest to buy, restore, and sell. And nothing compares with a top-down cruise on a warm summer afternoon. Avoid paying too much for a recent SL or buying one too soon. After initial depreciation, they begin appreciating. The trick is to buy just before the value rises.

Daily Drivers

For a daily driver, you'll have plenty of choices, but your big decision will be gasoline or diesel power. A Mercedes-Benz "driver" is not only safe, reliable, and comfortable, it can be a great long-term buy. Because recent models are so durable, you can keep them longer, use them more, and enjoy lower depreciation. You're better off buying a used Mercedes-Benz than a new Anything Else.

Find a good example of the model that you're considering, and drive it to see if it fits your needs and lives up to your expectations. Using it as you intend to use the car you'll buy provides a benchmark for judging similar cars later.

Sources and Signs

Finding a good Mercedes-Benz is no different from finding a good Ford. Actually, it's easier. Because Mercedes-Benz cars are higher quality and generally better cared for, many good cars await you. Most models are numerous enough so that you can find what you want nearby.

Private Parties

Private owners are a knowledgeable buyer's best source for good older cars. One advantage in buying from an owner is that you can get an idea of what kind of use and care it had. If he's a slob, look out. If he's meticulous, so much the better. How long has he owned the car? How did he use it, and where? Does he have service or restoration records? Why is he selling? If he can't or won't answer these questions clearly, beware. The drawback is that you normally get no guarantee.

To find private owners, check newspapers first; they offer the most current lists of cars for sale. A good car can justify an out-of-town trip. Before you travel, hire an appraiser or a good mechanic or persuade a friend nearby to check it out for you.

Dealers

If you're looking for a car less than 10 years old, Mercedes-Benz dealers tend to handle cars in the best condition, albeit at a price. They offer warranties on used cars and are usually convenient to deal with. Some dealers advertise collector models in national magazines such as *Auto Week* and in newspapers in larger cities.

Some independent used car dealers specialize in Mercedes-Benz. Visit those that have been around for a while. They can usually find cars not in stock, even out of town. Beware of ordinary used car lots, whose cars may come from unusual sources, including auctions, and may even be salvaged cars.

Check *Hemmings Motor News, Auto Week*, and club publications for specialist dealer ads. Ask owners and restorers which collector car dealers are best. Brokers can be difficult to deal with, because many take money from both buyer and seller.

This book is a guide to buying used cars, but if you're buying a new Mercedes-Benz, ask your dealer about the factory's excellent European delivery plan, which can save you money on a European vacation. The program applies only to models available in your country, but even Europeans like to pick up their new cars at the excellent Visitors Center at the Sindelfingen plant near Stuttgart.

Welcome to the Club

Joining a club gives you an edge. The Mercedes-Benz Club of America is the largest such club in the world. Its more than 30,000 members have owned examples of practically every model built. MBCA has 85 local sections, each publishing a newsletter (listing cars for sale). Its national magazine, *The Star*, carries ads for hundreds of cars in every issue. Smaller clubs exist for the 190SL and 300SL, but many of their members belong to MBCA, too, so it's the place to start.

A club's national experts can answer technical and restoration questions. Local members can point you to good cars before they even enter the market. You can examine good examples at car shows and chat with owners about what to look for when buying, what the cars are like to live with, and so on.

Auctions

The worst place to buy a Mercedes-Benz is at a typical collector car auction. The fast-paced, circus-like atmosphere may be exciting, and the cars may shine, but it's all show biz designed to exchange cars for money, strictly one way.

Auction scams are legendary, too many to repeat here. There's never enough time to check a car thoroughly. Can you drive the car before buying it? Do you know who actually owns it? Do you know who you're really bidding against? Is there a warranty? Will paperwork be properly processed?

Reported auction prices must be taken with a shovelful of salt. These numbers often bear no relation to a car's value. They may be run up artificially by a pair of wealthy egotists determined to beat the other guy. Cars are "bought-in" by auctioneers, their shills, or an owner who can't stand to sell for a low bid. This circus is no place for the novice.

Computerized Sales

Various computerized collector car sales services have appeared. Most have short lives, and some seem more interested in charging the owner for listing his or her car than in finding buyers. The most avid users of these services are likely to be computer hobbyists, not car hobbyists. Proceed with caution.

Buying by Remote Control

Some say you should never buy a car without seeing it, but with care you can do so successfully. But the opportunity to get nailed rises significantly when dealing by remote control.

Buying a car based on photos is a huge gamble. The owner isn't going to photograph the bad side, and he wiped off all the leaking coolant before he photographed the engine. Did he send photos of the entire interior? And the trunk? Did he shoot the car on a lift from underneath? You can't hear, feel, or drive the car in a photo. Cars always look better to a camera than they look through human eyes.

If you can't go to see, feel, listen to, and drive the car yourself, find someone knowledgeable to do it for you. The best at this are professional (*not* amateur) automotive appraisers. The next best are experienced mechanics or restorers, especially if they work on similar cars. For pay, they may be able to take the car to their shop and run a leakdown test. Brokers can also help, as long as they are working only for you, not the seller. If you belong to a nationwide car club, ask a nearby fellow member to look at the car or recommend someone who can do so.

The best course is to go and see for yourself. Even several expensive trips can be justified by finding the right car.

Gray Market Cars

Mercedes-Benz builds cars for many different markets. Until the 1970s, it didn't matter much whether a car was a U.S. version or a European model, but as emission and safety laws grew tougher, that became more important. U.S.-legal cars were equipped to meet these laws, and the government made it difficult to import nonconforming cars. An industry grew, converting European models to meet Environmental Protection Agency (EPA) and Department of Transportation (DOT) requirements. In the early 1980s the so-called gray market brought thousands of European Mercedes-Benz cars to the United States. Supposedly, all were made U.S.-legal. In fact, many were not, and many more were doctored in ways that make them poor risks.

The gray market offered some models before they became U.S. models. Others never came over otherwise. The 500SL, with more performance and more options than the contemporary U.S. 380SL, for less money, was probably the most popular gray market car.

Still, gray market cars invariably are worth far less than the equivalent U.S. models. They were often incorrectly converted or not converted at all. Many conversion companies were fly-by-night; few survive. Uncle Sam can still seize cars not meeting the law. Gray market cars are cheaper to buy, but when you sell one, it will not be worth as much as a U.S. model. Most dealers don't want them as trade-ins.

Some insurance companies will not insure a gray market car. Mechanics may refuse to work on them, and some parts are difficult to get. Owners manuals for European models can be difficult to find, but aftermarket literature suppliers may have them. European workshop manuals are generally unavailable. Owners and workshop manuals for U.S. models are available from Mercedes-Benz of North America and cover most but not all features and technical specifications of European models.

An improper conversion may leave you with a car that at best has some quirks and at worst is useless. If an equivalent U.S. model exists, a gray market car isn't worth the risk.

Converting a European model to U.S. specs varies in difficulty. Obvious items such as instruments and lights are easily changed. (Climate controls used Celsius markings even on some U.S. cars. European cars of the 1970s and 1980s were more likely to have velour interiors than leather or MB-tex.) Not so easy are substitutions of proper safety-related equipment. The smaller European bumpers on W116 sedans and SLs (the same as pre-1974 U.S. models) were often left in place, and side door beams were often a joke. Ignition and mechanical systems are even more difficult to convert. Some states now require all original emissions equipment to be present (whether the car passes their smog tests or not).

By 1986, Uncle Sam had cracked down on conversion shops, and European models had begun using catalytic converters. When European and U.S. versions began using the same engines, there was no power incentive to import German versions.

U.S. cars have a perforated sticker on the doorpost and the vehicle identification number (VIN) tag on the left windshield post. Gray market cars should have EPA and DOT papers documenting conversion, but don't assume that they will pass current emission tests. Velour upholstery, metric instruments, and European bumpers often betray partially converted gray market cars. Mercedes-Benz of North America's (MBNA) region offices have been known to check the VIN of a car and determine its origin.

Modified Cars

Mercedes-Benz owners tend to keep their cars in original configuration. Many frown on modified cars, perhaps because performance and appearance modifications are often done poorly. Appearance updates are a matter of taste. About the only tuner consistently able to provide well-integrated modifications was the German firm AMG, now closely affiliated with Daimler-Benz. Its power, handling, and aerodynamic modifications are widely seen in Europe, where cosmetic "improvements" are more common. In 1993, Mercedes-Benz dealers began selling AMG wheels and spoilers for current models.

Beauty is in the eye of the beholder, so if you want spoilers and air dams, that's your business. Be aware that most Americans think them silly on a dignified sedan, so the market value of such a car may be lowered. It's fun to customize your car to suit your own tastes, but it's a lousy investment. Wheels, body parts, and mechanical pieces cost more than for other makes, yet at sale time they subtract more from the price.

Avoid irreversible modifications. When looking at a modified car as a potential buyer, consider which changes you'll reverse to original and how you'll do so. The tougher that process will be, the more useful it is as a bargaining point.

Recent Mercedes-Benz models can often be updated with factory or aftermarket accessories. Owners find it easiest to replace sound systems and wheels. Aftermarket alloy wheels are not uncommon on 1970s and later models. Genuine factory alloy wheels—which have passed the tough German TUV tests—have the three-pointed star cast into them on the inside with a date of manufacture that should approximately match that of the car.

Suspension modifications generally come from German tuners. Typical kits include shorter and stiffer coil springs, stiffer shock absorbers, larger sway bars, and new bushings. Recent models with the excellent five-link rear suspension can shift from luxury toward performance. The factory's Sportline performance option, first appearing on 1992 models, is highly recommended for the enthusiast.

For ride comfort and less aquaplaning, original wheels tend to be narrower on U.S. models. Tires are relatively high-profile and slender. Since they are easy to switch, wider and larger-diameter wheels are common. Modestly broader wheels and tires capitalize on the potential of the excellent suspensions of recent models.

When considering a car with wider wheels and low-profile tires, check for unusual tire wear, vibration, harsh ride, and increased steering effort. Wheels differing much from stock offset cause wheel bearing wear or front-end misalignment. If tire diameter has been altered without recalibrating the speedometer, it will read incorrectly. Fuel mileage may suffer. Does the car have a suitable spare wheel and tire? Wide, low-profile tires grip better on dry pavement but ride more harshly and aquaplane more easily. Still, it's usually simple to return to stock configuration.

Mechanical modifications are more difficult and expensive to reverse. AMG and a few other tuners have done excellent engine work on 1980s and 1990s models, but there's real schlock out there, too. Avoid add-on turbochargers. Factory turbocharged models are designed to withstand the additional loads on engine, drivetrain, and cooling systems. Performance cams and exhaust headers are more durable. Count on zero warranty on any engine modification. With this stuff, it's once around the block or midnight, whichever comes first.

Even the best tuners have difficulties with drivability, reliability, and safety. Do the wheels, tires, brakes, and suspension of the modified car match its horsepower? Since DBAG now builds factory hot rods, you're better off with a 190E 2.3-16 or a 500E than with a locally modified car.

Be sure that the modified car is legal in your state, even in your own community. Many states now require that all original emission equipment be in place. Original smog gear is hard to find, and catalytic converters are expensive. If you're hoping to register an out-of-state car in California or another state with strict laws, be cautious. You can have a car tested elsewhere, but it still may not pass your local tests.

Agreeing on a Price

Although this book is not intended to be a price guide (real-world numbers change far too quickly for that), we can offer you some suggestions on negotiation.

Be prepared. Know how much you can spend, including possible restoration costs. Arrange a loan in advance. Some banks specialize in loans for collector cars.

Do your homework on typical prices. Price guides may reflect differences in condition, accessories, and other factors, but they usually don't cover geographic price differences. For example, convertibles are worth more in warmer climates; likewise, where the local economy is poor, Mercedes-Benz prices are likely to be low.

Refuse to be rushed. Don't be pressured by an owner telling you that another potential buyer is in the wings. If you lose the deal, you're no worse off than before you started, but if you let yourself be rushed, you may get a bad deal or a bad car.

Is the car's value rising or falling? The best time to buy a car is just as its depreciation stops

and appreciation begins. If you'll keep it, it's all right to pay a little too much for a car that will eventually be worth much more. Why lose a good car for $500 if you know that it's appreciating and that you'll keep it for 10 years?

Any car is worth what seller and buyer agree upon. Make an offer lower than what you would actually pay, then negotiate upward, but only up to your limit. If this doesn't work, walk away and tell the seller to call you if he changes his mind.

All of that said, it must be admitted that many lucky folks have successfully violated every rule. Sometimes the car speaks to you, sometimes there's no time for even a compression test, and sometimes the price is too low to wait when you know another serious buyer is half an hour behind you and approaching at flank speed.

For novices, though, caution is best. If you're reading this in a lather, dreaming about that gorgeous red 280SL that you're rushing off to look at, slow down. Enthusiasm is no substitute for experience and knowledge, and too much desire can get you into a bind. Don't plunge into anything until you know enough to judge a car properly. Buy what you can comfortably live with for years. You may have to do just that.

Practice by looking at as many cars as possible. Each one that you examine will teach you restraint and some useful facts which will prove valuable later on, when you find and check out a car that you *really* want.

Chapter 2

Checking the Car

Having found a candidate car, you're vulnerable. Desire can overcome reason. Be careful. Some of my most enjoyable days have been spent rushing off with trailer in tow, certified check in pocket, and hopes high. Some of the most tragic hours have been spent on arrival, when the object of lust finally appears in the flesh, a rust-holed shadow of its owner's glowing description.

This explanation of checking a car applies to most models; specific tips can be found in the appropriate chapters.

First, decide how particular you're going to be. If you're looking at a rare antique to restore completely, you'll be less critical about condition than if you're looking for a daily driver, you'll be less critical in some areas than you would be with a show car (and maybe more critical in other areas).

Line up the references you'll need to check chassis numbers, production numbers, current values, options, etc. Make sure the person you're dealing with has the right to sell the car. If a private party, does he or she actually own the car? It could be leased, or it could have an existing loan against it for more than the price. It could even be stolen. Look at the title, and check with anyone else listed as the owner. Make sure that the chassis number or VIN matches the title and registration documents.

Prewar cars usually have a stamped identification plate on the firewall. On post-1970 cars, the VIN is on the windshield post and elsewhere. A chassis identification plate is on the cross-member above the radiator of most recent models. Obviously, if the plate is missing or the numbers don't match the papers, steer clear. Plates have been known to be

Model identification plates fitted to the radiator top cross-member carry data regarding the individual car and its accessories. *DBAG*

switched or inexplicably "lost," and replacement plates have been available.

Check the service records. Mileage on recent invoices should conform to the odometer mileage. Don't rely totally on service records, though. An owner can conveniently misplace certain disastrous invoices. Look for mechanics' comments, particularly such telling phrases as "Customer declines."

Too often, potential Mercedes-Benz buyers are put off by high mileage. Some even make a fetish out of finding and preserving extremely low mileage cars at crazy prices. That's dumb. Lack of use kills a car; regular use and maintenance will best preserve one. Use this mileage phobia to your advantage. If the basic car is sound, almost any fault can be repaired to new or better condition.

Bodywork, Paint, and Trim

Daylight, preferably bright sunlight, best reveals bodywork and paint flaws. Look at the car (doors and lids closed) from the front, rear, and sides. Look at the tops of the fenders for dents caused by mechanics leaning on them. A dent in the hood will drive you crazy if you keep seeing it from behind the wheel. Dark-colored cars show body irregularities easily, but be careful when looking at light-colored cars, which can hide uneven bodywork.

Condition of trim is important because of the expense of replacing or repairing it properly. *FDB*

Does the car stand level? Do its panels line up? Are door, hood, and trunk gaps even? Is any trim missing? Do both bumpers fit properly? Is the paint consistent in color and gloss? Sight down the body sides, using reflections to show ripples, unnatural breaks in contour, and dull paint. In the paint, look for orange peel, grinder marks, overspray, shrinkage cracks, scratches, pinholes, chips, and rust spots. A good repaint is almost undetectable. New paint should be the same color throughout, including the underside of the engine and trunk lids, inside the engine compartment, the doorjambs, and other tough-to-paint areas.

Open the doors, hood, and trunk lid. How is the plating on the handles? Do the locks, latches, and hinges operate smoothly and quietly? Do the doors close smoothly with a proper thunk? Postwar engine hoods should close properly if simply dropped from a couple of feet. Are panel edges around doors and lids properly painted? How are the seals? Are the undersides of the lids properly finished, and are the door drain holes open? Nooks and crannies in the doorjambs tell you a lot. Tough to reach, they're the last area of a car to be cleaned well. If they are clean, that's a good sign.

Look at the inner and outer glass surfaces. Most postwar models have the trademark Sigla (or other German brand) etched into the glass. Is the windshield chipped, or has it been scratched by the wipers? Is the glass fogged at the edges? Is there overspray on the glass?

Exterior trim may be bent, scratched, loose, or even rusty. Replacement trim may not fit as well as the original or may show grinder marks or uneven plating. Thin, fragile trim is often bent or dented. Bumpers are expensive to straighten and replate. If rust has eaten into trim, replating may be infeasible, so it must be replaced.

Put the car on a lift—or at least a floor jack (with jackstands). Get underneath with a cloth, a screwdriver, and a flashlight. Check for rust in the panels behind each wheel where water, gravel, and rocks are thrown upward. Is the rocker panel paint the right pebbled texture? Are the floor panels dented? Do they have the factory-made indentations, or are they dead flat, indicating replacement? Check the footwells for rust. If new panels have been welded in, they should be butt-welded—joined edge to edge, not overlapped. Fresh paint or undercoating often hides rust or badly repaired sheet metal. As old factory undercoating lifts off the metal, rust forms beneath it.

Accident damage is usually easy to spot. At each corner of the underside, look for sheet metal that isn't shaped right (compare the shapes from side to side). If one side looks odd, it may have been straightened. Look for overspray and "too new" body parts. Newer cars have original spot-weld shapes that bodyshop welders don't duplicate. Run your hands around the inner lip of each wheel opening to detect rust or body filler.

Some expensive late models have another potential snag. Someone may have made one car out of two. With one car hit in the front, another hit in the back, it doesn't take a genius to figure out that the good ends can be joined, making one "good" car out of two wrecks. This was popular with S-class sedans. Pay attention to the body near the rear doors. If the doors don't fit well, that's a clue. Pull up the carpets. Fresh undercoating (or even a weld—some guys are more brazen than others) is an even bigger clue. Look for unusual wiring connections and paint that doesn't match in color or texture.

Mercedes-Benz exhaust systems are rust-prone, expensive, and hard to replace. Make sure pipes and mufflers are sound, properly shaped, and secured with factory brackets and fasteners. Most postwar systems are welded together, strapped in position by flexible rubber rings unlike U.S. replacement straps and hangers. Exhausts often corrode on rarely used cars from condensation. Aftermarket stainless-steel systems are available for most postwar models, usually at prices similar to those for original equipment exhaust parts. With the engine running, block the exhaust outlet for a few seconds and listen for exhaust leaks.

Look for bent suspension members, loose or leaky shock absorbers, old brake hoses, rusty fuel lines, and worn control cables. Check the insides of bumpers; rust eats them from the inside out. Look for body filler that has oozed through trim mounting holes. Look for rust around the jack points.

Look for fluid leaks from the cooling system, engine, fuel lines, transmission, power steering, and differential. A leak is almost always above and forward of the stain. Coolant is usually blue-green; it's poisonous, so don't taste it. Automatic transmission fluid is reddish, going to brown if it's old. Obviously, motor oil is black and slippery. Brake fluid is less viscous, clear to black, with a pungent smell. Ask a mechanic to demonstrate.

Look for leaks from front and rear oil seals on the engine and from the transmission. Look for brake fluid leaks at the master cylinder, slave cylinders, or calipers. Brake fluid should be clear. Check for fuel leaks around the carburetors or injection pump and the fuel pump, fuel lines, and filters.

All 1950s, 1960s, and 1970s Mercedes-Benz manual transmissions use automatic transmission fluid. Regular gear oil can allow damage to the needle bearings in these transmissions.

Seats, Upholstery, and Interior Trim

Good interior repair is expensive, so look for flaws. Usually the interior will be the best part of a Mercedes-Benz. The materials seem to last forever, and people take better care of what they can easily see and reach.

Look up at the headliner or convertible top. Does it fit, is it clean, will it need replacing? Check the wood, leather, or fabric trim. Is it dirty, scratched, or worn? Any signs of water leaks around the windows? Does the sunroof work?

Look at the panel between the rear seat and rear window. Check the window moldings for dirt and broken glass. Check door panels for dirt and wear, and try every window mechanism and door lock, especially on cars with power windows and locks. Vacuum locking systems are often weak, especially on older cars where the rubber diaphragms and hoses have perished.

Check the seats for wear at the edges and seams. Mercedes-Benz interiors can be cloth (velour), vinyl (called MB-tex), or leather. The MB-tex is the most durable, and 1960s and 1970s models often have almost perfect interiors. Cloth seat material in old models can be hard to match, and leather is expensive to replace, although it can be redyed well. Cloth interiors are common on 1970s and 1980s European models. Is the leather brittle and cracked? Is the seat stitching dry and strong, or is it rotted? If the seats have been reupholstered, was factory material used, or are they done in hide of the nauga? Sunlight and pets can ruin upholstery.

If the wood trim was damaged by sun fading or window leaks, it will be expensive and time consuming to restore correctly. Most Mercedes-Benz wood uses a veneer over a solid core. Any sanding almost immediately ruins the thin veneer, so amateur wood "refinishing" is usually to be avoided.

In recent models, look for holes and wires as evidence of poorly mounted telephones, sound systems, and alarms. Installed incorrectly, these can cause electrical problems as well as appearance flaws.

This 500SEC's clean engine compartment is the sign of a caring owner. *FDB*

If the ashtray's clean, you'll know the driver didn't smoke in the car—or else he replaced the ashtray.

Carpets should be reasonably clean. Diesel models invite tracking fuel inside the car, leaving the tell-tale smell. You'll probably cover the original carpet with floor mats anyway, so don't worry much about worn carpets on a daily driver. If the battery is above the passenger footwell, as on 1950s models, be sure that acid hasn't eaten through the battery box, allowing water (and acid) to drip into the footwell.

Accessories

Is the mirror glass clear? Does the radio antenna work? (Mercedes-Benz power antennae often fail.) Headlight, turn signal, driving/fog light, and tail-light lenses should be clear and uncracked; one inconsistently faded lens indicates a replacement, possibly because of an accident. Do interior, exterior, instrument, courtesy, indicator, and other lights work? This may sound trivial, but a current model may have as many as 100 light bulbs!

Original Mercedes-Benz convertible tops were usually made of tightly knit canvas fabric. If the fabric is stained, it will likely remain so. Does the convertible have a tonneau cover?

Does the car have an owners manual? It can help you to check the function of options, especially on older cars with unlabeled controls. Most models came with a parts picture catalog showing exploded views of all assemblies, including the engine, transmission, brakes, body, and trim.

Does the car have a spare wheel, an original jack, a lug wrench, and a tool kit? If the car has a central lubrication system, does it work? If not, suspension parts may be worn.

Engine

Because it's the most impressive, most expensive, and noisiest part of a car, most buyers spend too much time looking at the engine as if they expect it to say, "Hi, I'm fine." Or, "Damn, I feel like throwing a rod today." With the hood up, they stand there sagely listening to the engine idle, rev up a bit, then idle again. They'd be better off driving the car and listening for strange sounds. Better yet, they should drive it to a mechanic and let him or her do a leakdown test.

Unlike a compression test, a leakdown test determines not just whether the engine is worn, but where. The mechanic hooks up an air line to each spark plug hole, pumps air into the cylinder, and listens for it to exit the crankcase (worn rings), the valve cover (worn valve guides), or the intake and exhaust system (worn valves and valve seats). If you can't do this, pay someone to do it for you. It's worth it.

OK, if you must do a compression test, it's better than nothing. If you're looking at an ancient, frozen engine, don't waste time trying to free it enough to see if it will run. You're going to overhaul it anyway, so be patient, and try to avoid damaging it.

Don't put much stock in clean oil on the dipstick. Dirty oil is easy to change. Check the oil change records. Water droplets on the dipstick indicate coolant in the oil; overhaul time. Some white sludge on an oil filler cap is normal, especially in humid climes.

When the engine is cool, unscrew the radiator cap and look inside. (With a warm engine, the system will be under pressure, so unscrew the cap slowly with a rag on your hand.) Fresh coolant is blue-green; a gray mixture means that exhaust gas is getting into the coolant, possibly through a blown head gasket. An oily film means that oil is leaking into it, even more serious. Look for coolant leaks around the water pump, radiator (get underneath), hose joints, sensors, and heater fittings. On cars with early (1977–81) automatic climate control, check for coolant leaks at the servo, located in the engine compartment.

Electric fans in front of the radiator should come on automatically as the engine idles and warms up; as the engine cools, the fan should stop automatically (exact temperatures vary). The viscous fan drive on the fan behind the radiator should turn with slight resistance with the engine off. As the engine idles, the fan should turn normally; as rpm increase, the viscous clutch releases, and the fan coasts.

Has the engine fan hit the radiator? Is the water pump squealing due to a worn bearing? Are the drive belts cracked or frayed? Most are easy to replace. If you hear a squeal when you punch the throttle, a slipping accessory drive belt needs adjustment.

Does the engine smoke from the exhaust pipe? A little white fog of condensation is normal from a cold engine on a cold day, but persistent white smoke usually means a blown head gasket. If the smoke is blue, the valve guides or piston rings and cylinder walls may be worn. If smoke persists, a leakdown test can determine its cause. Black smoke is caused by a rich mixture on gasoline cars, indicating a need for carburetor or injection system work. Black smoke from a diesel engine is usually caused by a maladjusted or worn injection pump. Only prewar engines, with their looser clearances and more primitive carburetion, should smoke under normal operation.

How does the engine smell? If you smell raw gasoline, it may be running too rich or it may have a fuel leak. If you smell burning oil, an aged valve cover gasket may be allowing oil to leak onto the exhaust manifold; look for blue smoke. If you smell burning plastic, wiring may be overheating.

Engine, transmission, and subframe mounts often need replacement. Older rubber/metal sandwich-style engine mounts and the single rear transmission mount are best checked with the car on a lift. The 124-chassis engine mounts should have at least 10 millimeters (a finger-width) of clearance. If the rear of the car is lower than the front, the rear subframe mounts may be failing.

Electrical

Mainly you must rely on whether a given mechanism works to determine the state of the electrical system. Try out everything electrical: heater blower, radio, wipers and washers (windshield and headlight), power seats, power windows, sunroof, horn, power mirrors, station wagon tailgate closer, and so on. Older cars have fewer lights: headlights, parking lights, brake light(s), instrument lights, maybe turn signals, and interior lights.

Newer cars have dozens of lights. You can find over 100 in a current (pun intended) Mercedes-Benz. Most bulbs and switches are simple to replace, but a circuit that won't deliver power may indicate a major problem, such as improper accident damage repair or rust.

Do all instruments work properly, especially the tachometer? All 1981–1982 U.S. models had 85-mile per hour speedometers. Zero the trip odometer, then check it and the normal odometer after your test drive.

If you don't know how to operate the climate control, read the owners manual. Then try all heating and air conditioning modes and all fan modes. Air conditioning compressor noises indicate problems with belts, bearings, or seals. If it's the compressor, the noise will stop when the compressor stops. A foul smell in the car may be caused by algae in the condenser drain, which can be flushed by spraying disinfectant through the heater blower. Make sure the blower motor works; on some 1960s and 1970s models these are tough to replace.

Check the battery including electrolyte level, cables, connectors, clamps, and tray. The tray area should be clean, with no evidence of acid corrosion. Check the chassis end of the ground wire. Are all fuses intact?

Is all wiring stock and original, or did someone fit an alarm with wires strung across the exhaust manifold? Are the plug wires in good shape (old ones can cause an engine miss). Have wires been burned or patched? Are all original wire clamps in place?

Whines or rattles near the front of the engine can mean a worn timing chain and/or worn chain tensioners or belt tensioners.

Road Test

Road-testing a car reveals its condition and gives you an idea of what that model is like to drive. If the car is a nonrunner, or if you are unfamiliar with the model, try to find a good, running example that you can drive to see if this model is for you.

A car represented to be a runner should start and idle reasonably well, allowing for its age and technology. As a cold Mercedes-Benz engine starts, the oil pressure gauge should peg itself at the high end of the scale. As the oil warms, pressure will fall, but even at idle it shouldn't go below about 15 psi, about one atmosphere of pressure. Low oil pressure indicates worn bearings or a worn oil pump.

While driving, listen for knocks and whines. A knock on acceleration means worn main bearings. A knock on deceleration usually means worn rod bearings. A ping under heavy engine load is detonation, possibly due to poor fuel or incorrect ignition timing. A tapping sound can be due to loose valve lifters. A whine from the rear of the car can indicate worn differential gears, not an uncommon problem. A differential whine varies directly with the speed of the car and is usually most evident under power.

Check the cooling system while driving. Older models may overheat when idling in traffic on a hot day. Let the car idle for five minutes or so, and watch the temperature gauge. It may rise above boiling with no problem, but if it hits the red zone, a cooling problem exists. Overheating can indicate a worn water pump or more serious problems such as a blown head gasket or an engine rebuilt with insufficient clearances. Once overheated, any engine loses part of its useful life. Aluminum heads on Mercedes-Benz engines warp relatively easily.

Checking a manual transmission is mostly a matter of listening closely under acceleration and deceleration. If each gear works without whining, it's fine; noisy bearings need replacement. If shifts can be made without grinding, the synchromesh is in good shape. Bad synchros show up earliest in the lower gears. If the transmission jumps out of gear, usually high gear, either the internal parts or the linkage may need rebuilding.

The clutch should engage and release smoothly. Clutch chatter can be caused by oil leaking onto the clutch, wear, loose engine or transmission mounts, or driveline misalignment. A slipping clutch is easiest to detect in higher gears under heavy throttle. Punch the throttle going uphill in top gear. Some slip may be adjusted away but the clutch is more likely to need replacement, which may even include the flywheel. A dragging clutch grinds as you shift, especially going into reverse or first with the car stationary.

Until the 1980s, Mercedes-Benz automatic transmissions were less smooth than their U.S. counterparts. No matter how healthy any automatic seems, it can fail tomorrow. Likewise, it can feel bad but last a decade. Thoroughly testing a Mercedes-Benz automatic transmission requires connecting a set of special gauges, then driving the car through a prescribed routine. You're probably unable to do that, but you can make sure that the transmission functions reasonably well and doesn't leak. Open the hood, pull the automatic transmission dipstick, and smell the fluid. If it smells burned, you have a problem.

Drive off in each gear of an automatic. Slip or a significant delay in engagement means problems. Shift up and down manually; each gear should engage quickly, smoothly. Automatic shifts should be firm but not harsh, with no over-revving. Older Mercedes-Benz automatics with fluid couplings instead of torque converters are known for hard shifting. Harsh shifting in diesels is commonly caused by loss of vacuum pressure. The modulator pressure valve of most automatics can be checked and adjusted to reduce hard shifting.

When you floor the accelerator at a reasonable speed, the transmission should shift down. Most pre-1980s transmissions are slow to do so. Early examples (1960s models) can be downright clunky. If the model was available with a manual gearbox, try one before making a buying decision.

Feel a vibration in the drivetrain? Many models have two-piece driveshafts with a center bearing. Wear here or at the universal joints or flex disks causes vibration. If vibration persists when the car is coasting, out of gear, the problem may be in the driveshaft, bearing, or joints. If vibration ceases when coasting out of gear, the problem is more likely in the engine or clutch.

If the car has cruise control, try it for more than just a few seconds. Mercedes-Benz cruise control systems are not exactly synonymous with total reliability, especially on diesels, and fixing them can be expensive. But then, real drivers like you don't use cruise control, do they?

Suspension, Steering, and Brakes

Other than looking for obvious problems under the car, or feeling for loose wheel bearings with the wheels off the ground, your judgment of the suspension system will come mainly from driving the car.

Check the tires. Make sure they carry the recommended pressures (modern models list pressures on the fuel filler door and in the owners manual). If the tread is worn in unusual patterns, wheel alignment may be incorrect, a matter of adjustment or possibly due to worn suspension bushings. Make sure the speed rating of the tires suits the top speed of the car. Some owners try to save money by replacing VR or even ZR tires with cheaper ones. The owners manual lists the original speed rating.

Wider wheels and tires must clear the bodywork throughout the entire steering range and suspension travel. Driving the car into a steep driveway with the front wheels turned sharply usually reveals clearance problems. Look for tire chafe marks on inner fender panels, brake lines, and suspension parts.

On the road, does the car maintain a straight line without constant steering corrections? If the steering wheel pulls to one side on rutted asphalt, front camber may be excessive. (If the car pulls to one side under braking, chances are the cause is a brake problem.) If the steering shimmies, especially on bumps, then steering and front suspension joints may be worn. A mild steering wheel vibration is usually due to wheel/tire imbalance, and is easier to fix.

Testing shock absorbers via the old "bounce up and down on the bumper" method isn't valid. You're better off checking the service records to see when shocks were last renewed. Drive on a bumpy road and see if the shocks work. A frozen shock absorber can cause a jarring ride. Shock absorbers are relatively easy and inexpensive to replace.

Most large 1950s to 1970s models with coil-spring suspension (not air suspension) used a rear compensating spring above the differential to supplement the springs at each rear wheel. If the rear sags, this spring either needs replacement or has been improperly replaced. Air suspension is covered in detail in Chapter 12.

Many 1950s and 1960s Mercedes-Benz cars have vacuum-assisted brakes fed by a large, circular brake booster, usually on the firewall. If the brakes need high pedal pressure, the booster may need to be rebuilt. To test it find a long hill (trust us) where you can safely coast the car, with the engine off. As you ride downward, apply the brakes maybe a dozen times, to use up any available vacuum. Note how much force the pedal requires. Now, start the engine, go back to the top of the hill, and do the whole thing again but with the engine running and the transmission in neutral. If less pedal pressure is needed this time, the booster works.

With your hands just off the steering wheel, and the front tire pressures equal, brake to see whether the car pulls to one side. If the brakes drag and don't release properly, the usual cause (in older cars) is clogged brake hoses. Flexible rubber brake hoses deteriorate internally. Broken-up lining material clogs them, preventing brake fluid pressure from releasing, and causing brake drag. If enough drag occurs, the fluid will boil, rendering that brake unit temporarily ineffective. Feeling each wheel hub to see if one is hotter than the others can pinpoint the trouble, but if this happens at one wheel, all flexible brake hoses should probably be replaced.

After your test drive, look under the hood and under the car for leaks. See if brake backing plates or the back of the tires are wet with brake fluid.

This isn't the end of your job. Specific items to check on various models are included in the appropriate chapters.

Chapter 3

Antique Mercedes and Benzes 1886–1926

Building the best cars in the world is not new for Mercedes-Benz. They have been doing so since the company's pioneering cars of 1886.

Joint credit is given to Carl Benz and Gottlieb Daimler for inventing practical automobiles in 1886, but Benz deserves the most. Daimler adapted his engine to an existing carriage, but Benz designed and built an entire car. By 1900, Daimler had caught up, as evidenced by his new Mercedes, which set the pattern for future automobiles.

This 1893 Benz Victoria with a one-cylinder engine of 4.5 horsepower could do about 20 miles per hour.

The early years involved minuscule production numbers. Not until 1934 did Daimler-Benz annual production exceed 10,000 cars. Some prewar cars thus come onto the market rarely; the rarest may appear only once in a lifetime. You're more likely to find an early Benz than a Daimler or a Mercedes. For instance, in 1900, as the world's largest automaker, Benz built 603 cars, Daimler 96. Total 1908 to 1926 production of Benz cars was just over 27,000. In this time Daimler built fewer than 20,000, but more of his Mercedes cars have survived.

Benz Veterans 1886–1914 ★★★★★

Benz started it all with his three-wheeled Patent Motorwagen of 1886. Its one-cylinder, 954-cc, water-cooled, horizontal engine ran on the equivalent of cleaning fluid. His first car was the sole Model 1, but starting in 1888 about 25 of the similar Models 2 and 3 left the workshop. Benz's wife, Berta, drove the car on its first long trip, in 1888. Having driven a replica, we can report that the sensation involves a lack of power and stability. Hills cause major concern, and in sharp turns you worry about the high three-wheeler tipping. Visibility and ventilation are unbeatable!

For the company's 1986 centennial, Daimler-Benz built 11 1886/1986 replicas, and an English company made several more, so despite the rarity of the real thing (only one is known to exist), the Patent Motorwagen is the earliest collectible model, albeit in replica form.

In 1892, the Benz Victoria and Vis-a-Vis models appeared, and in 1893 the first Benz came to the

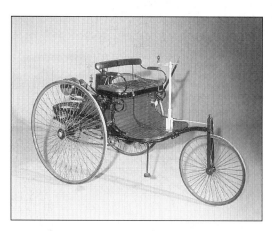

Benz's first car was a tube-framed three-wheeler. *DBAG*

United States. The world's first production car was the Benz Velo; about 1,200 were built between 1894 and 1899, so these are the most common today. Its one-cylinder, 1.5-horsepower engine gave it a 12-mile per hour top speed. The car was somewhat practical for the real world, but most were sold to wealthy folks as toys. The Velo was developed into the 1896–1901 Benz Comfortable. The Benz Dos-A-Dos seated four back to back, hence its name, using a horizontally opposed twin-cylinder engine.

After 1900, Benz cars had front engines, and the 1903–1904 Parsifal model used some new design principles demonstrated by Mercedes. The best Benz was the 40-horsepower 1906 Double-Phaeton for Prince Henry of Prussia. (Even then Benz had sales outlets in foreign countries, so cars turn up in unexpected places.)

Daimler Veterans 1886–1914 ★★★★★

Daimler was more adventurous than the traditional Benz. He and his associates went on to develop such features as the vee-twin engine, mechanical inlet valves, the use of ball bearings, and low-tension magneto ignition.

Daimler's first car was a horse-drawn carriage with his air-cooled 1.5-horsepower single-cylinder engine driving the rear wheels through a two-speed transmission. Water cooling, a four-speed transmission, and an all-metal car were early improvements; the 1889 car's twin-cylinder engine, metal frame, and wire wheels abandoned the carriage chassis.

Daimler powerplants powered boats, rail vehicles, buses, trucks, and even early lighter-than-air craft. Daimler licensed others to build engines and cars in France and Britain. (The resulting Daimler cars from England eventually developed separately and bore no real connection to their forefather.)

By 1896, Daimler had built the world's first front-engined vehicle, epitomized in the Phoenix. He is credited with the world's first truck and bus, plus many marine engines, electrical generators, an early fire pumper, and the first rail car.

Daimler's landmark model—for the entire automotive world—came just after the turn of the century. His 1901 Mercedes was the first car to look like what we now think a car should look like: lowslung, with a honeycomb radiator up front and an inline, upright, four-cylinder engine behind it, all on two steel channel frame rails. From 5.9 liters, the engine made 35 horsepower, giving the light car good performance. Instead of relying on suction to draw in the fuel, it had the first mechanically operated intake valves, controlled by an external camshaft.

A flywheel fan drew cooling air through the radiator and engine compartment, and a water pump circulated coolant. The H-pattern shift lever operated the coil-spring clutch and the gearbox shafts. The weak spot was probably the underdeveloped four-speed transmission, which drove the rear wheels via chains. Leaf springs supported each corner of the tapered channel steel frame, and internally expanding drum brakes were fitted at the rear.

For 1902, an improved 6.5-liter engine made 40 horsepower, and a 60-horsepower version appeared for 1903. When the 90-horsepower factory racers were demolished in a fire, this 60-horsepower car became legendary by winning the 1903 Gordon Bennett race in production form against all-out racers. Today, the three 60-horsepower cars known to exist are among the most desirable Daimler antique models.

Daimler Motoren Gesellschaft then led the automotive design world, and its inventions were widely copied. By 1906, Mercedes cars grew larger, more powerful, and faster, mainly thanks to a new six-cylinder engine generating up to 95 horsepower. Even this

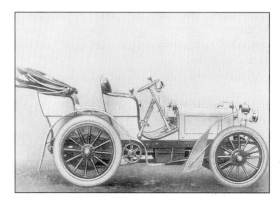

The 1901 Mercedes set new standards for future cars. *DBAG*

Daimler's first car, built in 1886, was carriage-like, midengined, and leaf-sprung. *DBAG*

Cross-section of the Knight sleeve-valve engine reveals the complicated system of sliding sleeves that served as valves. Poor lubrication and wear caused problems. *DBAG*

smoother power unit continued to use total-loss lubrication; adjustable sight-glasses on the dashboard meant that driving required mechanical knowledge. Four-cylinder models, from the 2.6-liter 10/20 on up, continued with smaller bodies. All engines had huge one-piece cylinders and heads cast in pairs, slid down over the pistons, and bolted to a cast crankcase.

By 1908, buyers could choose either chain (*Kettenantrieb*) or the new shaft (*Kardanantrieb*) drive, the latter with a differential featuring two ring gears, set at an angle to allow proper positive camber at each rear wheel. This choice continued until at least 1914. Mercedes abandoned the cone clutch for a metal-to-metal plated unit, allowing smoother starts and shifts.

Windshields began to appear in 1910, and the cars became heavier and faster. The last big chaindrive Mercedes was the 90-horsepower model introduced in 1910. Its advanced engine had three overhead valves per cylinder. Most of these cars were fitted with limousine or touring car bodies. Four-cylinder models were named for their horsepowers—15/20, 25/30, 35/40, 45/50, and 65/70—capped by the six-cylinder 75/80.

In 1914 came the luxurious Mercedes 28/95, but only 25 were built before World War I; 574 more were built by 1924. The 28/95 used an aircraft-derived six-cylinder, 7.2-liter motor and shaft drive, as well as a vee-shaped radiator and outside exhaust pipes. Front-wheel brakes were fitted.

In 1915, Daimler Motoren-Gesellschaft (DMG) celebrated its 25th anniversary, but just a year afterward, car production was halted by war, not to resume until 1920.

Between 1910 and 1924, DMG also built Mercedes-Knight cars with sleeve-valve engines. Their advantages were quiet operation and low-end power, but they were followed by clouds of oil smoke. Despite a racing version finishing fifth in the 1913 Indianapolis 500, the production cars were a financial failure. The best Mercedes-Knights were probably the 16/40, 16/45, and 16/50 models.

American Mercedes ★★★★★

In 1905, American Mercedes cars were built by piano maker Steinway in Long Island City, New York. Financial complications and a fire wiped out the whole plot, or things might be different today. The American Mercedes was built to the design and standards of its German equivalent. Its 6,785-cc, T-head, four-cylinder engine made 45 horsepower at 1,100 rpm.

Various castings and forgings came from Germany; many gears and shafts were machined in America of German steel. A metal spiral spring clutch ran in oil, final drive was by chain, and 60 miles per hour was guaranteed. Seven-passenger

This 1902 Mercedes Simplex used a four-cylinder, 5.0-liter engine to make 37 miles per hour; racing versions were faster. *DBAG*

The 1910 Mercedes-Knight used a sleeve-valve engine, which emitted plenty of smoke but not much power.

This Mercedes 90-horsepower touring car was sold by the American importers in 1912.

This is the only known surviving American Mercedes, built by Steinway in 1905. *FDB*

bodies, sheet aluminum over a wooden frame, were built and trimmed by Brewster. Two wheelbases—3,225- and 3279-millimeter—were offered.

The number of American Mercedes produced is unlikely to have exceeded 100. Today the only known survivor, restored in 1985, graces the lobby of Mercedes-Benz of North America's headquarters in Montvale, New Jersey.

Racing Versions ★★★★★

Mercedes racers came to America to compete for the Vanderbilt Cup. Ironically, these hard-used cars survived in greater proportion to production models, perhaps because they were more treasured. The 1908 racers that gave Daimler its first Grand Prix win are the most desirable early race cars. Several survive, along with the other famous Mercedes racers, the 1914 Grand Prix cars.

Meanwhile, the Blitzen Benz made Americans aware of the skills of German auto engineers. Under Barney Oldfield and Bob Burman, it raced all over the country. Today the car is preserved in the Mercedes-Benz Museum. In 1915, after a disappointing failure the previous year, a Mercedes driven by Ralph De Palma won the Indianapolis 500.

The Early 1920s ★★★★

After Germany emerged from World War I, only the clever could build cars, and only the wealthy could afford them. Daimler and Benz engineers had learned from their aircraft engine work, but the scarcity of good raw materials and the need to keep prices low meant that the first post-World War I cars were small and simple.

Not until 1921 did racing resume, led by Max Sailer's Targa Florio success in the 28/95. A production roadster was built, and three are known to survive. Derived from the DF80 aircraft engine, their six-cylinder, 7.3-liter power plant must have influenced W. O. Bentley, whose designs bore a similar gear-driven overhead cam.

The 1923 Mercedes 10/40/65 boasted the first supercharger on a production car; this 2.6-liter four-cylinder sports model soon gained front-wheel brakes. The Roots supercharger, driven from the crankshaft via a clutch, was activated only when the driver floored the accelerator. It forced air into the carburetor, designed to operate under pressure.

The 4.0-liter 15/70/100 and 6.0-liter 24/100/140 Mercedes were the most sophisticated DMG cars before the 1926 merger with Benz. Not

Supercharged 1923 Mercedes Targa Florio Roadster helped to get DMG back into international competition after World War I. *FDB*

only did these six-cylinder models make great touring cars, but they did well in competition, too.

What to Look For

If the car you are looking at has been restored, as most have, your main concern is authenticity. An antique car is mostly gauged by its historic value, so it had better be the real thing. Provenance is important. Ask for documentation on owners, restoration, or shows. A car may be a "confection" of new and old parts. If another example exists that is known to be genuine, compare the two. If you will drive the car occasionally, try it. Rather than adapting these cars to your driving needs, you must adapt to their abilities.

When looking at an unrestored original, authenticity remains important, but the difficulty of restoration becomes paramount. Your restorer should examine the car before purchase to estimate the task's cost and complexity.

Restoration

Owners and restorers of these early antiques are responsible for preserving automotive history. Winning an award takes a back seat. Few restorers are qualified to take this approach, so finding one with a good record is critical.

If the car has a wood-framed body, determine its condition by polite probing; sagging doors and ill-fitting panels can mean that the wood below them is crumbling. Replacement is labor intensive and demands special skills.

Be prepared to fabricate your own parts. Sometimes it's possible to find others who need parts to jointly fund a production run. An informal international network of veteran Mercedes-Benz owners enjoys Daimler-Benz assistance, but prepare for great expense and effort in restoration.

Summary

Apart from the racing models, the 1902–1903 Mercedes is the most significant pre-1926 model. It inspired other car designers and set the standard by which their products were judged. If you plan to drive an early car, try a 1920s model; the bigger the engine, the better. Performance and drivability are secondary. These historic artifacts should be preserved for future generations. Their owners are more caretakers than users.

Chapter 4

Vintage to Classic 1926–1940

By 1926, Daimler and Benz could not survive in competition with each other, so they merged, effective June 1926, into Daimler-Benz. Afterward, differing philosophies and old rivalries stifled creativity. During the 1930s, though, engineering and styling bloomed, yielding some cherished classics.

Luxury and Sport Models
Type K ★★★★★

The Type K replaced the 28/95. Based on the 630 (24/100/140), the K (for Kurz, or short) had a shorter wheelbase but more power—110 horsepower unblown, 160 horsepower blown—from its 6.24-liter, overhead-cam, inline six. The four-speed transmission could be coupled with several optional rear-end ratios. Type Ks were heavy; a bare chassis weighed about 3,400 pounds, and complete cars usually exceeded 5,000 pounds. Top speed was said to be 90 miles per hour, but brakes were marginal. A typical touring version sold for $16,000 in the United States in 1927, ensuring that the cars would always be rare. Before production ended in 1929, only about 1,150 Ks had been built.

Type K used either spoke or wooden wheels; the inline six was supercharged, but the blower cannot be used continuously. *FDB*

Type S, SS, SSK, and SSKL
1928–1934 ★★★★★

Strong-willed Ferdinand Porsche shook up the design department. His talent and effort created the classic 1927–1928 Type S sports car. Thanks to its supercharger, dual carburetors, and dual ignition, the Type S 6.7-liter engine made 120 horsepower unblown, 180 blown. A four-speed transmission was used, and the huge drum brakes were vacuum-assisted on some cars. Underslung rear springs and a lighter frame arched over the axles to lower the car and improve handling. Production models could touch 100 miles per hour, and race versions pushed 120.

Besides the factory-built Sindelfingen bodies, the production Type S was dressed by Saoutchik, Van den Plas, Zietz, D'Ieteren, Freestone & Webb—even Murphy. The 7.1-liter SS, which followed, has a higher engine hood and 225 horsepower. The shorter-chassis, 170–225-horsepower SSK followed in 1928 and the extremely rare, lightened SSKL in 1929.

Only 146 Type S cars were built, followed by 111 SS and 33 SSK models. Production ceased about 1934. Pseudo-SSKs and SSKLs were confected during the 1950s and 1960s, so insist on documented provenance. Because the replicas are known, owners of genuine cars are prepared to prove their history.

380, 500K, and 540K 1933–1943 ★★★★★

The scream of the supercharger made these cars legendary, but their excellence goes beyond that. This luxurious line commenced in 1933 with the 380, with four-wheel, coil-spring independent suspension. Its new overhead-valve straight-eight displaced 3,820 cc and was supercharged, but the 380 never had the "K" appended to its name. In a year only 154 were built; the car was underpowered, especially with a large formal body.

Next came the 1934 500K, the "K" denoting Kompressor, or supercharger. Boring and stroking the engine to 5,019 cc boosted output to 160 horsepower with supercharger engaged. Wheelbase stretched to 129.5 inches, and gleaming exhaust pipes cascaded from the right side of the hood. In 1935 and early 1936, a handful of 500Ks were fitted

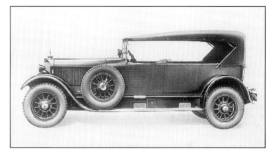

Most Type Ks carried mundane but spacious bodies. *DBAG*

with early 5.4-liter eights, but the 180-horsepower 540K was officially introduced for 1936.

The 380, 500K, and 540K used wood-framed bodies, making them labor-intensive to build (and to restore). Other features included a 12-volt electrical system, central lubrication, vacuum-assisted hydraulic brakes, and electric windshield wipers. Transmissions were either a three-speed with overdrive (*Schnellgang*), a four-speed without overdrive, and finally a four-speed with overdrive, all with synchronized second and higher gears. In good condition, these cars are easier to drive than most people think, about on a level with a big 1950s American car. A typical 540K demanded a gallon of fuel every 10 miles, making good use of its 29-gallon tank.

The 540K was then the fastest production automobile, and 406 were built with bodies ranging from four-door sedans to Special Roadsters and a few Special Coupes. Most are Cabriolets—the A (two-seater), B (four-seater, two side windows on each side), and the C (four-seater, one side window). The factory's Sindelfingen bodyworks built eight models: a sedan, an open tourer, Cabriolets A, B, and C, a Coupe, a Convertible Coupe, and a sensational Special Roadster, the most sought-after prewar model. Most were on a 3,290-millimeter (129.5-inch) wheelbase, but a few sportier versions used a 2,980-millimeter (117.3-inch) chassis. Apart from Sindelfingen selections, some were bodied by Erdmann & Rossi, but other coachbuilders were engaged. Only 25 Special Roadsters were built, and only 3 Special Coupes. A series of *Aktion P* armored 540Ks was built during World War II.

Model	1933	1934	1935	1936	1937	1938	1939	Total
380	93	61	—	—	—	—	—	154
500K	—	105	190	59	—	—	—	354
540K	—	—	—	97	145	95	69	406

380, 500K, and 540K Production Figures

Sindelfingen-bodied S tourer has classic sports car lines; engine hood was lower than that of the SS, SSK, and SSKL that followed it. *DBAG*

Whitewall tires on chrome-plated wheel spokes and rims make this Type S appear over-restored compared to what was originally available in 1927. *Dennis Adler*

Most 540Ks had a single wide rubber strip in the bumper, and most 500Ks had two narrow strips, but exceptions exist. Custom features were common, and the cars could be right-hand drive or the more usual left-hand drive. Four-wheel independent suspension used coil springs. Fuel consumption was roughly 8 miles per gallon, 0–60 miles per hour required about 16 seconds, and top speed might be 105 miles per hour, all depending on the body.

Grosser Mercedes: The 770
1930–1943 ★★★★

Even more imposing than a 500 or 540K is the 770, built in two series of long-wheelbase models, bodied as limousines or open cars for parade use.

The first series, with the W07 chassis and 7.7-liter M07 inline eight-cylinder motor, was built from 1930 through 1938 and included 117 cars. These used a box-section frame, leaf springs, beam axles,

continued on page 34

About to be delivered, this 500K Cabriolet A has twin flagstaffs, possibly indicating that it was intended for a prominent owner. *DBAG*

The Special Roadster is the most desirable 500K or 540K body style. *FDB*

The six-cylinder, 3.7-liter flathead engine of the 370S makes 75 horsepower; brakes are vacuum-assisted. *FDB*

This 1932 370S Mannheim Cabriolet Sport has a two-seater factory body and is capable of about 80 miles per hour. *DBAG*

This short-wheelbase 1936 290 Cabriolet A is almost a scaled-down 500K. Its six-cylinder engine made 68 horsepower. *FDB*

Introduced in 1935, the long-wheelbase 290 Cabriolet A is a bit more streamlined than the car above and with minor changes would become a 320; horns and fog lights on this restored car appear to be from earlier and later decades, respectively. *Dennis Adler*

Designed to sell as a moderately priced model, the late 1920s Stuttgart used six-cylinder engines in sober bodywork. *DBAG*

Continued from page 30

and a 150-horsepower engine; an optional supercharger raised power to 200 horsepower. The tall, upright bodies were clearly styled in the late 1920s, with wooden artillery wheels or wire-spoked wheels.

The later series, on the W150 chassis with the M150 inline eight, ran from 1938 to 1943, with 88 built. This lower, sleeker 770 was redesigned on a tubular frame with coil-spring independent suspension, disc wheels, and a five-speed transmission. Built only with a supercharger, the engine made 155–230 horsepower. Many of these cars were armored.

More myths have developed around the 770 than any other Mercedes-Benz. Almost every one is said to have been used or owned by one potentate or another. Be skeptical.

Apart from military vehicles, wartime automobile production was almost zero. The last 770 was built in 1943, and although a V-12 version was being developed, none apparently survive.

Midrange Models 1926–1940 ★★★

The Stuttgart and Mannheim medium-priced models from the late 1920s and early 1930s were named for cities where Daimler-Benz had plants, but the larger Nürburg was named for the Nürburgring race circuit. Except in sports-bodied form, these cars were fairly mundane. Their normally aspirated, side-valve engines provided utility, not performance, and most were bodied as heavy sedans. Many more were made than the luxury and sporting models, but fewer survive.

The six-cylinder Stuttgart 200 and 260; the Type 300, 320, and 350; the Mannheim 350, 370, and 370S; and the eight-cylinder Nürburg 460 and 500 were mid-1920s designs with beam front axles and mechanical brakes. (Before hydraulic brakes, Daimler-Benz employed the Bosch-Dewandre system, using engine vacuum to boost the mechanical brakes.) These models used conventional chassis and side-valve (flathead) engines. Typical sedans were tall and boxy. The Nürburgs were impressive; the Nürburg 500 was actually built until 1939 in small numbers, but it was a utilitarian car, less advanced than the 500K, 540K, and 770.

Open models, especially with custom coachwork, are attractive restoration candidates. The 370S Mannheim Roadster and Sports Cabriolet are quite desirable. The Stuttgarts were modest, but a Sports Roadster would be a find. Total production of these series was only about 23,000 units.

290 and 320 1933–1942 ★★★

Fully independent suspension graced the 290 and its successor the 320. These cars could be bodied in myriad short- or long-wheelbase variations—

The world's first diesel-powered passenger car, the 260D was designed as a commercial vehicle but appealed to private owners as well. *DBAG*

sedans, touring cars, Cabriolets (A, B, C, D, or F), plus at least one Roadster and by 1938 even military vehicles. Bodies emulated the bigger cars, with a broad choice of options.

The 290's 2.8-liter, side-valve six made either 60 or 68 horsepower. Its chassis used three front springs: one transverse leaf and two inboard coils, the latter acted upon by rocker arms. DBAG quoted top speed as 70 miles per hour; 0–60 miles per hour required 44 seconds.

The 290 and 320 are substantial-appearing classics with styling flair at less cost than a 540K. Short-wheelbase, five-passenger 290s seem short for their bulk, and the massive Cabriolet F and Pullman Limousine are ponderous. Look for excellent originals with sound bodies needing minimal work. The streamlined and special-bodied sedans are rare.

Late 320s have a 3.4-liter engine and overdrive—*schnellgang*, which lowers engine rpm. The 320 Cabriolet A and Roadster (long- and short-wheelbase) are rare and desirable. The handsome long-wheelbase 320 Cabriolet B and Cabriolet D have dual side-mounted spare tires and split windshields.

200, 230, and 260D 1933–1943 ★★★

Numerous bodies were built on the 200 and 230, on long (3,050-millimeter) and short (2,700-millimeter) wheelbases. There were as many as four Cabriolet A models, three long-, and one short-chassis. Two-seat models are most desired. Short-chassis models have a shorter wheelbase than the 170V and stand higher at the beltline, making them tall for their length. The Cabriolet A and Roadster look good. The late 1939–1943 230 (W153) got a lighter X-plan frame. Five-passenger W153 cars had all-steel bodies, a first for Mercedes-Benz.

Daimler-Benz marketed the first diesel passenger car, the four-cylinder 260D, in 1936. Its body was derived from the gasoline-powered 230. Using Bosch mechanical fuel injection, its overhead valve (cam-in-block) 45-horsepower engine got the car to 55–60 miles per hour and averaged over 20 miles per gallon. Most 260Ds became taxis and limousines, but some were sold as family cars. Most collectors consider the 260DX the only diesel car of serious historic interest.

Mercedes for the Masses: 170 and 170V 1931–1942 ★★★

In 1931, the unpretentious 170 economy model brought four-wheel independent suspension to Mercedes-Benz production cars. Despite the Depression, this 1.7-liter, six-cylinder car boasted central lubrication, four-wheel hydraulic brakes, pressed steel wheels, and (maybe because of the Depression) an antitheft steering lock. The 170 began as a sedan, a Cabriolet A, and a Cabriolet B.

In 1936, the 170 was superseded by the 170V. Despite replacing the six with a four, this is the best pre-war 170. The ladder frame was replaced by an oval cross-section, tubular frame. Power rose, and a four-speed transmission appeared. Body styles blossomed into 10 varieties, including the rare and desirable Roadster. A coal-burning 170V made its debut in 1939.

Between 1931 and 1939, about 83,000 170s were built. Early six-cylinders are scarce, so the 170V is the most available. The Roadster and Cabriolet A are beautifully styled and well worth restoring. When considering a prewar 170 sedan, remember that a postwar 170V looks the same but has improvements, which make it easier to restore, maintain, and use. Many prewar 170Vs were retro-fitted with postwar engines. An original engine is a mixed blessing because replacement of its babbitt bearings requires an expert. Thin-wall bearing inserts in postwar engines provide better fit, heat dissipation, and life.

Rear-Engined 130H, 150H, and 170H 1934–1938 ★★★

The most unusual production Mercedes-Benz models ever, the 1934–1938 130H, 150H, and 170H, were rear-engined on a central-tube frame. Volkswagen-like in appearance, these small four-place cars used inline four-cylinder engines hung out behind the rear axle. The alloy, air-cooled, VW engine was light enough for this, but the H's tall, cast-iron, water-cooled unit unbalanced the car. Rear swing-axles used coil springs, and the front suspension had a transverse leaf spring; four-wheel hydraulic brakes were fitted.

In five years only 5,816 were sold, as a sedan or as a semi-cabriolet with a roll-back fabric roof. A 26-horsepower 130H or a 38-horsepower 170H is interesting—and usually modestly priced—but these cars are best appreciated as historic artifacts.

An unusual model was the streamlined 1934 150 Sports Roadster. With its 55-horsepower, four-cylinder engine mounted amidships and driving via an automatic overdrive, it was ahead of its time. Few survive.

What to Look For

As prices of the glamorous cars rose, collectors with modest budgets turned to unsupercharged models. Today, even some owners know little about these cars, so they are often mis-described. Check identification plates carefully.

Parts can be difficult to find—and expensive—so finding a complete car is important. Even in poor condition, an assembled car provides a reference point. Photographs and organized disassembly make reassembly easier than puzzling over boxes of parts.

The wooden structure supporting the sheet metal requires skill to repair properly, so its condition is critical. Is there evidence of botched repairs or rotted wood? Do the doors sag or twist? Do the engine hood and top fit well? A tired original body can provide patterns, but a botched repair can destroy evidence of what the original wood looked like.

Restoration

It's unusual to find an unrestored 1930s Mercedes-Benz; you're more likely to find one that needs re-restoring. Because of the high standards of classic restoration, your most important decision will be choosing a restorer. Two factors make a prewar restoration project more difficult than a postwar restoration.

First, original parts are scarce. Except for the 170V, no prewar model was produced again after the war, so postwar parts interchangeability is practically nonexistent.

Second, most prewar cars have wood-framed bodies, which will need repair. An advanced amateur with woodworking skills and equipment can tackle the job, but this exacting work requires patience. Wood-framed bodies are rare enough these days that even a good restorer may send you elsewhere; bad restorers may just let your project gather dust.

Get involved in the restoration. Research authenticity, find parts and materials, and oversee the job. Restorers charge for research and parts locating, so you gain more than knowledge by being an expert on your own car.

Summary

Not all 1920s and 1930s cars measure up to the top models. The latter have skewed most people's judgment of the desirability of the mid-range and economy models. Not every 1930s Mercedes-Benz is comparable to a 540K.

Power, style, and engineering count. Open cars are preferred, especially those with independent suspension, hydraulic brakes, and overhead valve engines—the more cylinders, the better. To spend less, move into the sedans. If you're a contrarian, find a 260D diesel or a 170H.

Consider postwar models with similar vintage styling but all-steel bodies and better parts availability. It is usually less expensive to buy a properly restored car than to restore an original.

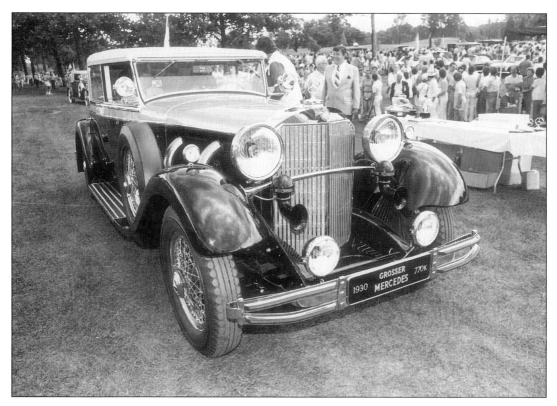

An early 770 makes an impressive concours d'elegance entry. *FDB*

The sportiest 170V is this 2+2 Roadster, with its second seat covered by the folding lid. *DBAG*

Production Figures

Model	Years	Engine Type	Chassis Type	Engine Specs	Production (Approx.)
400 (15/70/100 hp)	1926–1929	—	—	6-cyl/3,920 cc	911
630 (24/100/140 hp)	1926–1929	—	—	6-cyl/6,240 cc	508
Model K	1926–1929	—	—	6-cyl/6,240 cc	150
630 with K engine	1928–1932	—	—	6-cyl/6,240 cc	117
8/38 hp	1926–1929	—	—	6-cyl/1,988 cc	9,105
300 (12/55 hp)	1926–1927	W03	—	6-cyl/2,968 cc	834
300 (12/55 hp)	1927–1928	W04	M03	6-cyl/3,030 cc	2,485
320 (12/55 hp)	1928	W04	M04	6-cyl/3,131 cc	202
350 (14/60 hp)	1928	W05	M09	6-cyl/3,444 cc	355
350 (14/60 hp)	1928–1929	W09	M09	6-cyl/3,444 cc	358
460, Nürburg	1928–1929	W08	M08	8-cyl/4,622 cc	1,385
Type S	1927–1928	W06	M06	6-cyl/6,800 cc	146
Type SS	1928–1933	W06	M06	6-cyl/7,065 cc	111
Type SSK	1928–1932	WS06	MS06	6-cyl/7,065 cc	33
200, Stuttgart	1929–1933	W02	M02	6-cyl/1,988 cc	6,452
260, Stuttgart	1928–1934	W11	M11	6-cyl/2,581 cc	6,757
260L, Stuttgart	1933	W11L	M11	6-cyl/2,581 cc	50
350 Mannheim	1929–1930	W10	M10	6-cyl/3,444 cc	65
370 Mannheim	1929–1934	W10	M10II	6-cyl/3,689 cc	213
370K Mannheim	1931–1933	W10	M10II	6-cyl/3,689 cc	1,162
370S Mannheim	1931–1933	WS10	MS10	6-cyl/3,689 cc	183
460 Nürburg	1929–1933	W08	M08	8-cyl/4,622 cc	1,508
500 Nürburg	1931–1939	W08	M08II	8-cyl/4,918 cc	931
380	1933–1934	W22	M22	8-cyl/3,820 cc	154
500K	1934–1936	W29	M24I	8-cyl/5,018 cc	354
540K	1936–1939	W29	M24II	8-cyl/5,401 cc	406
770	1930–1938	W07 (K)	M07 (K)	8-cyl/7,655 cc	117
770	1934–1939	W150	M150	8-cyl/7,655 cc	88
170	1931–1936	W15	M15	6-cyl/1,692 cc	13,775
200	1932–1936	W21	M21	6-cyl/1,961 cc	9,281
200 Long	1934–1936	W21	M21	6-cyl/1,961 cc	6,341
290	1933–1936	W18	M18	6-cyl/2,867 cc	3,476
290 Long	1934–1937	W18II	M18II	6-cyl/2,867 cc	3,929
260D	1935–1940	W38	OM138	4-cyl/2,545 cc	1,967
130H	1933–1936	W23	M23	4-cyl/1,308 cc	4,298
150H Roadster	1934–1935	W30	M30	4-cyl/1,598 cc	5
150H Sport	1934	W130	M30	4-cyl/1,598 cc	16
150V Sport	1934–1935	W130II	M30	4-cyl/1,598 cc	11
170H	1935–1939	W28	M28II	4-cyl/1,697 cc	1,507
170V	1935–1942	W136	M136	4-cyl/1,697 cc	71,973
200V	1938–1939	W149II	M149II	4-cyl/2,007 cc	31
230	1936–1937	W143	M143	6-cyl/2,229 cc	966
230L	1936–1941	M143	M143	6-cyl/2,229 cc	19,324
230	1938–1943	W153	M153	6-cyl/2,229 cc	4,210
230SV Sports Roadster	1938	W153	M143S	6-cyl/2,229 cc	33
230 Sports sedan	1939	W153	M153S	6-cyl/2,289 cc	19
320	1937–1942	W142	M142	6-cyl/3,208-3,405 cc	5,097

Chapter 5

Beginning Again: 170 and 220 Sedan, Coupe, and Cabriolet 1946-1955

To satisfy a rebuilding nation needing basic transport, the first Mercedes-Benz back on the production line in 1946 was largely a prewar design.

170V, 170Va, and 170Vb 1946–1953 ★★

Had DBAG started from scratch in 1945 with an all-new car, it couldn't have created anything more appropriate. The simple, inexpensive 170 models were descendants of the 170V that appeared in 1936. These postwar rebirths had flat-head four-cylinder gasoline or diesel engines, with a four-speed transmission. In 1946, body styles varied from a police car to ambulances *(krankenwagen)*, trucks, and vans. The charming little four-door sedans appeared in mid-1947.

The 170Va, introduced in 1950, brought improvements such as insert crankshaft bearings, a trunk lid, integral heating and ventilation; bigger brakes, front spindles, and wheel bearings; and wider tires. More displacement (1,767 cc) and more power (45 horsepower) boosted top speed to 72 miles per hour.

The suspension still used twin transverse leaf springs up front and a coil-spring rear swing axle. The updated 1952 170Vb had a hypoid rear axle, horizontal instead of vertical hood louvers, a larger windshield, and front bumpers that began to wrap around the fenders.

Postwar 170Va four-cylinder sedans were intended as basic, economical transportation. *DBAG*

170S and 170Sb 1949–1953 ★★★

In 1949, Mercedes-Benz introduced its first new postwar models, the 52-horsepower 170S sedan, Cabriolet A, and Cabriolet B. Refinements included a downdraft Solex carburetor; a larger fuel tank in the rear instead of under the hood; and coil-spring front suspension instead of the transverse leaf spring. The spare tire moved into the trunk, allowing the lid to hinge at the top instead of the bottom.

The 170S body was slightly larger than the 170V, but more important, it was all-steel on the sedan and Cabriolet B. The Cabriolet A still used structural wood. The sedan was also sold with a canvas sunroof.

In 1952, the 170Sb took over, with a shifter on the column instead of the floor. The 170S Cabriolet models were dropped in 1951.

170D, 170Da, 170Db, and 170DS 1949–1953 ★★

Postwar diesel 170s included the 170D, from May 1949, then the 170Da, 170Db, 170DS, and 170S-D. Diesels used the new OM636 engine. This 1.7-liter overhead valve unit, with 19:1 compression and Bosch fuel injection, pumped out 38 horsepower and 71 lb-ft of torque. Maximum speed was 62 miles per hour, fuel consumption about 30 miles per gallon.

The 1950 170Da, with 40 horsepower and the same improvements as the 170Va, was superseded by the 170Db in 1952; the latter was also sold as an ambulance, a taxi, and a station wagon, usually bodied by outside coachbuilders. In 1952–1953, a diesel version of the 170S, the 170DS, became available.

The most Spartan model, the 170D OTP (*Offen Tourenwagen, Polizei,* Open Touring, Police),

| Technical Specifications (1950) | | | |
Model	170Va	170a	170S
Engine			
Type	Inline side-valve four	Inline OHV four	Inline side-valve four
Engine No. prefix	M136VI	OM636VI	M136III
Displacement	1,767 cc (all)		
Bore x stroke	75x100 mm (all)		
Compression ratio	6.5:1	19:1	6.5:1
DIN horsepower	45 hp @ 3,600 rpm	40 hp @ 3,200 rpm	52 hp @ 4,000 rpm
Torque	11 mkg @ 1,800 rpm	10.3 mkg @ 2,000 rpm	11.4 mkg @ 1,800 rpm
Fuel system	Solex 30 BFLVS	Fuel injection	Solex 32 PICB
Fuel required	Regular	Diesel	Regular
Coolant capacity	9.5 qt	9.5 qt	11.1 qt
Chassis			
Type	Tube (all)		
Body	Steel, wood-framed	Steel, wood framed	All-steel
Chassis No. prefix	W136 (all)		
Transmission	4-speed manual (all)		
Rear-axle ratio	4.125:1		4.375:1
Rear suspension	Swing-axle; coil springs	(Same)	
Front suspension	Transverse leaf springs	Transverse leaf springs	A-arms, coil springs
Wheels	3.50x16 in.	3.50x16 in.	4x5x15 in.
Tires	5.50x16 in.	5.50x16 in.	6.40x15 in.
Brakes	Drum (all)		
Fuel capacity	11.1 gal	9.8 gal	12.4 gal
Weight	2,612 lb (sedan)	2,756 lb	2,690 lb (sedan)
Performance			
0-60 mph	32 sec	45 sec	30 sec
Top speed	72 mph	65 mph	76 mph
Fuel consumption	20–24 mpg	24–32 mpg	20–26 mpg

This 1952 170DS interior is fitted with a steering-column-mounted four-speed gearshift and cloth upholstery. *DBAG*

was built mainly for German police departments from May 1950 to April 1952. This four-door, can-vas-topped device had a 40-horsepower OM636 diesel engine (OM means *oel motor*), a folding wind-shield, painted trim, and bench seats.

170S-V and 170S-D 1953–1955 ★

Except for these stripped-down versions, the 170's final model year was 1953. The 170S-V and the 170S-D, mating the all-steel 170S body with the V (gas) or D (diesel) engine, were priced below the new unibody 180 and the earlier 170S and DS. Built on the older chassis, the S-V and S-D were strictly economy cars. Collectors prefer the better-appointed S and DS.

What to Look For

On postwar steel bodies built on a wooden frame, age and the elements can cause the suicide doors (the front doors are hinged at the rear) to sag. Proper wooden-frame rebuilding is difficult and expensive. Look for leaks and wood damage along the drip rail and the molding between rear deck and roof. Look for poor-fitting doors, loose striker plates, and door hinges. Be wary of new paint over a patched-up, weak body structure.

On 170 models with all-steel bodies, watch for rusted box channels in the lower body, rust in the trunk floor, and—on Cabriolets—in the lower quarter panels. Since the 170S Cabriolet A still used wood framing, the above warnings apply. The front suspension may be worn due to clogged central lubrication lines; front-end parts are rare. Try for a complete car including the correct lights, bumpers, bumper guards, interior hardware, and instruments—especially sun visors and rearview mirrors on Cabriolets. An original radio is a bonus.

Early 1950s 220 sedans look old fashioned but were technically advanced, with a six-cylinder overhead-cam engine and four-wheel independent suspension. *Dennis Frick*

170 Production		
Years	Model	Production
1947–1953	170V sedan	45,741
1949–1953	170D sedan	26,758
1949–1952	170S sedan	28,708
1949–1951	170S Cabriolet A	830
1949–1951	170S Cabriolet B	1,603
1952–1953	170Sb sedan	8,080
1952–1953	170DS sedan	12,857
1953–1955	170S-V sedan	3,122
1953–1955	170S-D sedan	11,800

Restoration

Few of the 150,000 170s were exported. Today they aren't exactly considered classics, but they are rare and inexpensive. Touches like flip-up orange turn-signal trafficators give them an endearing personality. Some folks have sunk money into fancy restorations on Cabriolets, even the lowly 170D OTP, gilding the lily with fancy color combinations and whitewall tires. These cars were never plush, colorful, fast, or luxurious. Their modest colors and low power fit their quiet personalities, and they appear best that way.

Parts for the 170V are only moderately difficult to obtain. An OTP is Spartan; consider a more attractive prewar 170V Cabriolet B (wood-framed body) or an all-steel 170S Cabriolet B. They cost more to restore but are more comfortable and better finished, with bucket seats, roll-up windows, and padded tops.

A 170S is a good choice for a vintage look (free-standing headlights, running boards) with better parts supply than prewar cars. Reproduction wood parts are available. Its wood-framed body makes a Cabriolet A tough to restore, but its value can justify the cost.

The 170S Cabriolet B, overshadowed by the more stylish Cabriolet A, should not be overlooked. It has an all-steel body and a roomy back seat. If a Cabriolet B can be bought for little more than a sedan, only the leather versus cloth upholstery and the convertible top will cost more to restore, yet a finished Cabriolet B could be worth two sedans.

220 Sedan 1951–1955 ★★

By 1951, DBAG had designed the 220, with a new, six-cylinder overhead-cam 2.2-liter engine, smoother and providing more usable performance. The 220 was sold as a sedan, Cabriolet A, Cabriolet B, Coupe, and as the Open Touring Police car.

The oval tube chassis was retained with a new hypoid rear axle and improved brakes. The grille moved forward to accommodate the longer engine, resulting in a longer hood, improving the body's proportions. Instead of being free-standing, the headlights were finally built into the fenders, an easy way to tell a 220 from a 170. All window glass was flat, and the 220s were the last Mercedes-Benz with rear-hinged front doors.

Swing-axle rear suspension continued, as did the central lubrication and the column-shifted, all-synchromesh four-speed transmission. With a 6.5:1 compression ratio, the new single-carburetor six gave 80 horsepower DIN at 4,850 rpm, a major improvement. This power may seem meager, but the cars were relatively light. Drum brakes were hydraulic but unboosted, and the electrical system still ran on 6 volts.

The 220 sedans were trimmed sparsely, the usual upholstery being broadcloth with a floor mat of molded rubber. Square-weave carpet like that of early VWs (and 300SLs) was used on the rear floors and seat risers. The trunk had rubber mats on the floor and the luggage shelf, with black cardboard side walls.

Solid wood (as opposed to veneer) forms the dashboard top, but the fascia is stamped sheet metal. Regardless of trim color, both wood and metal were dark brown. The wood was not stained but colored with a tinted varnish for a near opaque finish. Headliners were felt-like cotton cloth. Knotted tassels on the pillars between the doors served as hand grips in fast corners. Rounding out the Victorian decor were the fine looking but low-fi Telefunken or Becker vacuum-tube radio and the trafficators.

Trafficators were outside-mounted signal arms. Rotating the horn ring left or right caused one to spring upward from its recess, light up, and sit there until canceled. Trafficators in good condition are rare. The dash includes an ignition timing control.

Sedans came without fog lights, trim rings on the wheels, or luggage. Leather was an option, but other embellishments were few. The small, nippled hubcaps are different from the domed style on 300SLs and later sedans. The hood star was rigid, part of the radiator cap that screws into the grille shell, and scaled to the 200. Early 220s had a vertical crank handle hole in the lower grille shell, with a chromed cover. A full-length fabric sunroof was optional. Other options included a passenger-side headrest, a radiator roller blind, fitted luggage, various radios, an underhood light, a heater blower, a spare parts kit, and a reclining front seat.

Technical Specifications

Model	220	Transmission	4-speed manual
Years	1951-1955	Rear-axle ratio	4.44:1
Engine		Rear suspension	Swing-axle, coil springs
Type	Inline ohc six	Front suspension	A-arms, coil springs
Engine No. prefix	M180	Wheels	4.5x15 inch
Displacement	2,195 cc	Tires	6.40x15 inch
Bore x stroke	80x72.8 mm	Brakes	Drum
Compression ratio	6.5:1	Fuel capacity	17.2 gal
DIN horsepower	80 hp @ 4,850 rpm	Weight	2,975 lb (sedan)
Torque	14.5 mkg @ 2,500 rpm		3,175 lb (Cabriolet)
Fuel system	One two-barrel Solex 30 PAAJ	**Performance**	
Fuel required	Premium	0-60 mph	20 sec
Coolant capacity	16 qt	Top speed	87–90 mph
Chassis		Fuel consumption	15–20 mpg
Type	Unibody; steel		
Chassis No. prefix	W187		

Note: Performance figures, based on original factory information and new car test reports, are approximate and depend on the individual car, options, driving conditions, and other factors.

Production

Years	Model	Production	Chassis prefix
1951–1954	220 sedan	16,066	187011
1951–1953	220 Cabriolet B	997	187013
1951–1953	220 Cabriolet A	978	187012
1954–1955	220 Cabriolet A	300	187024
1954–1955	220 Coupe	85	187023
1953–1954	220 4-door Convertible (OTP)	41	187015

Typical 220 chassis numbers: 18701202532/51 (early); 1870244500046 (late)
Typical 220 engine numbers: 18092001234/51 (early); 1809234501234 (late)

220 Cabriolet A 1951–1955 ★★★

The 220 was also built as a Cabriolet A and a Cabriolet B. Following tradition, the Cabriolet A was a two-passenger Convertible with a jump seat in the rear, distinguished from the four-passenger Cabriolet B by having only one side window. The padded top had chromed landau bars.

An optional external spare tire increased trunk space. Fog lights and wheel trim rings were standard on Cabriolets, and fitted luggage was offered. Windshield wipers are electrical. The interior rearview mirror is on a clever swivel so that it can be raised to allow a view over the bulky folded top.

Cabriolet A and Coupe interiors were trimmed differently from other 220s. The dash fascia was leather-covered in a color matching the seats. The dash top had veneered wood trim matching the windowsills in burled elm, burled walnut, or rosewood, matching seat color. A short, cut-pile wool carpet, usually referred to as Wilton, covered the risers and kick panels, and the rear floor. The carpet was bound in scived leather matching seat color except in the case of off-white leather, used with gray or "salt and pepper" carpet. Rubber mats covered the front floor.

The trunk carpet was the same color as the interior, but cars with the optional fitted luggage had tan carpet to match it. A horizontal spare tire and wheel, with jack and tools, dominated the trunk. A shelf above accommodated fitted suitcases.

A 220 Cabriolet A is pretty, a sort of scaled-down 300S but friendlier. The Cabriolet A is the most valuable 220 today. Economy and good cruising performance from the 80-horsepower engine are reasons to choose this as an only collector car. If you want a collectible for tours and club outings, this is your 220.

220 Cabriolet B 1951–1955 ★★★

The 220 Cabriolet B body is all-steel, like the sedan's. The four-passenger B has a roomy bench back seat and rear side windows. Its rear window is a small chrome-framed glass unit, like the Cabriolet A's. Interior trim details are the same as the sedan, except that leather upholstery was standard. The soft top was the usual padded affair, bulkier than the Cabriolet A, and it lay atop the rear deck when folded. A top boot made from top fabric was trimmed in leather matching the seats. An outside spare tire was optional. Positive camber was evident in the rear suspension of an empty car.

Controls of the 220 sedan were straightforward with no frills.

220 Cabriolet and Coupe 1954–1955 ★★★

By early 1954, the 220 sedan and Cabriolet B were replaced by the completely new unibody 220a, but the old 220 Cabriolet A and a new Coupe were assembled through 1955. The 1954–1955 Cabriolet A and Coupe can be distinguished by their curved windshields.

These so-called "second series" 220 Cabriolet A models were given 187024 chassis numbers

---

Driving Impressions: 220 Sedan

The 220 can be driven comfortably at highway speeds for long distances. Alex Dearborn drove a 1954 220 sedan all through the 1970s and recalls no trouble cruising at 70 miles per hour. The rear swing-axles were not yet the low-pivot version, so surprise oversteer lurked. The 220 had 7-plus inches of ground clearance and had positive camber built into the rear alignment in anticipation of heavy loads, so an unladen one was a challenge in fast corners.

Unassisted drum brakes require fairly high pedal pressure. Top speeds of the Coupe and the Cabriolets are in the high 80s, with 0-60 miles per hour requiring about 20 seconds.

The 1954-1955 220 Cabriolet A has a curved windshield and was one of the last Mercedes-Benz models to use a wood-framed body. *DBAG*

but were little changed from the 187012 chassis cars. The curved windshield is a nice distinction, but only if it's not cracked. Records show 85 Coupes produced, 13 with a sunroof, making them rare. The 1951–1955 220 Cabriolet A cars numbered 1,278; perhaps 300 were second-series cars. Incidentally, the 220 Cabriolet A is not a 220A, as it is often mislabeled. The Coupe was pretty, resembling the 300S Coupe, with the added cachet of being rarer.

220 OTP ★★

DBAG made a police variant called the 220 OTP (Open Touring, Police), following the lines of the 170D OTP. The car was sparsely trimmed; its top was not padded or even lined. This was a four-door utility vehicle for transporting personnel. Compared to its predecessor, the 170D OTP, the 220 was a less modest performer. With dual Solex carburetors as later fitted to the 220SD, the 220 OTP must have worried the bad guys a little more than the 170 had.

Rare today, the 220 OTP was a military-style vehicle. It would be a crime to tart one up.

This is a jeans-and-mud, dogs-in-the-back-seat kind of collectible.

What to Look For

Because the 220 was so similar in construction to the 170S, caveats listed for that model apply here.

First, look for rust. The 220's rugged backbone frame has stringers going out to the jacking points. We have never seen a seriously rusted frame, but the body channels above it are another story. A sheet-metal box section runs parallel to the door sills, fore and aft, on each side. Examine these box-section channels for rust or rust cover-up; we have seen these parts made of cardboard with undercoating as camouflage.

The 220 Cabriolet A and Coupe have wood body framing, including the door frames, door hinge posts and front latch posts, doorsills, and the rear compartment frame at the base of the convertible top. To determine the condition of doorsill wood, open and close the driver's door. If the door has to be lifted into place, then there is deterioration in the door structure or in the door hinge posts. Many "restored" Cabriolets have sagging doors, usually because the wood is rotten or weak. Remove the

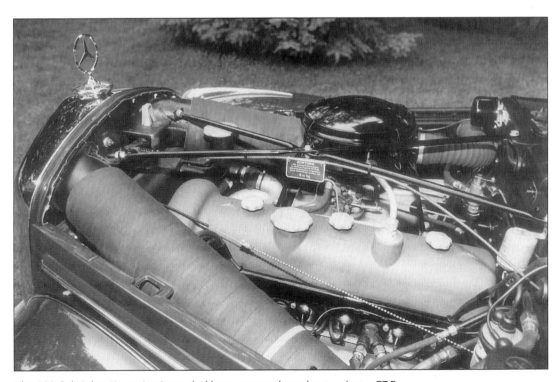

The 220 Cabriolet A's engine is nestled between two large heater ducts. *FDB*

Rarest 220 is the elegant Coupe, here with the particularly desirable sunroof. The 220 was the last Mercedes-Benz with suicide doors. *DBAG*

chromed doorsill plates to expose the wood structure. Wood pieces are being replicated. The higher value of this model might justify the expense of replacing the wood framing, but it can only be done with the car totally apart.

All 1951–56 220 models—the sedan, Cabriolets A and B, and Coupe—should have chassis numbers starting with 187 and engines number starting with 180.

Restoration

Which 220 do you choose? The sedans are the least expensive and the most practical. Made in large quantity, they will never be rare. Still, they're seldom seen. Sedans are cheaper to restore than the Cabriolet A, and parts are fairly obtainable, used or new. A 220 sedan is affordable. Look for a good complete unabused original. A sunroof is a lucky find.

Expect to replace or rebuild most mechanical parts. Many cars were the victims of indifferent care and limited parts availability. Now, specialists provide new-old-stock and reproduction parts. Used

parts are available through restorers and collectors.

The 220 engine remained in production until the mid-1960s, so parts are easily available. The original cast-iron heads are prone to cracking. Many have been replaced; if not, an aluminum head from the late 1950s is recommended.

Before an extensive restoration of a 220 sedan, consider moving up to a Cabriolet B. These are rarer than the A (997 versus 1,278 produced), and with no structural woodwork, are easier to restore than a Cabriolet A.

The handsome 220 Cabriolet A is one of the more desirable Mercedes-Benz 1950s collectibles. Structural woodwork is an obstacle, but replacement wood is available. Because of the engine, the 220 is preferred over the 170S by most collectors. If you plan to restore a Cabriolet A, the 220 is a safer investment than the 170S.

The 220's purchase price will be higher, but restoration costs will be the same as an equivalent 170. If you'll do the restoration yourself and can't afford a

The 220 Cabriolet A trunk could accommodate factory-fitted luggage and even a spare parts kit in a wooden box. *Alex Dearborn*

220 Cabriolet A, a 170S Cabriolet A might be in your range. If performance isn't a concern, you will have a fine car when finished, the same quality as a 220.

Summary

These charming small cars are sound buys when they need little or no restoration. Otherwise you can invest more than they are worth, but if you're going to keep and enjoy the car, so what?

The 220 models can be enjoyed on today's roads. In styling they look prewar, but mechanically they incorporate many practical improvements. Best buys are the 220 sedans, with prices a fraction of the more glamorous, lower-production models. As usual, most collectors prefer the Cabriolets. The graceful and rarer 220 Coupe is probably the most sought-after 220, especially with a sunroof.

Chapter 6

The Luxurious 300s of the 1950s

Because they had historically catered to luxury car buyers, DBAG introduced upscale models as soon as possible after World War II, not only to satisfy the reemerging need but to protect its position in that profitable market.

By 1952, using a new 3.0-liter, overhead-cam six, Mercedes-Benz was building newly designed four-door luxury sedans and convertibles plus smaller numbers of 300S and 300Sc two-door Cabriolets, Roadsters, and Coupes on oval-tube chassis.

Larger and with more luxurious features, these 300 models were much heavier and more complex than the utilitarian 170s and 220s. Low volume and high quality mean that parts cost more, but these were the most elegant automobiles of the 1950s.

300, 300b, 300c, and 300d
1951–1962 ★★★

The 300 four-door sedan (practically a limousine) appeared in late 1951, followed by the elegant four-door Convertible (sometimes called a Cabriolet or a Cabriolet D) in April 1952. With a compression ratio of 6.4:1 (for poor postwar fuel) and two Solex 40 PBJC single-barrel carburetors, the overhead-cam six made 115 horsepower DIN. The four-speed manual transmission had its shifter on the column or on the floor (rare). A self-leveling rear suspension was fitted, along with central lubrication operated by a plunger beside the accelerator pedal; both were operated by the 12-volt electrical system. The taillights were tiny horizontal slots just above the bumper.

The 300s were miles ahead of other luxury cars in engineering and taste. Despite fresh memories of the Recent Unpleasantness, these German luxury models became popular around the world. Besides show business personalities and heads of state, they were owned by refined persons who preferred to avoid the ostentation of a Rolls-Royce or a Cadillac. Because the 300 served German Chancellor Konrad Adenauer, it soon became known as the "Adenauer" model, a nickname that stuck to it almost as well as "Gullwing" has stuck to the 300SL.

The 300b, introduced in 1954, had front vent windows, a pair of Solex two-barrel carburetors, higher compression, more power, and larger brakes. The 300c, built from September 1955 through July 1957, brought more carburetor improvements and an automatic transmission option, a first for Mercedes-Benz.

The three-speed automatic, built by Borg-Warner, was also offered in the succeeding 300d. This ultimate 1950s luxury car was introduced in 1957 on a 4-inch longer wheelbase (124-inch) than the 300c, subtly restyled in more modern fashion. Besides a wider grille, larger windows, longer rear fenders, larger upright taillights, and a new roofline, the sedan abandoned the center pillar and became, in effect, a four-door hardtop. Removable rear quarter windows make the side view more dashing. The 300d's mechanical fuel injectors were in the intake ports rather than in the cylinders, like those of the 300SL. The engine made 160 horsepower.

Between July 1957 and early 1962, 300d production included 3,077 sedans but only 65 Convertibles. Custom bodies included parade cars (often with raised rooflines in sedan and Convertibles), ambulances, even hearses. All 300s appear elegant and conservative, but the 300d is undoubtedly the most attractive.

Technical Specifications

Model	300	300b	300c	300d
Years	1951-1954	1954-1955	1955-1957	1957-1962
Engine				
Type	Inline ohc six (all)			
Engine No. prefix	186	186 II	186 II	189
Displacement	2,996 cc (182.8 ci) (all)			
Bore x stroke	85x88 mm (all)			
Compression ratio	6.4:1	7.4 or 7.5:1	7.4 or 7.5:1	8.55:1
DIN horsepower	115 hp @ 4,600 rpm	125 hp @ 4 500 rpm	125 hp @ 4,500 rpm	160 hp @ 5,300 rpm
Torque	20 mkg @ 2,500 rpm	22.5 mkg @ 2,600 rpm	22.5 mkg @ 2,600 rpm	24.2 0 mkg @4,200 rpm
Fuel system	2 Solex 40 PBJC	2 Solex 32 PAITA carburetors	2 Solex 32 PAITA carburetors	Mechanical fuel injection
Coolant capacity	21.1 qt	22.2 qt	22.2 qt	22.2 qt
Chassis				
Type	Oval tube, steel body (all)			
Chassis No. prefix	186 II	186 II	186 IV	189
Transmission	4-speed manual (all)			(3-speed auto optional)
Rear-axle ratio	4.44:1	4.67:1	4.67:1	4.67:1
Rear suspension	Swing-axle, coil springs (all)			
Front suspension	A-arms, coil springs (all)			
Wheels	5x15 in.	5x15 in.	5.5x15 in.	5.5x15 in.
Tires	7.10x15 in.	7.10x15 in.	7.00x15 in.	7.60x15 in.
Brakes	Drum	Vacuum-assisted after 1954		
Fuel capacity	19.0 gal (all)			
Weight	3,924 lb (sedan) 4,034 lb (con)	3,924 lb (sedan) 4,034 lb (con)	4,100 lb (sedan) 4,211 lb (con)	4,299 lb (sedan) 4,409 lb (con) Add 88 lb for automatic
Performance				
0-60 mph	18 sec	17 sec	17–18 sec	17–18 sec
Top speed	99 mph	101 mph	96–99 mph	103–105 mph
Fuel consumption	14 mpg	15 mpg	14–15 mpg	13–15 mpg

Driving Impressions: 300 Sedan

Despite feeling cumbersome, the big 300 sedans and Convertibles move along well once you get them rolling. Performance was adequate, but who cares? These cars exuded presence, not speed.

Braking requires planning ahead, especially without vacuum-boosted brakes. The automatic transmission is probably best avoided in favor of the more reliable and enjoyable four-speed manual gearbox.

If you plan to drive the car much, we recommend a 300d, which has more power, by far the best visibility, and is more refined and better developed.

The 1952 300 sedan's six-cylinder overhead-cam engine made 115 horsepower and went on to greater things in the 300S, 300Sc, and 300SL. *DBAG*

Restoration

Since the 707 Convertibles built are valued far more highly than the 10,723 sedans, the latter can be a bargain if it doesn't need restoration. Many of these cars were maintained well, so finding one requiring minimal restoration is not difficult.

Avoid cars requiring total restoration. These big, rare, and complex cars are expensive to restore. Many people restoring a 300 find it best to buy a parts car. Engine and drivetrain overhaul are relatively simple, but the size and complexity of the body, trim, and interior are something else. The Convertible's top is another challenge.

300S 1951–1955 ★★★★

The 300S was a two-door, grand touring model based on the 300 sedan. All three body styles—Coupe, Cabriolet, and Roadster—shared the same chassis and basic shape, shorter yet more voluptuous than the sedan. Their 3.0-liter, single overhead-cam, six-cylinder engine was uprated from the sedan's with higher compression and three Solex 40 PBJC carburetors instead of two. This gave 150 horsepower and a top speed of 110 miles per hour. Central lubrication was also fitted.

The hand-assembled 300S was rare and expensive. Only 560 were made. Most chrome-plated trim parts were solid brass, test-fitted to each car, then removed for final plating and reinstalled. Radio

choices were Becker and Grundig, all tube-types. Until 1955, when the small face-plate of the 1960s and 1970s was first used, radios had large face-plates.

Early 300S cars cost about $6,500 in the United States, twice the price of a Cadillac. By 1955, all three body styles were priced at $12,457 FOB California, almost double the price of a 300SL. The lucky owners were surrounded by the best leathers and wood-veneered panels. Their weekend clothes could be packed in custom suitcases fitting the curves of the trunk. Additional fitted suitcases were available for the folding rear occasional seats.

Two oval frame tubes ran the length of the car. Four-wheel, coil spring independent suspension (swing-axles at the rear) gave a supple ride with little roll. The four-speed manual gearbox was shifted via a column-mounted lever. Some cars were fitted or retrofitted with floorshifts. Rear-axle ratio was 4.125:1. Neither an automatic transmission nor power steering was offered. Finned aluminum brake drums, vent windows, different heater boxes, and vacuum-assisted brakes were fitted to 1954 and later cars, sometimes known as the 300Sb.

Options were few, but lighting changed depending on country of destination. German bulb-type headlights had narrow rims and large, round, fluted glass covers. U.S. headlights had wide chrome-plated rims to accommodate the smaller, 7-inch sealed-beam units.

Technical Specifications

Model	300S	300Sc
Years	1951-1955	1955-1958
Engine		
Type	Inline ohc six (all)	
Engine No. prefix	188	199
Displacement	2,996 cc (182.8 ci) (all)	
Bore x stroke	85x88 mm (all)	
Compression ratio	7.8:1	8.55:1
DIN horsepower	150 hp @ 5,000 rpm	175 hp @ 5,300 rpm
Torque	23.5 mkg @ 3,800 rpm	26 mkg @ 4,300 rpm
Fuel system	3 Solex 40 PBJC carburetors	Mechanical fuel injection
Coolant capacity	20.6 qt	21.1 qt
Chassis		
Type	Oval tube, steel body (all)	
Chassis No. prefix	188I	188II
Transmission	4-speed manual (all)	
Rear-axle ratio	4.125:1	4.44:1
Rear suspension	Swing-axle, coil springs (all)	
Front suspension	A-arms, coil springs (all)	
Wheels	5x15 in. (all)	
Tires	6.70x15 in. (all)	
Brakes	Drum, vacuum-assisted after 1954 (all)	
Fuel capacity	22.5 gal (all)	
Weight	3,880 lb	3,924 lb
Performance		
0–60 mph	15 sec	14 sec
Top speed	109 mph	112 mph
Fuel consumption	14-16 mpg (all)	

300S Production 1951-1955

Years	Model	Production	Chassis prefix
1951-1955	Coupe	216	188011
1951-1955	Cabriolet	203	188010
1951-1955	Roadster	141	188012

W188 chassis, M188 engine
Typical chassis numbers: 18801000074/52 (early); 1880105500006 (late)
Typical engine numbers: 18892000162/52 (early); 1889205500098 (late)

300Sc Production 1955-1958

Years	Model	Production	Chassis prefix
1955-1958	Coupe	98	188014
1955-1958	Roadster	53	188015
1955-1958	Cabriolet	49	188013

W188 chassis, M199 engine
Typical chassis number: 1880137500009
Typical engine number: 1999807500023

300Sc 1955–1958 ★★★★★

In late 1955, the 300Sc brought a few trim embellishments over the previous 300S, but all three body styles continued with nearly unchanged sheet metal. The plain chrome bumpers no longer had a rubber strip set in chromed brass channel as on the 300S. The "300S" lettering remained on the trunk lid, but the new model was identified by the large chromed letters *"EINSPRITZMOTOR"* in the rear bumper. Underneath, the Sc's cowl was

A 300c Convertible, as it was called in America, was often known as a 300c Cabriolet D to European buyers. *DBAG*

Top down, the 300c Convertible still makes a great parade car. This one has a pair of unusual spotlights; its folded top recalls 1930s designs. *DBAG*

The 300's final iteration was the 300d, modernized with a 180-horsepower SAE fuel-injected engine, sleeker roofline, removable rear quarter windows, upright taillights, and more. *DBAG*

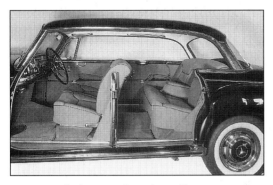

Interior of the 300d sedan allows generous legroom front and rear. Visibility was much improved over the earlier 300s. *DBAG*

better supported, and the transmission cover is not removable. Central lubrication continued. Other differences involve the fuel tank and radiator.

The big news was Bosch direct-port fuel injection. Similar to that on the 300SL, it boosted power from 150 to 175 horsepower. The engine block continued as cast iron with an aluminum head. The 300SL production engine produced more power and was canted in the engine bay, but the upright 300S/Sc design was similar. Like the 300SL, 300Sc engines used a dry-sump lubrication system, providing an additional 2.5 quarts of capacity over the 300S's wet-sump system.

Exterior changes included two chrome horizontal spears on the sides of the engine hood; the 300S had none. Chromed steel wheels replaced the painted wheels on the 300S. Body-color hubcaps were interchangeable with the 300SL. Chromed brass wheelwell moldings were used for the first time.

Interior trim and layout remained as per the 300S. Radios were almost all Becker, with the familiar small face-plate. The only notable body change

Driving Impressions: 300S and 300Sc

These cars were grand touring predecessors of the S-Class of the 1990s. Sports car buffs would be better satisfied by the 300SL. Still, power of the 300S was on a par with the better American cars, and roadholding was remarkable for a car of 3,700 pounds.

The 300Sc could run in the fast lane in 1955. It may be the best all-around car made in the 1950s. Driving one today tempts comparison with expensive modern cars. The power-to-weight ratio compares favorably with the 1969 280SE Coupe. Zero to 60 takes about 14 seconds, and the car will do 112 miles per hour. The fuel injection is reliable, and collectors prefer it to the tri-carb 300S setup.

was a larger plastic rear window for the Roadster. A sunroof was optional for the Coupe. Various other options involved lights, keys, and so forth, but since these cars were often built to order, establishing an options list is folly.

Low-pivot swing-axle rear suspension, replacing the older swing-axle of the 300S, improved cornering power and stability. Rear-axle ratios were 4.44:1 for U.S. cars, 4.11:1 for European. Drum brakes were retained.

Before the 300Sc line stopped in April 1958, only 200 were built, fewer than half as many as the 300S.

What to Look For

Look for undamaged, complete, original examples with their trim intact. Items such as headlight doors, fog lamps, and grille shells were special to these cars and are hard to find. Apart from certain chassis parts, only such minor parts as fasteners were shared with the 300 sedan.

Rust is usually minimal, as the bodies were separate from the frames. The subframe box sections under the doorsills were apt to rust but are fairly easy to repair with the car apart. Check for rust under the headlights and in the trunk floor.

Engine numbers begin with 188 (300S) or 199 (300Sc), but do not match chassis numbers. Neither car had self-leveling rear suspension.

All 300S models had dense wool cut-pile carpet trimmed in leather the same color as the seats. Interiors were trimmed in 4.0-ounce leather supplied to DBAG by the German leather company Roser. Lightweight, more supple leathers don't match the

This 300S Roadster has painted wheels and European headlights; when lowered, its top disappears completely. Later 300S and 300Sc Roadsters have vent windows. *DBAG*

The early (no vent windows) 300S Cabriolet uses landau bars; when lowered, its bulkier top stands above the rear deck. U.S. versions have sealed-beam headlights inset into plated spacer rings. *DBAG*

original appearance or give the firmness of the original cushions. The trunk carpet was normally dark tan, anticipating the tan fitted luggage, secured by a single belt with a chrome-plated roller buckle. Replica fitted luggage has been made.

Interior wood was usually rosewood veneer on an ash core. In cars with black or red leather, the rose-wood was apt to be dark; with blue leather, it was usually light-colored. Burled walnut veneer was used in cars with tan or brown leather. This color and wood matching continued, with minor changes, in Mercedes-Benz cabriolets and convertibles through 1971.

The underside and engine compartment were finished in near-glossy black paint, not body color.

This handsome 1955 300Sc Coupe has a plain front bumper, horizontal trim on the sides of the engine compartment, chrome-plated fender trim, and chrome-plated wheels. *DBAG*

Matched 300Sc Coupe and Cabriolet (rear). The 300Sc used "300S" model designation on its trunk, supplemented by the *EINSPRITZMOTOR* set into the bumper. *FDB*

Fitted luggage for the 300S and 300Sc is now being reproduced to high quality. *Dennis Adler*

The body-color tag on the firewall, near the chassis number plate, listed a two- or three-digit number ending in G or H (for example, 40G was black paint made by Glasurit).

The 300S and 300Sc Coupes were available with a factory-installed steel sunroof; some early ones had glass wind deflectors overlapping part of the side windows. Late cars (sometimes known as "b" models) had vent windows instead. Chromed brass plates cover the doorjambs.

The Cabriolet's padded top uses a horsehair mat over the top bows, under several layers of jute and the outer fabric. A loosely woven fabric headliner was light gray, light beige, or light tan. The top gave excellent sound insulation but is expensive to restore properly. A correctly restored top will be smoothly filled out, with the outline of the bows not easily visible. The top takes a little care to fold properly. Down, it rests in a stack on the rear deck and is covered by a large boot made from top fabric trimmed in leather to match the seats. A

swing-up bracket allows the interior rearview mirror to be raised to allow rearward vision.

With the top up, rear vision is through a small, chrome-rimmed glass window. Chromed landau bars provide bracing and serve as an identification point for Cabriolet-spotters.

The 300S and 300Sc Roadsters used the Cabriolet body with minor changes. Its unpadded top has no headliner and stows in a well, covered by a leather boot color-matched to the seats and attached by chromed Tenax fasteners.

On the 300Sc, look for the chassis number on the plate on the firewall. The body number plate in the driver's doorjamb should have a stamped number beginning with A 188. Body number will not match chassis number. Subtle differences exist between the fuel injection of the 300Sc and that of the 300d; for instance, the d's intake manifold has a clearance problem in the Sc. The 300Sc used the same trim and color combinations as the 300S.

Lower the Roadster's top and it disappears into a well behind the seats; only 53 of these 300Sc Roadsters were built. *DBAG*

The 300S engine uses three Solex carburetors and has an unusual slanted head-block joint relating to the similar engine in the 300SL.

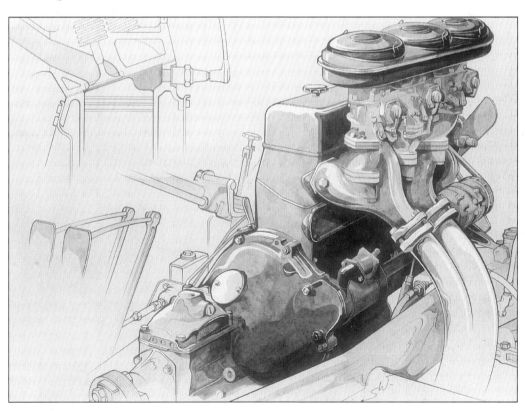

Chapter 7

The Pontons 1953–1960

These round-body 1950s four- and six-cylinder cars formed the first postwar armada of Mercedes-Benz exports and established the company's overseas markets. Today they remain easy to find and to own.

The German word *ponton* translates as "pontoon," describing the rounded shape of these uni-body models. The four-cylinder 180 and 190 were strictly utilitarian four-door sedans (DBAG has never marketed a two-door sedan). The slightly more upscale sixes included the 219 (single-carburetor), 220S (dual-carburetor), and the 220SED (mechanical fuel injection).

The pontons were sensible cars with few unusual variants or options. Plentiful and simple, they are ideal for the beginning collector or restorer, yet they possess character. The earliest models that can be used every day, the 220s are overlooked collector cars.

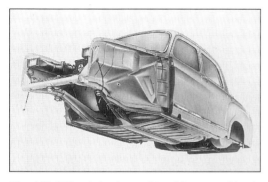

The 180-220 unit-body combined frame and body into one unit. Note the three rubber mounting points for the engine subframe. *DBAG*

180 and 190 1953–1960 ★★

In late 1953, the four-cylinder 180 began the ponton generation. The first low-priced Mercedes-Benz unibody, it went beyond the old-fashioned separate chassis and body, using sheet-metal body panels, resulting in a lighter yet stronger, simpler structure, now without running boards.

The 180's gasoline engine was the same side-valve unit as in the previous 170S, with 52 horsepower, but in 1957 this was swapped for an overhead-cam unit churning out 65 horsepower. The 190 emerged for 1956, boasting an overhead-cam engine with a heady 80 horsepower.

Mercedes-Benz built the workhorse 180 and 190 only as sedans, although they did supply chassis to coachbuilders for conversion to ambulances and station wagons. Economical and reliable, the 180 and 190 are appreciated far more as faithful servants than as collectibles.

Gasoline-fired examples included the 180, 180a, 180b, and 180c, but the 180 was more popular in diesel form as the 180D, 180Db, and 180Dc. The 190 was built in fewer models—the gasoline 190 and 190b and the diesel 190D and 190Db. For more on diesels, see Chapter 18.

The 180's brightest claim to fame is that it set the official world's record for high mileage. In 1979, a 1957 180D owned and driven by Robert O'Reilly of Tacoma, Washington, was found to have reached 1,184,000 miles and thus entered the *Guinness Book of World Records*. The car still exists, although not with Mr. O'Reilly.

Updated with a new engine hood and grille in 1959, the ponton 190 continued into the 1960s, beyond the debut of the fin-back models. Most

Technical Specifications			
Model	190	220S	220SE
Years	1956-1959	1956-1959	1958-1960
Engine			
Type	Inline ohc six (all)		
Engine No. prefix	M121B I	M180 III	M127 I
Displacement	1,897 cc (115.8 ci)	2,195 cc (133.9 ci)	2 195 cc (133.9 ci)
Bore x stroke	85x83.6 mm	80x72.8 mm	80x72.8 mm
Compression ratio	7.5:1	8.7:1	8.7:1
DIN horsepower	75 hp @ 4,600 rpm	106 hp @ 5,200 rpm	115 hp @ 4,800 rpm
Torque	13.9 mkg @ 2,800 rpm	17.5 mkg @ 3,500 rpm	19 mkg @ 3,800 rpm
Fuel system	1 Solex 32 PAITA carburetor	2 Solex carburetors	Bosch mechanical fuel injection
Fuel required	Regular	Premium	Premium
Chassis			
Type	Unibody; steel (all)		
Chassis No. prefix	121	180II	128
Transmission	4-speed manual (all)		
Rear-axle ratio	4.10:1 (all)		
Rear suspension	Swing-axle, coil springs (all)		
Front suspension	Unequal-length A-arms, coil (all)		
Wheels	4.5x13 in.	5x13 in.	6.70x13 in.
Tires	6.40x13 in.	6.70x13 in.	6.70x13 in.
Brakes	Drum, vacuum-assisted (optional)	Drum, vacuum-assisted	Drum, vacuum-assisted
Fuel capacity	14.8 gal	16.9 gal	16.4 gal
Weight	2,734 lb	2,976 lb (sedan)	3,020 lb (sedan)
	3,108 lb (Convertible)	3,241 lb (Convertible	
Performance			
0-60 mph	20.5 sec	17 sec	15 sec
Top speed	86 mph	99 mph	99 mph
Fuel consumption	20–22 mpg	17–20 mpg	18–20 mpg

Note: The 220S specifications cover cars built after August 1957; earlier cars had slightly less power.

180s and 190s are now extremely well worn. Few remain in daily use, and even fewer have been restored, but this is likely to change.

220a, 1954–1956 ★★

Using a single Solex 32 PAIA carburetor on its M180 inline overhead-cam six, and usually upholstered in cloth rather than leather, the 220a was spartan; although few exist today, they are less than prized. With 85 horsepower DIN (about 100 SAE), this model appeared only as a sedan, not a Cabriolet or Coupe, mainly for the German market. But for the lack of chrome trim along the front fender crease and door, it looks much like the later, more popular 220S.

219, 1956–1959 ★★

The 219, another economy sedan, used the 220, a single-carburetor engine in the 180/190 body, its engine bay having been lengthened to accommodate the six instead of a four. This low-priced 85 horsepower alternative to the 220S has a shorter wheelbase than that car, hence less rear legroom. Instruments are similar to those of the 180/190 (a round speedometer, for instance). The dash is capped with a token strip of wood, but the window surrounds and other interior trim are dull bakelite. You'll find no leather upholstery here, either. Given a choice, the more powerful, roomier, and luxurious 220S and 220SE are better all-around cars for the driver—and more interesting for the collector. (The author enjoyed his 219 but likes his 220SE even more.)

220S and 220SE Sedan, Coupe, and Convertible 1956–1960 ★★★

Body styles for the better-known 220S and 220SE included an elegant sedan plus the more exclusive Convertible and the Coupe. Options included fitted luggage, two-tone paint, a front bench seat instead of two large buckets, reclining seats, whitewall tires, and more. Convertibles

Production Years	Model	Production
1956-1959	219 sedan	27,845
1956-1959	220S sedan	55,000+
1956-1959	220S Convertible	2,178
1956-1959	220S Coupe	1,251
1959	220SE sedan	1,974
1959-1960	220SE Convertible	1,112
1959-1960	220SE Coupe	830

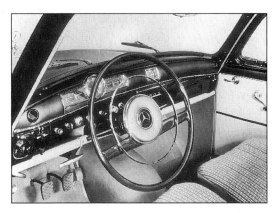

The 1959 update to the 180 introduced this padded steering wheel hub, widely used in other models into the 1970s. Gearshift lever is on the column. *DBAG*

could have either a fold-down rear jump seat or an optional bench seat. Sedans occasionally can be found with a huge, folding fabric sunroof, and a few Coupes had a metal sunroof.

By now radios were common, usually Becker and Blaupunkt. Most were multiband (AM, FM, and short wave) with some optional signal-seeking models. If the radio doesn't work, don't fret; these vacuum-tube units can still be repaired.

These were among the last Mercedes-Benz cars offering only a manual transmission, a four-speed with the lever on the steering column. The Hydrak option included a vacuum-operated clutch, electrically activated whenever the shift lever was touched. A fluid coupling allowed stopping and idling without disengaging the clutch. Available after August 1957, Hydrak found little favor, and conversions to a normal clutch were common. Factory air conditioning was unavailable, but a few cars had it as a dealer-installed option.

Most collectible are the Convertible and Coupe. Both were made in smaller numbers than the sedan, with more amenities. Built on a 4.7-inch shorter wheelbase than the sedan, the Convertible and Coupe looked similar to it at the front. At the rear, an extended trunk lid and near-finned rear fenders with larger taillights set off these two models. Inside, the two-door cars had much more elaborate woodwork and leather, plus chrome-plated covers on the doorjambs.

The 2,195-cc, single-overhead-cam M180 III six of the 220S used two Solex 32 PAJTA carburetors and 8.7:1 compression to raise 106 horsepower DIN (124 horsepower SAE). Thanks to two-plunger Bosch mechanical fuel injection, the 1958-on 220SE made 115 horsepower DIN (134 horsepower SAE). These durable engines usually make 100,000 miles before blue smoke signals worn valve guides. Water pumps and engine mounts often need replacement. A clever device on the distributor permits easy timing adjustment to accommodate poor fuel, and the mechanical

fuel pump's lever allows hand pumping. Fuel-injected cars have an additional electric pump near the tank. Their characteristic cylindrical cast-alloy air intake plenum and long intake pipes are unmistakable. Compression of most cars (1958 and 1959 models) is 8.7:1, so they benefit from premium fuel.

The original 6.70x13 inch tires (on 5x13 inch wheels) are uncommon, but antique tire dealers handle equivalent sizes. Hubcaps are full wheel covers, and the star's background should be painted in body color. Brakes are vacuum-assisted drums with cast-in cooling fins. The 12-volt electrical system powers bulb and reflector headlights on European cars; U.S. versions got sealed beams. European cars used orange lenses in the fender-top turn signal lights; U.S. cars used clear ones. Since clear lenses were unavailable for years, orange ones were fitted to many U.S. cars. Home market cars had red reflectors in their rear bumper guards; U.S. cars got small body-mounted reflectors, too.

Performance wasn't the forte of these 3,000–3,200-pound cars, but they can hold their own with contemporaries. Top speeds of the 220S and 220SE were around 100 miles per hour.

The fuel-injected 220SE sedan, Coupe, and Convertible began as 1959 models. The 220SE sedan was built only for that year, but the Coupe and the Convertible rolled on into late 1960 because the new fin-back cars offered no such variations. The Coupe and Convertible are four-

This four-cylinder 180 is a 1959 model, with wider grille than earlier cars. *DBAG*

seater cars; small rear seats fold to accommodate custom factory luggage.

What to Look For

Mechanically, the 1956–1960 220S and 220SE are predictable. All eventually need water pumps and engine mounts. As the result of improper repair or broken hangers, their exhaust systems often hang low. Door locks are frequently worn, and windshield wipers may be sluggish.

Body-wise, it's rust again. Look at the inner fender panels in the engine compartment near the headlights. Check beneath the battery (acid eats this panel and can eventually drip into the passenger-side footwell). Open the rear doors and look for rust in the rounded panel in front of the rear wheel. Check the trunk floor, the spare wheelwells, and the front passenger compartment floor. If the car has a sunroof, its floor is more likely to be rusty. Make sure that the longitudinal arms from the rear suspension are securely attached to the body at their forward end; these mounts are vulnerable to rust.

Good bumpers (and bumper guards) are rare; bent ones can be restored, but rusty ones are tough to rescue. The chrome-plated grille surround is expensive to restore or replace. Trim strips along the rocker panel are hard to find in good shape. Convertibles with two-tone paint used a short, curved piece of chrome-plated trim behind and below the headlight that's extremely tough to find, and their lower body trim is likewise expensive to repair. The sedan's optional cloth sunroof has an intricate mechanism, so try it. Driving lights are expensive to replace. Because the hubcaps protrude beyond the tires, they have often been "curbed"; replacements should be painted.

The two-piece steering column is linked by a flexible fiber joint exposed to heat and oil in the engine compartment. As this joint ages, it can gradually separate. If you notice excessive steering play, the joint may be failing. Stop immediately and check it. The white steering wheel is a desirable option. Can't find the turn-signal lever? Turn the horn ring!

These cars' drum brakes use friction discs in the automatic adjusters to position the brake shoes. If the brakes require pumping, or if they pull to one side, the shoes may be retracting too far as a result of these discs being broken, incorrectly installed, or having been greased rather than left dry.

The 219 melded the front body and engine of the 220 with the rear body of the 180/190, creating the lowest-priced six-cylinder car. *DBAG*

The 220S/SE sedan was dressed with chrome trim; this rare fuel-injected 1959 220SE is identical in appearance to the carbureted 220S. *FDB*

The 220S/SE Convertible (Cabriolet to Europeans) seats four in a more luxurious interior than the sedan; rear fenders and taillights are similar to those of the upscale 300d. *FDB*

Brakes—drums on all these models—may pull to one side due to fluid or grease on the shoes or because of clogging of internally deteriorated rubber brake lines. If brake pedal pressure is unusually high, the vacuum booster may need to be rebuilt. See Chapter 2 for a method of testing the booster.

The optional Hydrak automatic clutch depends on a mixture of vacuum and electrical components to function; the potential for wear and other problems is high. Hydrak can be repaired or replaced by a standard clutch.

The six-cylinder 220 engines run about 100,000 miles before needing attention beyond normal maintenance. Trouble usually begins in the cylinder head, with valve guide wear evidenced by smoking. If the coolant has not been

Top down, the 220S/SE Convertible epitomizes growing German prosperity of the 1950s. *DBAG*

The steel top of the 220S/SE Coupe was fixed, not removable; few were fitted with a sunroof. Chrome lower fender trim is similar to that of the Convertible. *DBAG*

The 220S/SE Convertible interior is all leather, wool, wood, and chrome; veneered wood requires skill to restore properly. Sedans had a much simpler dash and rubber floor mats. *FDB*

The 220SE engine is instantly recognizable by the huge intake manifold used with its mechanical fuel injection; power output was 130 horsepower DIN. Note the heater duct and windshield washer bag (left foreground). Notice the two different types of clamps on cooling hoses in the foreground of this original factory photograph. *DBAG*

changed regularly, the aluminum head can corrode internally, transforming it into expensive junk.

Check the condition of the heat exchanger ducts on each side of the engine compartment. These gather fresh air at the front and run it through a heat exchanger to warm it. The ducts were pressed cardboard, so they deteriorate. Fiberglass replacements don't look shabby enough to be original. Dash levers control coolant valves atop each heat exchanger. These tend to corrode and jam. The valves can be freed, but a stuck cable is more difficult to replace.

Look for a patched-together exhaust system, and check it carefully for leaks.

Restoration

The ponton-bodied 220S and SE models are among the simplest to restore with few difficulties if the body is sound. Sedans form a good source of used parts for the rarer Coupes and Convertibles.

Most mechanical parts remain available from Mercedes-Benz dealers and specialists, but external trim is another story.

The entire engine and front subframe can be wheeled out as a unit, making front suspension and engine compartment restoration easier. Replace the subframe mounts when you do this.

Proper tires can be hard to find, but later 14-inch steel (or even alloy) wheels fit. Taillights are easy to find for sedans. Replacements for the clear fender-top lenses were not made for years but are now being reproduced.

The 220 ponton sedans are fine, enjoyable cars, but they may be worth less than the cost of a thorough restoration. Rejuvenating a Coupe or Convertible is easier to justify economically but will cost much more because you're expected to restore it to show standards. Based on our own experience, we recommend the 220 sedans to anyone who wants an economical car with character to drive and enjoy.

Summary

The 180 and 190 pontons are charming but will never be sought after, especially as diesels. Many dismiss the 1950s 220 sedans, but these are more elegant and more usable cars. We've enjoyed a 220SE for thousands of miles with few problems. These are some of the simplest, most durable, and economical collector cars for the beginning or low-budget enthusiast.

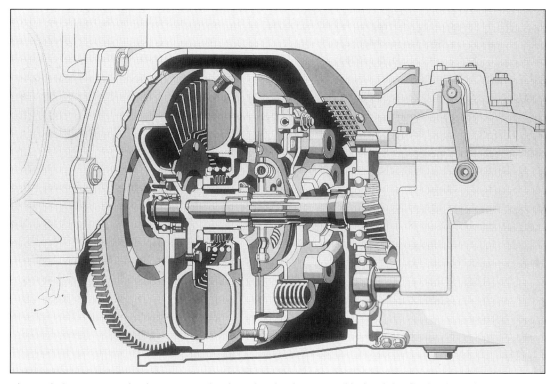

The Hydrak automatic clutch uses a single-plate dry clutch mounted behind the flywheel and hydraulic coupler. The clutch releases and engages when the driver touches and releases the gearshift lever. This was as close as the 220S/SE got to an automatic transmission.

Driving Impressions: 219, 220S, 220SE

The 180 and 190 sedans are decent drivers, but the 220S and 220SE are best for more extensive driving. The most usable is the fuel-injected 220SE, although vapor lock can be a snag. Fuel injection makes the 220SE more flexible and smoother to drive, with good torque over a wide rpm range.

Looking out through the shallow windshield, you see the clearly old-fashioned shape of the hood and front fenders. Most people will guess that this is a car of the 1940s rather than the 1950s.

Controls on the dash are unlabeled; read the owners manual. Some models used the horn ring to activate the turn signals. If the fuel and ignition systems are in good shape, poor starting and rough idling can indicate a burned valve, not uncommon.

The 220 models (and the 219) had their shifter on the steering column. The shift pattern is the usual H, with reverse outside it, up and toward you. The shifter isn't as precise as a floorshift, but compared to clunky automatics in other models, the manual transmission and clutch allow smooth shifts up and down. Be alert for vibrations; the two-piece driveshaft's center bearing can wear.

The front end must be in top shape for precise steering. Under the hood, on the left side, check the fabric joint between the upper and lower steering column; it can rot with age.

The drum brakes are effective and reasonably fade-resistant but lack the bite of good discs. The front end dives under braking. Don't follow too closely; grilles and front bumpers are expensive. These cars handle well on dry roads, and a 220S or SE can keep pace with today's traffic on interstate highways or back roads. For years, a 1959 220SE sedan was our daily driver.

The rear swing-axle has no load-compensating spring, so if you overload the car, the rear sags, and the wheels take on heavy negative camber. Ride should be quiet and smooth, without rattles, thumps, or squeaks. Interior comfort is good. Many of these cars lack seatbelts, but that's easily rectified. Heating, cooling, and ventilation are primitive by today's standards.

Chapter 8

300SL 1954–1963

After World War II the 300SL announced to the performance world that Daimler-Benz was back and a force to be reckoned with. Using expensive materials in a hand-assembled, low-volume, complicated car probably never made DBAG a pfennig, but the money could not have been invested in any more impressive or enduring form of publicity.

Early Competition Versions ★★★★★

The first 300SLs were race versions built in 1952, a year after the first 300 sedan on which the drivetrain was loosely based. The factory raced 10 or 11 "W194" cars then; records are unclear. The coupes' doors opened only into the roof (later into the lower body), and some were open cars. Several were raced with different bodies, and at least two were later rebodied as semi-production cars. The originals had Rudge knock-off wheels and smooth, rounded bodywork, free of wind-catching details.

Innovations included a light but stiff multi-tube space frame and a 3-liter engine based on the single-overhead-cam unit of the 300 sedan but tuned for 171 horsepower DIN instead of 115. Using a dry-sump oiling system, the engine was canted leftward to reduce frontal area and fitted with three Solex downdraft carburetors. Wind-tunnel tests helped aerodynamics, and various induction systems were tried, including Weber carburetors and even, briefly, a supercharger.

This production 300SL has the sought-after Rudge knock-off wheel hubs. Wheels are painted body color. *DBAG*

Only the driver's side of the 300SL has "Mercedes-Benz" trim. Compare side vent trim, headlights, and other features with those of the 300SL Roadster. *DBAG*

The 300SL with its famous "Gullwing" doors raised. Only left-hand drive 300SLs were built.

Early 300SL had plaid wool cloth seats. Fitted luggage is an attractive option resulting from lack of trunk space in the Coupe. *Paul Russell*

A 300SL leather interior. *Alex Dearborn*

The 300SL proved fast and reliable. Its successes, including Carrera Panamericana and Le Mans wins, are legendary. Several racing cars were later fitted with production bodies and sold to the public; no W194 cars are known to exist in private hands with all-original bodywork, but at least two are unaccounted for.

Production 300SL 1954–1957 ★★★★

The production 300SL Coupe introduced in 1954 was a street version of the W194 300SL racing cars. DBAG at first hesitated to build it, but in response to demand sensed by U.S. importer Max Hoffman and others, the 300SL premiered at the International Motor Sports Show in New York in 1954. Fittingly, about three-quarters of all new 300SLs were sold in the United States.

This was one production car that made more power than its racing predecessor. With the newly developed Bosch direct-port mechanical fuel injection, the W198 engine gave 215 horsepower DIN at 5,700 rpm and 213 lb-ft of torque at 4,500 rpm. The electrical system was 12-volt, with its generator cleverly linked to drive the water pump, too.

Production bodies had eyebrows over the wheel openings, and larger doors eased entry and exit. Because the doors opened upward, the coupe was soon nicknamed the Gullwing. The factory called it neither a coupe nor a Gullwing, just "300SL," but the nickname stuck. The main body was steel, with the large rocker panels, hood, trunk, and doors being aluminum. Exceptions were the 29 all-aluminum-bodies cars produced in 1955 and 1956, about 175 pounds lighter than the steel-bodied coupes.

The first production coupes, built in early 1954, had a few features different from later cars. Their long, bent shift levers entered the floor ahead of the dashboard; later cars moved the lever back on the tunnel. Early cars also used Treadle-Vac brake boosters instead of the later ATE T-50 unit and had fender welting between eyebrows and fenders. Instead of the later Mercedes-Benz box, ZF steering went on the first 151 cars.

The 300SL was the first production car to use gasoline fuel injection, with a six-plunger mechanical pump forcing gasoline directly into its cylinders. Unusual even now, the dry-sump oil system used pumps to scavenge oil from the crankcase, run it through a cooler, dump it into a tank, then pump it back into the engine. This ensured an oil supply uninterrupted by cornering forces.

The engine's 50-degree tilt was necessary to fit the inline unit under the low hood. The block/head joint is angled to level it, so the combustion chamber extends beyond the head into round pockets in the block. Although the engine is related to that of the contemporary 300 models, it is not even close to being interchangeable.

300SL Production and Chassis Prefix Numbers

Years	Model	Production	Chassis Prefix
1952-1953	300SL (racing)	10–11	194010
1954-1957	300SL (production coupe)	1,374	198040
1955-1956	300SL (aluminum coupe)	29	198043
1957-1964	300SL Roadster	1,858	198042

Chassis type: 198
Engine type: 198
Typical chassis numbers: 1980404500057 (coupe); 1980427500694 (early Roadster); 19804210003168 (late Roadster)

Technical Specifications

Model	300SL	300SL Roadster
Years	1953–57	1957–63
Engine		
Type	Inline ohc six (all)	
Engine No. prefix	M198 (all)	
Displacement	2,996 cc (all)	
Bore x stroke	85x88 mm (all)	
Compression ratio	8.55:1 (all)	
DIN horsepower	215 hp @ 5,800 rpm	235 hp (approx.)
Torque	28 mkg @ 4,600 rpm (all)	
Fuel system	Bosch six-plunger mechanical fuel injection (all)	
Fuel required	Premium (all)	
Coolant capacity	27 qt	21 qt
Chassis		
Type	Multi-tubular; steel body, aluminum doors, engine lid, trunk lid, rocker panels	
Chassis No. prefix	W198 I	W198 II
Transmission	4-speed manual (all)	
Rear-axle ratio	3.64:1 (options: 3.25, 3.42, 3.89, 4.11:1) (all)	
Rear suspension	Swing-axle, coil springs	Low-pivot swing-axle, coil springs
Front suspension	A-arms, coil springs (all)	
Wheels	5x15 in.	5.5x15 in.
Tires	6.50x15 in.	6.70x15 in.
Brakes	Alfin drum	Alfin drum Dunlop disc (March 1961)
Fuel capacity	34.3 gal	26.4 gal
Weight	2,888 lb	3,130 lb; 3,219 lb w/hardtop
Performance		
0-60 mph	8–9 sec (all)	
Top speed	146–161 mph	137–155 mph
Fuel consumption	15–20 mpg hwy (all)	

To fit beneath the low hood and lower the 300SL's center of gravity, the engine was tilted 50 degrees to the left. *Alex Dearborn*

A four-speed, fully synchronized transmission feeds power through a ZF limited-slip differential; rear-axle ratios were 4.11:1, 3.89:1 (standard on U.S. cars), 3.64:1 (standard on European cars), 3.42:1, and 3.25:1. Depending on gearing, a 300SL can reach 60 miles per hour in about 8 seconds and go on to 150 miles per hour or more. Much of the coil-spring suspension was adapted from the sedan. Brakes were specially developed finned drums with linings over 3.5 inches wide; the ATE T-50 vacuum booster is similar to that of the sedans. At 2,849 pounds, the 300SL Coupe's power-to-weight ratio is almost the same as that of the heavier but more powerful 1994 600SL (11.85 pounds/horsepower vs. 11.45 pounds/horsepower).

This 300SL Roadster has European headlights. From the Coupe, the gas filler was moved from inside the trunk to the left rear fender; windows now roll up; taillights are larger. Jack hole in rocker panel had no cover. *DBAG*

The optional removable hardtop made the 300SL Roadster into an all-weather car. *DBAG*

Gullwing Spotter's Guide

Chassis numbers are on a plate riveted to the driver's side firewall and, consistent with Mercedes-Benz practice, on the left front frame rail below the engine. Below the plate on the firewall is a smaller plate with the paint color code, a two- or three-digit number ending in "G" or "H." Standard colors were: 040, black; 050, white; 158, white gray; 166, blue gray; 180, silver gray; 190, graphite gray; 334, light blue; 534, fire engine red; 543, strawberry metallic; and 608, ivory.

Interiors were available in MB-tex combined with plaid wool. The plaid fabric was blue (as in the factory racing cars), red, or green. This plaid appeared only on the seat facings, presumably for better grip while cornering and for better breathing. Full leather was optional, available in red, tan, beige, dark blue, gray-blue, light gray, black, green, or white. These colors were from the Mercedes-Benz family palette, but the hides were heavier than those in the sedans and quite smooth in texture.

The 300SL Roadster's U.S. headlights, shown here, differed from the glass-covered European units. *Dennis Adler*

Other coupe options included fitted luggage (replicas are available), bumper guards, chrome wheels, windshield washers, Rudge knock-off wheels and hubs, the rear-axle ratio, a sport cam, stiffer springs and shock absorbers, a Becker Mexico radio, a Becker short-wave adapter, a cold weather radiator blind, and a spare parts travel kit. Not all were available in any one year, and some cars were built with custom touches for special customers, mostly involving exterior color and interior trim.

Headliners, gray or beige fuzzy cotton, extend down to the windowsills. A chrome luggage rail runs around the area behind the seats, where the luggage fit (the trunk was filled by the 34-gallon fuel tank and a spare tire). In this luggage area was an access door for the battery. Floors got square-weave carpeting on the tunnel and trunk floor. The two footwells had ribbed rubber mats.

The outside door handles are unique; push in at the back, and a flush-mounted lever appears out of the slot. The lightweight doors are supported by spring cylinders. Originality buffs look for a concave star in the center of the grille instead of the later flat star. The concave original was phased out as a spare part; many restored cars have a flat one, which looks fine, so the difference is only for cocktail party discussions or a tie-breaker at concours events.

Bumper guards were standard, but many have been removed for a cleaner look. Certain European-delivery cars likely had no guards. The jacking hole in each rocker panel never had a plug.

The 300SL's wheels were light-alloy 5x15-inch rims with either Rudge knock-off centers or bolt-on steel wheels. Rudge wheels, which add value, had either painted or chromed centers; with the latter, the rims were polished aluminum. Bolt-on wheels had painted hubcaps and either painted or polished rims. Rudge wheels were unavailable with disc brakes. Putting knock-off wheels on a car that originally had bolt-on wheels is not simple, requiring changing front hubs and rear axles, but Rudge wheels were often retrofitted.

Alloy-Bodied Cars ★★★★★

The 29 aluminum-bodied coupes had Rudge wheels, plaid seat covers, plexiglass windows, and

Roadster interior and dash were developed from the Coupe. The radio mounts below the dash. *Dennis Adler*

"NSL" engines. They were said to have been made as customer racers to help amateurs win production-car races and rallies.

The NSL engines were simply the best-running of a batch. They were dynamometer-tested, then fitted with a sport cam, worth perhaps 20 horsepower. The letters "NSL" appear on a small boss near the cam cover on engines so equipped. Since the standard engine can be blueprinted at rebuild time, then fitted with the Roadster cam, the same as the sport cam, there is little value in an NSL engine.

Production 300SLs did well in competition, mostly on an amateur basis, but by the late 1950s they were outmoded by lighter, more purpose-built race cars. Production stopped in 1957 with about 1,400 made, and the Roadster took over.

300SL Roadster 1957–1964 ★★★★

The 300SL Roadster that replaced the 300SL (coupe) in 1957 was more refined, less of a racer. Doors opened conventionally, so access was easier, and since the side windows rolled down instead of popping out, ventilation improved.

Despite its snug-fitting soft top and roll-up windows, this car was known as the 300SL Roadster. First it was sold with only a convertible top, but for 1958 and beyond, it was available with either a soft top, a hardtop, or both. The hardtop didn't fit over the soft top, so either the soft top's metal boot or the hardtop had to be left at home. Check that these parts are included with the car. Among the few other Roadster options were fitted luggage and a white or black steering wheel.

The Roadster's multi-tube space frame was similar to that of the coupe but with lower doorsills. Its engine was basically that of the coupe but with the sport cam. Wheelbase was the same, but rear overhang was longer; fuel capacity was reduced to 22 gallons, creating more trunk space. The fuel filler moved from inside the trunk to the left rear fender, and the Roadster's side trim was a bit more elaborate.

One could see which rear-axle ratio was fitted by looking down into the lower edge of the Roadster speedometer for the numbers. A 3.64:1 ratio was standard on U.S. models.

The Roadster's low-pivot rear swing-axle reduced jacking and camber change, and therefore, oversteer.

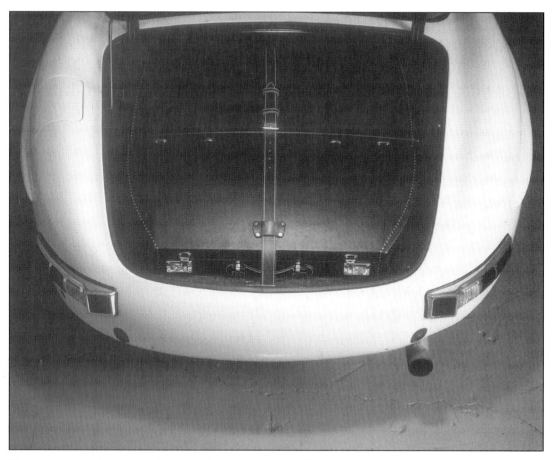

The Roadster trunk accommodates two fitted suitcases. *Paul Russell*

A horizontal compensating spring softened the ride, too. The transmission whine and the ratchety limited-slip differential action familiar in the coupe were gone. Weight was up, offsetting the power improvement.

The Roadster offered further subtle improvements over the coupe. Taillights, for instance, are larger, for better visibility. Headlight units incorporate turn signals and parking lights in one-piece housings. European Roadsters used a sleek glass headlight cover, but U.S. cars simply had chrome trim around both lights. The revised instrument panel uses a vertical combination gauge instead of the coupe's round dials.

Rudge knock-off wheels were optional on 1957–1958 Roadsters. The Alfin drum brakes were improved for 1960, then replaced in March 1961 by four-wheel Dunlop-licensed discs, although the drums were always more than adequate for stopping the car.

For 1962, DBAG phased in aluminum engine blocks, which looked identical to the iron blocks and had the same specifications. The aluminum engine is identified by an engine number beginning with 198982. These engines were deemed "unrebuildable at the dealership level" by the factory, and factory bulletins suggested that worn engines be traded for new ones at dealerships.

This exchange system authorized new aluminum blocks to be re-marked with the original engine's number, although this wasn't always done. To further confound numbers fanatics, a customer could trade his worn iron-block coupe or Roadster engine at a dealership. Since 300SLs chassis and engine numbers never matched, such an exchange is no deterrent to buying a car with any proper 300SL engine. A dealer's invoice for replacement gives a replacement engine the same value as an original.

The 300SL requires no unusual preparation to become a good vintage racer, and can easily be driven to and from the track. *FDB*

Although official production ceased in 1963, the final 300SLs were three Roadsters built in 1964. By then the 300SL was twice the price of the Jaguar E-Type, yet slower. The unibody sports car was about to appear. With 1,858 300SL Roadsters built, production ended, and the 230SL took over as the sporting Mercedes-Benz.

What to Look For

Look for the usual rust and bondo, especially in the headlight and grille area. The aluminum rocker panels unbolt and are still available, so if they are hopelessly full of filler or dents, they can be replaced. There is no exposed frame for a floor jack, so insert the factory jack through the rocker panel into the jacking hole. The coupe's removable, louvered, aluminum belly pans were often misplaced during mechanical work, but reproductions are available. Rust occurs in the headlight buckets, the sheet metal behind the rear wheels, and the rear roof posts of the coupe.

The frame is unlikely to rust, but any corrosion will be hard to repair, requiring a proper frame jig. Coupe doors were built and fitted with quality. In spite of hinges in the roof, they should open and close precisely and fit snugly all around. Look for cracked paint in the roof around the hinges as a sign of prior damage.

Under the hood, check oil quality by smelling for gasoline. Oil diluted by gasoline won't lubricate well. The fuel injection system may leak gas into the oil, and the oil seldom gets hot enough to evaporate it. The oil tank is in the engine bay, behind the left wheel. The cap has the dipstick

Easily the most recognized Mercedes-Benz collector car, the 300SL is supported by an active international owners group that even helps to supply rare parts. *FDB*

attached. Its bottom line indicates the 12-quart level; the top mark is for 18. If the oil cooler is connected, this large quantity never gets hot, so savvy owners bypass the cooler for normal driving. Oil pressure should be 65–75 psi at speed and at least 20 psi at warm idle.

Although some have been polished, the intake manifold was originally a bare metal casting, and the valve cover was painted black.

The engine should run smoothly and strongly. Set up by a knowledgeable mechanic, these cars need minimum tuning. Only three reasons exist for poor running: (1) the car was tuned by someone unfamiliar with the specs; (2) the gasoline has gone stale and/or the fuel system is clogged; or (3) it's just plain worn out. The fuel injection system can deteriorate if the car has not been driven regularly. A separate, driver-controlled electric fuel pump helps to overcome vapor lock.

Restoration

Although you might think that by now few 300SLs exist in seedy enough condition to need restoration, forgotten examples continue to surface. Restoration standards rise, too, boosting cost. Excellent professional restorers of the 300SL can

be counted on the fingers of two hands, so at least you have some choice. To reduce costs, mechanically inclined owners use the pros for high-skill jobs (bodywork, paint, interiors, engine overhauls) and do the disassembly and reassembly themselves.

Few parts are truly difficult to obtain. Most mechanical parts remain available from factory and aftermarket sources. Mercedes-Benz kept many parts in production and is reviving others in a vintage parts program. The Gull Wing Group has contracted for the manufacture of some crucial parts, and their technical literature is useful.

Summary

The 300SL is the most popular Mercedes-Benz collector car and will remain so. Professionals with the skills to restore and maintain the cars make ownership relatively easy, even for those not mechanically inclined. The big hurdle is the initial purchase, but handle that successfully, and you'll never look back.

No trailer queen, a 300SL can be a dependable, appealing driver, a car that you can enjoy using, even hard. The car's few quirks give it character. The 300SL will forever be seen as one of the finest products of Daimler-Benz.

Chapter 9

190SL 1955–1963

The 300SL tempted only those able to afford it. The 190SL was a lower-priced sports car with broader allure. In styling, the 190SL emulated the 300SL, but otherwise it was a shadow of its senior. Unlike the tube-frame 300SL Coupe and Roadster, the unit-body 190SL was solely a Roadster (more on that later). Its simpler, less energetic engine was DBAG's first overhead-cam four, similar to engines in the 180 and 190 sedans.

Origins

A prototype 190SL with "racing" accessories made its U.S. debut alongside the 300SL at the New York Auto Show in February 1954, but the assembly line didn't roll until May 1955. The 190SL set the stage for future SL models, particularly in America, proving to DBAG that its future sports cars would be more successful if they were designed for the boulevard rather than for the racetrack. A total of 25,881 were built until February 1963, when the all-new, six-cylinder 230SLs took over.

In comparison to its peers, the 190SL was a sophisticated sports car. Its top didn't leak, it was comfortable, quiet, dependable, warm in the winter, and everything worked all of the time. The 190SL could be serviced painlessly, and parts arrived with dispatch.

Some consider the 190SL fairly dull. It enjoyed only a minuscule competition career—it was heavy and lacked tuning potential. The 1.9-liter, four-

The removable 190SL hardtop's rounded shape, reminiscent of earlier Mercedes-Benz coupes, is well integrated with the rest of the car. Chrome trim on fender strakes and rocker panel indicates that this is a 1956 or later car. *DBAG*

Soft top folded, this 190SL clearly shows the vertical seams in the rocker panel. European headlights are non-sealed-beam. Unusually, this car's hubcaps are unpainted; perhaps the DBAG press office was in a hurry to shoot this picture. *DBAG*

Early 190SL lacks chrome trim on fenders and rocker panel but has small-window hardtop, sedan-style hubcaps, and an unusual ski rack. *DBAG*

The four-cylinder 190SL engine is almost surrounded by an elaborate induction system; vacuum brake booster is at right. *FDB*

This 1957 190SL has U.S. headlights and bumper guards. *FDB*

Prototype 190SL was first shown with cut-down doors, hood scoop, racing windshield, and other sporting features. *DBAG*

cylinder engine has only three main bearings, so souping it up was risky. Judson sold a supercharger for the 190SL, but most who installed them found cause to regret it. The only factory competition venture with the 190SL used a diesel engine, to set a standing-start, 1-kilometer record of 61.3 miles per hour.

No 190SL history would be complete without the obligatory reference to one John Moore and his 190SL, winners of the Islander Race at the 1957 Nassau Speed Weeks. They beat a Jaguar, an Austin-Healey, and a Triumph TR-2, no less. Fame may be fleeting, but John lives on in the hearts of 190SL devotees.

The first unit-body SL from Mercedes-Benz, the 190SL used a steel chassis with aluminum doors, trunk lid, engine hood, dash, and a few other parts. It still weighed nearly 2,600 pounds, light today but leaden for a 1950s sports car. A Porsche Speedster weighed nearly 800 pounds less.

A subframe holds the front suspension and engine, and the entire assembly can be unbolted and rolled out from under the car, but few actually do so. The subframe mounts, similar to engine mounts, must be in good condition. At the rear is a swing-axle, with coil springs fitted all around. The aluminum brake drums were cast with fins for cooling, and an ATE T-50 vacuum brake booster was fitted to all but a few early cars.

Nit-pickers will tell you that the 190SL was sold as a Roadster (with soft top only, chassis number 121.042 . . .) or a Coupe (with hardtop only, chassis number 121.040 . . .), but rarely are they described and sold with the optional hardtop. Coupes are basically the same, with minor differences relating to the tops. Most people call the car a 190SL and leave it at that.

190SL ★★★

The 190SL experienced myriad running changes throughout its life. The most, over 100, occurred for the 1956 model year, at or near chassis number 01115. After that, chrome-plated trim was added on the fender moldings above the wheelwells, on the rocker panels, and as stone guards in front of each rear wheel, along with a glovebox door lock.

Hardtops came in two types. Early ones had a small rear window, late ones a much larger one, changing in September 1959 at chassis number 121.040.95.015061. For better visibility, most prefer the late version, which fits any 190SL. Most U.S.-delivered cars had front bumper guards. Chrome-plated headlight rims should carry an engraved Bosch or Hella logo. The red rear reflectors, moved from below the bumper upward to the body for 1958 and later cars sold in the United States, are often missing.

Most 190SLs were powered by engine type 121.921, but in mid-1961 an improved 121.928 version appeared. Besides its 1-millimeter larger diameter wrist pin, an 8.7:1 compression ratio, and a slightly different timing chain, the later engine changed camshaft lubrication from internal to external and had a slightly different valve adjustment arrangement. A variety of Bosch distributors used one-piece points until mid-1962, two-piece later. Early engines used knurled knobs to fasten the valve cover; late ones used hex-head bolts. To compensate for varying fuel quality, ignition timing was adjustable via a knurled knob on the distributor base; early cars had a cable leading to a knob on the dash. A three-point engine mounting system was used until 1956, when it was replaced with a four-point system.

Early seats were similar to the 300SL buckets, but in 1956 a wider, more padded style was installed, with pivoting brackets for package area access. Upholstery was usually vinyl (MB-tex), with leather and a transverse rear jump seat optional. Other options included skid plates, right-side sun visor, fog lights, heavy-duty springs, and a wind-up clock in the glovebox door (late 1956 onward). Also offered were an automatic antenna, a short-wave adapter, various horns,

undercoating, radiator shutters, and heavy-duty cooling and suspension systems for "tropical" use.

Until mid-1957, a rotating horn ring operated the turn signals. During 1958 production, a steering lock was first fitted. Original radios included Becker, Telefunken, and Grundig. Some post-1958 Becker Mexicos, the grandest, had a signal-seeking feature. Technically, dealer-installed air conditioning was an option, but we've never seen it.

One of the rarest options is the fitted luggage by Karl Baisch or Hepco (replica pieces are available). Three pieces fit the trunk, while two more rest behind the seats. Most of these suitcases had a vinyl fabric covering, but matching leather is not unknown. Even rarer would be a set of cut-down doors and a low windshield, factory-modified for racing. In 30 years, we've never seen these in original form, so maybe they exist only in the imagination of a few.

Floors were covered by rubber mats, with carpets in the rear. The first trunk handle combined a finger lift and the lock, but after chassis number 018346, handle and lock were separate. In 1956, the small taillight lenses were replaced by larger ones similar to those on the sedans. In 1957, the license plate lights moved from the body to the bumper guards. During 1958, the front parking lights switched to a three-prong, twist-in lens. If only one back-up light works, don't fret. That's how it was designed.

A floorshift controls the four-speed manual transmission; shift knobs were threaded on until sometime in 1958, when DBAG switched to a push-on type. Various windshield washing systems were fitted—hand pump, foot pump, and a few electric pumps—with various styles of washer bags. For 1957 production, the nozzle was moved from the cowl to the hood.

The 190SL's bias-ply tires were small, 6.40x13 on 5-inch wheels; whitewalls were optional. Hubcap centers were painted body color and set off by a larger, separate trim ring. Early cars had a 3.70:1 rear axle; to aid acceleration, later ones used 3.90:1, and 4.10:1 was an option. With a redline of 6,000 rpm, top speed was about 105 miles per hour, and 0–60 miles per hour took about 13 seconds.

What to Look For

Rust.

Starting at the front, look carefully at the grille and front bumper. How do they fit against

Technical Specifications

Model	**190SL**
Years	1955–1963
Engine	
Type	Inline ohc four; three main bearings
Engine No. prefix	M121BII
Displacement	1897 cc
Bore x stroke	85x83.6 mm
Compression ratio	8.5:1 after September 1959 (engine No.65.03804) 8.8:1; 8.7:1 with 121.928 engine (summer 1961 and later)
DIN horsepower	105 hp @ 5,700 rpm (120 hp SAE)
Torque	14.5 mkg @ 3,200 rpm (105 lb-ft)
Fuel system	Dual Solex 44 PHH carburetors
Fuel required	Premium
Coolant capacity	10.5 qt
Chassis	
Type	Steel unibody, aluminum doors, engine lid, trunk lid
Chassis No. prefix	W121
Transmission	4-speed manual
Rear-axle ratio	3.90:1 (3.70:1 early, 4.10:1 option)
Rear suspension	Low-pivot swing-axle, coil springs
Front suspension	A-arms, coil springs
Wheels	5x13 in.
Tires	6.40x13 in.
Brakes	Alfin drum, vacuum booster
Fuel capacity	17 gal
Weight	2,557 lb, plus 44 lb hardtop
Performance	
0–60 mph	13–14 sec
Top speed	106 mph
Fuel consumption	19–25 mpg
ID Numbers	
Chassis type: 121	
Engine type: 121	

Typical chassis numbers: Roadster (soft top only) 121.042; Coupe (hardtop only) 121.040

Production

Years	Model	Production
1955-1963	190SL	25,881

the surrounding sheet metal? Front sheet-metal damage is common on 190SLs. Is there evidence of accident repair? Does everything fit together neatly, without unusual gaps, either between panels or from bumper to fender, or different contours on each side? Remove the headlights and look inside their buckets for rust or evidence of repair (overspray, primer, and so on).

How does the engine hood fit? Is the gap even all around? Does the hood contour match the surrounding panels? In the rocker panel, behind each door, a vertical seam should be visible. If not, someone has covered it with bondo. How do the doors fit? Are the gaps even, or do the doors sag?

As you jack up the car, be careful. Jackpoints at either side frequently rust so much that they

crumble when the factory jack is used. More seriously, the rear suspension is located by trailing arms that run forward and mount to the floor pan. These mountings often rust, loosening the arms. You can buy reproduction floor pans and weld them in and install new bushings for the trailing arm mounts, but it's no weekend job. Make sure the chassis is solid around the top mounting of the rear coil springs.

Look for leaky axle boots, transmission seals, brake cylinders, and shock absorbers. Does the car sag on collapsed springs? Are any shock absorbers seized? Has any of the floor pan been replaced, or will it need to be? The floor pan should have pressed-in stiffening indentations; if the metal is flat, it's probably a replacement. The 190SL uses

As a show car or as an enjoyable driver, the 190SL's popularity endures. *FDB*

wooden floorboards; water can collect under them and rust the floors.

The box sections at the outer edges of the floors are notable for internal rust. The wheelwell "eyebrows" are equally susceptible to rust and to poor repairs, usually with body filler instead of new metal. Look for rust in the lip under the trunk seal and around the trunk floor.

Bumpers on an unrestored car may be dented and bent. Bumper parts are expensive to repair and replate properly. It's not unusual for a complete bumper to run into the thousands of dollars.

Check the engine number carefully. It's easy to substitute a sedan engine. The number should begin with 121.921 or 121.928; the change fell in mid-1961. The compression ratio is cast into the head, either at the rear or on the left side, above the coolant outlet. In 1959, the compression ratio changed from 8.5:1 to 8.8:1. The 121.928 engine's ratio was 8.7:1. You probably won't find the trouble light that plugs into the socket near the fusebox.

What carburetors are fitted? The 190SL originally had two side-draft, dual-throat Solex 44 PHH carburetors that dwarfed the engine in size and complexity. These heavy carburetors had a large, cast-metal air intake box hung way out to the right and braced from below. The metal brace is difficult to reinstall, so some people just left it off, which stressed the manifold and often led to air leaks at its gasketed block joint. Correctly adjusted, Solexes should allow a smooth, even idle and acceleration, even from low rpm, without hesitation.

Many owners gave up trying to keep the Solexes synchronized and in tune. These carburetors depend on vacuum to open the second barrel, so vacuum leaks, age, and other variables (temperature, humidity, barometric pressure) can upset them. Throttle shafts wear into the carburetor body, making a smooth idle difficult to obtain. Thus, you may see the less fussy Weber 40 DCOE or others in their place. If you're planning to just drive the car, this is fine, but if you'll show it seriously, the original

The 190SL dash is quite simple; optional clock is not easy to find. *FDB*

Solexes will improve your score. With time, patient effort, and an overhaul kit, they can work properly. On the other hand, Webers are easier to tune, hold a tune longer, and make the car perform a little better. Take your choice.

Pressed cardboard heater ducts along both sides of the engine compartment were easily damaged. Fiberglass reproductions are available, but they are an obvious replacement. Cable-controlled by dash levers, the brass valves atop these air ducts direct coolant through heat exchangers in the ducts. Unless exercised, these valves corrode and seize. Look for corrosion under the battery and the brake booster.

To test the brake booster, find a hill on a lightly traveled road. Starting from the top, push in the clutch and let the engine idle as you descend at a reasonable speed. Use the brakes several times. They should work with the same effort for several applications. If the system is losing vacuum, pedal effort will increase as it leaks. Bringing the engine up to normal operating rpm should restore the vacuum and ease pedal pressure again. Leaky brake boosters can be rebuilt.

The 190SL interior should be either all-vinyl or all-leather. Replacement leather is often thinner and softer than the original surface-dyed material,

usually supplied by the German firm of Roser. Doorsill and transmission tunnel rubber mats are tough to find, so check their condition. If hard, they can be softened with a vinyl treatment such as Armorall, but tears are tough to hide.

Is the car complete? Some trim parts such as bumpers are extremely expensive to replace. While driving, watch the temperature gauge for signs of overheating.

Restoration

The 190SL has proven popular to restore. A cottage industry has grown up around 190SL restoration, furnishing nearly all of the necessary parts and services.

The 190SL's worst enemy over the years has been rust. Its steel body was never well protected when new, and corrosion is time-consuming to repair properly on any unit-body car. Most steel panels remain available, either from the factory or as reproductions. Unfortunately, these must be properly fitted and welded on rather than simply bolted on. Every part that rusts (floor pan, fenders, inner panels) requires extensive labor.

Do you want a nice street car or a show winner? To avoid wasted time and money, decide before work starts. Will you use the car as a driver or show it? Can you do the work yourself? Will you choose a local shop or a top-notch Mercedes-Benz restorer? These cars are not simple, so a proper restoration can easily exceed a finished car's value.

The mechanical aspects of restoration are relatively simple. Any restoration shop that does much Mercedes-Benz work has probably restored several 190SLs. Ask the shop for names of references with similar cars, then contact them.

Summary

The 190SL's appeal is based largely on its superficial resemblance to the more sophisticated 300SL. Judged on its own merits, it's actually prettier than a 300SL. The simpler 190SL is easily attainable and practical for the average owner.

The restoration industry support the 190SL well, and you'll have plenty of fellow owners to chat with. The 190SL is tractable, dependable, even economical, and those who see it and own it love it.

Chapter 10

230, 250, and 280SL 1963–1971

The 230, 250, and 280SL models are for enthusiasts who want to use their collector sports car for pleasure *and* for practical pursuits. These cars can be shown on Sunday, then driven to work on Monday. They are straightforward to maintain, and sufficient numbers were built so that parts as well as expert mechanics and restorers will remain in good supply well into the future.

Origins

The angular 230SL succeeded two traditional 1950s models, the 190SL and the 300SL. It constituted an unusually fortunate compromise, which still works for those who want to drive their SL or those who wish to show the car. The 230, 250, and 280SL models are uniquely styled yet thoroughly practical two-seaters. They are more advanced, more powerful, better handling, more comfortable, safer, easier to maintain, and more fun to drive than the 190SL—for about the same price on today's market.

The three models, known collectively by the 113 chassis designation, are renowned for their totally fresh look. The crisp, pagoda-roof styling has endured well, and the cars look equally attractive with the soft top folded beneath their flush metal deck. The only postwar Mercedes-Benz production cars styled outside the company, by Paul Bracq, the cars made their debut at the March 1963 Geneva Auto Show and became instantly popular as grand touring sports cars.

The 230, 250, and 280SLs had no significant competition career, beyond Eugen Böhringer's win in

The 230SL, 250SL, and 280SLs are nearly identical; this 280SL has the U.S.-mandated side reflectors, no trim beneath the license plate (as on European 230, 250, and 280SLs), and flat hubcaps. *FDB*

Technical Specifications

Model	230SL	250SL	280SL
Years	1963–1966	1966–1968	1968–1971
Engine			
Type	Inline ohc six (all)		
Engine No. prefix	127.981	129.982	130.983
Displacement	2,306 cc (140.7 ci)	2,496 cc (152.3 ci)	2,778 cc (169.5 ci)
Bore x stroke	82x72.8 mm	82x78.8 mm	86.5x78.8 mm
Compression ratio	9.3:1	9.5:1	9.5:1
DIN horsepower	150 hp @ 5,500 rpm	160 hp @ 5,500 rpm	170 hp @ 5,750 rpm
Torque	20 mkg @ 4,200 rpm	22 mkg @ 4,200 rpm	42.5 mkg @ 4,250 rpm
Fuel system	Bosch six-plunger mechanical fuel injection (all)		
Fuel required	Premium (all)		
Chassis			
Type	Unibody; steel with aluminum doors, engine lid, trunk lid, tonneau (all)		
Chassis No. prefix	113.042	113.043	113.044
Transmission	4-speed manual or 4-speed automatic (280SL 5-speed manual rare) (all)		
Rear-axle ratio	3.75:1	3.69:1	4.08:1 (Europe: 3.92:1, 3.69)
Rear suspension	Swing-axle, coil springs (all)		
Front suspension	Strut, coil springs (all)		
Wheels	Steel, 5.5x14 in.	6x14 in.	6x14 in.
Tires	185HR14 (all)		
Brakes	F disc, R drum	F&R disc	F&R disc
Fuel capacity	17.2 gal	21.7 gal	21.7 gal
Weight (add 176 lb for hardtop, 88 lb for automatic transmission)	2,866 lb	2,998 lb	2,998 lb
Performance			
0–60 mph	11 sec (13 auto)	12 sec (13 auto)	11 sec (12 auto)
Top speed	124 mph (121 auto)	121 mph (118 auto)	124 mph (121 auto)
Fuel consumption	16 mpg (15 auto)	15 mpg (14 auto)	14 mpg (13 auto)

Production

Years	Model	Production
1963–1967	230SL	19,831
1966–1968	250SL	5,196
1967–1971	280SL	23,885

the Liége-Sofia-Liége Rally, but competition was not the point. It proved far more significant that the cars were the first Mercedes-Benz sports cars to be available with dealer-installed air conditioning and an automatic transmission. The purists fumed, but the cars sold well.

230SL, 250SL, and 280SL ★★★

The 230SL emerged as a 1963 model, and despite a plethora of mechanical improvements and interior updates, this SL's W113 unit-body chassis changed only slightly until the last 280SL left the factory in March 1971.

All three models used an inline overhead-cam six, similar to those in contemporary Mercedes-Benz sedans. The 230SL used the trusty M127 II, making 150 horsepower DIN (170 horsepower SAE)—midway between the 190SL's 105 horsepower DIN and the 300SL's 215 horsepower DIN. The 250SL used a new M129 engine with seven main bearings (up from four in the 230SL) and higher coolant capacity. Besides a 10 percent boost in torque, the 250SL made 10 more horsepower—160 DIN. The 250's oil cooler used coolant as a medium; the 280's used air. To improve cooling ability, the 280SL's improved

Upon its introduction as a 1963 model, the 230SL, here with European headlights and hardtop in place, was immediately recognized for its styling and handling abilities. *DBAG*

M130 engine differed in cylinder spacing. Thanks to higher compression and a few other changes, and despite its new emission controls, the U.S.-version 280SL made 170 horsepower DIN (195 horsepower SAE) and another 10 percent more torque. All engines had Bosch mechanical fuel injection.

All three SLs also used disc brakes at the front (Girling on the 230, ATE on the 250 and 280), and when the 250SL appeared, discs replaced the 230SL's finned aluminum rear drums. Brakes are vacuum-assisted and operate on dual circuits for safety. The 230SL was the first SL to be introduced with radial tires, and much was made of its wide track, 8 inches wider than the Jaguar E-Type.

Visual clues to the 230SL in the engine compartment include the flat radiator expansion tank; the 250SL and 280SL have cylindrical tanks. Only 230SLs and early 250SLs had rubber covers over the subframe mounts.

All 230, 250, and 280SLs could be bought with a four-speed manual or a four-speed automatic transmission. In 1969, a ZF five-speed manual was first offered as an option, but it is rare. The 250 and 280SL have a 21.6-gallon fuel tank, up from 17.1 in the 230SL. The 280SL has a self-adjusting clutch and a hydraulic rear compensator above the rear swing-axle instead of the compensating spring used on the earlier cars.

In March 1966, the 250SL took over from the 230SL; 5,196 were built before January 1968, when 280SL production began. By then the car had evolved more toward luxurious touring than sporting use. Sixty percent of 230SLs had manual transmissions, and air conditioning was then unavailable. A 280SL was far more likely to have an automatic transmission—and Frigiking air conditioning.

Because the SL's weight increased along with power, performance changed little throughout the series, although the added displacement made the 280SL more flexible. Today's performance depends more on the condition and tune of a given engine than on which model you're driving.

One subtle model designation deserves mention. The 230/250/280SL could be bought new with a soft top, a metal hardtop, or both. With the soft top only, the car was sometimes called a Roadster. With the hardtop only, a Coupe. With both, it was infrequently referred to as a Coupe-Roadster or

Unusual in a sports car, these SLs have wide doors for easy entry and exit, a roomy interior, good outer vision, comfortable seats, and excellent weatherproofing. The exhaust note defines the entire car—nicely sporty, but tasteful. Performance and handling are excellent for their day, but the rear swing-axle suffers from camber change, especially under heavy braking. The nose dives, the rear end rises, and rear camber goes from negative to positive. Braking hard from high speeds into a sharp and/or slippery curve, this can lead to oversteer, but you'll rarely drive this grand tourer that hard. Under other conditions, the car has excellent grip, and the steering can be accurate and light (tire choice and inflation pressures play a role).

There is not much difference in handling among the three. A 280SL can exceed 3,000 pounds in weight, so the lighter 230SL feels more nimble. The car's track is wide, so it feels quite stable. Zero to 60 miles per hour takes about 10 seconds, and top speed was almost 125 miles per hour for the 230SL; the 250 and 280SL were slightly but not significantly slower. Added displacement makes the 280SL torquier than a 230SL at lower rpm, and the smaller-engined car needs to be revved a bit more. Fuel mileage is reasonable, in the high teens or better, depending on mechanical condition. In top gear with stock tires, a 280SL engine turns at about 19 miles per hour per 1,000 rpm.

The color of the painted dash should match the exterior color. The soft top operates easily, but you'll need a friend and/or a hardtop winch to remove or replace the hardtop. One false move, and you can scratch or dent the aluminum tonneau cover.

even a Roadster-Coupe. Just call it an SL.

Major options included the soft top and hardtop, a transverse rear bench seat, manual or automatic transmission, power steering (optional on 230SLs, standard on late U.S. 280SLs), air conditioning, leather interior, whitewall tires, bumper guards, various radios, and more. Rare options include fitted luggage, a hardtop with a sunroof (very rare), ski and luggage racks, different rear-axle ratios, and the ZF five-speed transmission. Rubber mats covered the floors of the 230 and 250SL, but the 280SL had carpet. The 280SL lacked the horizontal trim strip below the 230 and 250SL license plate. New safety requirements for 1968 models meant changes in control knobs, logos, and exterior lights.

All three SLs originally had steel wheels and hubcaps, the 230 and 250 with a small center cap with a separate chrome-plated trim ring, the 280 with larger and flatter one-piece cap over the entire wheel. In 1968, wheels were widened from 5.5 to 6.0 inches. Hubcaps were painted in hardtop color. If the hubcaps are unpainted, they're probably replacements, which came that way. The early 230SL spare tire stands upright; others lie nearly flat and take up more trunk space.

Many owners have fitted Mercedes-Benz alloy wheels, usually 6x14 inches. Introduced in late 1969, these wheels are technically correct only for late 280SLs, which could have had them dealer-installed or as a special option. The car looks handsome with them, so many owners forgo originality in favor of personal preference.

Minor changes were blended into production as they were needed and developed. To satisfy U.S. safety regulations, the 1968 250SL had side reflectors, and 280SLs had lights in these units. From 1963 to 1971, nearly 100 running changes can be documented. For a list, see *Vintage Reprint #1, The 230/250/280SL*, available through the Mercedes-Benz Club of America. For color and interior samples, see the Mercedes-Benz *Refinishing Manual*, circulated to dealers by Mercedes-Benz of North America. It goes back to 1963.

European versions often found their way across the Atlantic. Because the law didn't require it, few pre-1967 European cars were converted to U.S. specifications. Apart from their chassis numbers, they are usually distinguished by metric instruments and their one-piece, glass headlight covers.

Which is best for you, the 230, 250 or 280SL? The last of a series usually seems more desirable to collectors, and the more numerous (23,885 produced) 280SLs are likely to have more options and updates. The 280SL is the newest, quietest, most comfortable, and most developed of the trio. The 250SL's lower production numbers make it neither more nor less desirable. If anything, the 230SL is undervalued. It's a good buy if you can live without the improved engine, and no evidence exists that these engines are any less reliable than the later ones. Rear disc brakes can be retrofitted to the 230SL, but unless you're driving hard in autocrosses and time trials, you'll never miss them.

What to Look For

As usual, rust is the main enemy. When using a magnet to check for body filler, remember the aluminum panels: doors, engine hood, trunk lid, and

The 230, 250, and 280SLs seem to look cleaner without the optional front bumper guards. Note the U.S. headlights. *FDB*

Hinged aluminum boot neatly hides soft top. *FDB*

Even without the optional child seat, an SL can seat three in a pinch. Factory alloy wheels update the car's style. *FDB*

tonneau cover. These parts may not rust, but they are easy to dent, expensive to replace, and more difficult than steel panels to repair properly.

Areas most susceptible to rust are the front fenders (around the headlights, along the inner engine compartment panels at the top of the fenders, and at the seams of the closing panels behind the wheels) and the rear fenders (along the bottom edge and around the taillights). Check inside the engine compartment for rust along the inner fender panels and in the recesses above the subframe mounts.

Underneath the car and ahead of the rear wheels are a couple of traps for dirt and rust; lift the carpet behind the seats and look for holes. Check the chassis just outboard and forward of the rear springs. Look closely at all fender lips. Check the front cross-member, which is exposed to road salt and often distorted when incorrectly used to jack up the car. Look under the trunk mat and in the spare wheelwell on early 230SLs; leaky trunk seals let in water. Poke at the rocker panels and floor pan, especially around the pedal and seat mounting areas.

Look closely at the grille and surrounding sheet metal, often improperly repaired after accidents. Does the grille fit evenly against the body? Condition of the grille and bumpers is important, because they are particularly expensive to replace. Dents can be fixed, but rust is more difficult to stop and replate over. The sheet metal behind the grille should be painted black, not body color; looking into the grille, all you should see is black. Along the inner edge of the headlight's plated trim ring, where it has a small bump, you should see a matching short (1/2-inch) horizontal crease in the steel fender. Replacement fenders don't have this crease. If the fender has no crease, a body man has either filled it on an original fender or failed to build it on a replacement.

The hardtop is time-consuming to restore, so make sure the headliner is in good shape and that there's no rust in the lower rear quarters; drain holes should be clear. Replacement soft tops are reasonably priced, especially if you're willing to accept something less than show-quality material. Check the plastic rear window for fogging and scratches, sometimes removable via plastic cleaner. Be sure that the hand levers to operate the top latches are with the car; replacements are available.

Under the hood, first see that the engine is the right type. Because the contemporary sedans used similar engines, it's easy to swap them into an SL. Engine numbers should include the M-codes 127.981 (230SL), 129.982 (250SL), or 130.983 (280SL). A 250SL should have a bayonet oil filler cap rather than the earlier threaded type. All valve covers had a fine sand-grained natural finish and were unpolished.

Main engine areas of concern are the cooling system, fuel injection, timing chain, and cylinder head; any may have been neglected. The aluminum head may corrode from incorrect or infrequently changed

Even the trunk lid model designations resemble each other (this is a 280SL). Top, with plastic window, is easy to operate. *Dennis Adler*

The 280SL dash has rounded control knobs; original radios such as this Blaupunkt are a plus. *FDB*

coolant, often causing blown head gaskets (steam out of the tailpipe) and overheating. Valve guides are generally the first top-end part to wear out, with blue smoke when starting as evidence. Timing chains stretch, and chain tensioners should be replaced along with them. Cam lobe wear can result from infrequent oil changes. Water pumps and motor mounts don't last forever, either. Check the viscous fan drive on the 250 and 280SL. The mechanical fuel injection pump is expensive to rebuild, but done properly it's a once-in-a-lifetime job.

If the engine won't start and run smoothly, and nothing is wrong with the ignition, suspect the fuel injection. With today's higher-volatility fuels, hot weather can cause vapor lock, which can be cured by activating the cold-start switch so that it also works when the engine is hot (via a momentary switch or a factory relay). A mechanic without proper equipment, knowledge, and experience can cause more fuel injection problems than he or she solves, so repair is best left to experts. To keep the fuel injection system working properly, drive the car regularly rather than letting it stand.

If the engine oil smells like gasoline, the fuel injection pump is probably set far too rich and is thus pumping fuel through the cylinders and into the sump, diluting the engine oil. This problem may be indicated by a higher than normal oil level. Bearings won't last long in a gas-oil mixture. About the only place these engines leak oil is at the front crankshaft seal. Oil pressure at hot idle may seem low, but around 2,000 rpm or so, the oil pressure gauge needle should rise and become pegged at its top reading.

These engines have a normal life of about 100,000 miles, although a well-maintained unit may go much farther. Original and factory replacement exhaust systems tend to rust, but stainless-steel replacements are available.

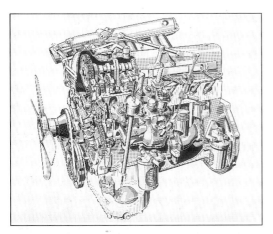

Except for its earlier two-plunger fuel-injection pump, this 220SE inline six is similar to the M127 engine that powers the 230SL, which used a six-plunger pump. *DBAG*

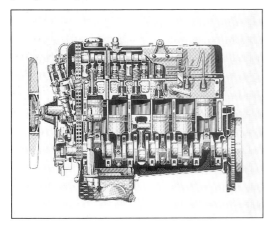

Cross-section view of the M129 engine of the 250SL. *DBAG*

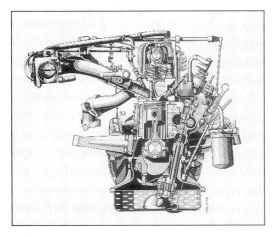

Original tire size on the 280SL's 6-inch-wide steel wheels was 185HR14, an 80-series profile designed for a smooth ride, light steering, and minimal aquaplaning. Today's best equivalent size is 205/70HR14. Since the car's four gears are widely spaced, a too small or too tall tire can have a major effect. Some opine that the stock gearing is low, but this is a revving six, not a lumbering V-8. The automatic transmissions shift firmly; proper linkage adjustment may reduce hard thumps, but not to 1990s levels. The suspension requires lubrication, so look for clean grease nipples.

Newer radios are popular, but original 1960s Beckers are obtainable and can be repaired. The original air conditioners never iced anyone's nose, but with a top that drops, who cares? If hot air enters the interior with the heater off, the air control flaps need to be rebuilt and readjusted. Heater controls and the wiper works, entombed in the cowl, are difficult to reach. If the wipers don't work, you'll have a tough time repairing them.

The 1967 and earlier cars had unmarked heater controls with hard knobs; 1968 and later models had symbols on the rubber knobs. The interior rearview mirror finish changed from chrome to black plastic at about the same time. Interior wood is usually sunfaded. To determine the true wood color, check the wood trim on the inside of the hardtop's rear window, where the sun rarely hits it.

Restoration

Any worn but sound example is a good restoration candidate, but so many good original cars survive that it pays to be patient. Find a good one, and avoid restoration altogether!

Because so many 230, 250, and 280SLs were built (48,912), and the cars have remained popular, an industry has developed around their restoration. For instance, sun visors used to be impossible to find, but now they're being made again. Specialty parts and services are easy to find, and more good reproduction parts appear regularly.

Most mechanical and major body parts remain available from Mercedes-Benz. Trim is more difficult to find and is expensive, particularly the front bumpers and grille. The aluminum panels are also not cheap, but fenders and other steel body parts are reasonably priced. Since the fenders are welded on, not bolted on, they require skilled labor to replace

The M130 engine of the 280SL. *DBAG*

Pininfarina rebodied this 1965 230SL into a coupe with a permanent top. *Dennis Adler*

One of the SL's rarest options is this manually operated sunroof in the factory hardtop. *FDB*

Presence of this small crease in the headlight rim and fender is a clue to an original body—or good bodywork.

correctly. Mechanical parts shared with the sedans can be found new or used. Used hardtops are available but not cheap, so use the lack of a hardtop as a bargaining point. Try to get the soft top frame with the car; used ones are expensive.

Before restoration, decide whether you want the car to be a nice driver, a national show winner, or something in between. Changing goals in mid-restoration is expensive and frustrating. A 230, 250, or 280SL is moderately easy to restore, but being a convertible, you have a soft top to replace and a hardtop to restore. Interior wood trim is minimal but vulnerable to sun damage. Most cars had MB-tex upholstery rather than leather.

Since these cars are so frequently restored, professional restorers have had a lot of experience with them. This also means that there are more good cars for you to pick from and avoid restoration altogether.

Summary

In numbers, style, usability, and affordability, the 230, 250, and 280SL models are the most collectible SLs. They drive well, they're appreciating in value, and they're reasonably simple to restore. What more can you ask? If you want a good car at a fair price, go for an early model. You'll pay a premium for the slight mechanical and psychological advantages of the last model year. Whichever you choose, you'll own one of the prettiest Mercedes-Benz models, and if you don't like it, you can always find someone else who does. But we can practically guarantee that you'll enjoy these cars—a lot.

Chapter 11

Fin-Backs, Coupes, and Convertibles 1960s

If one Mercedes-Benz model series has been unfairly reviled, it is surely the be-finned (and berated) sedans of the early 1960s. Underneath the skin, though, they are excellent cars. Alongside the finned sedans, these years also brought a subtle line of Coupes and Convertibles.

Suddenly, It's 1960

OK, let's get it over with and move on. Some think the finned 1960s sedans are ugly. Even if their tacked-on tailfins were designed to appeal to some German marketer's misperceived tastes of American buyers, these ugly ducklings only grow rarer and more collectible. Good "fin-backs" are tough to find.

The fin-back's body/chassis was completely new, with emphasis on safety, visibility, and space. Before regulations required it, these were the first Mercedes-Benz cars to be crash-tested. They used a variety of diesel and gasoline engines, from the 60-horsepower, four-cylinder 190 diesels to the 195-horsepower, six-cylinder gasoline 300s. These cars marked the first widespread use of gasoline fuel injection. One basic chassis served as everything from an economical taxi to a luxurious limousine.

190 and 200 Sedans 1961–1968 ★★

The four-cylinder fin-backs were plain and functional, built to provide inexpensive but reliable transportation. These are taxicabs, not collector

Proudly presented to the world for the 1960 model year, the sleek new 220S was billed as "the elegant car with the 124 SAE horsepower engine." Nowadays it's mostly called the fin-back. *DBAG*

Years	Model	Chassis Prefix	Engine Prefix	Description
1961-1965	190c	110	121	4-cyl gas, 90 hp
1961-1965	190Dc	110	OM621	4-cyl diesel, 60 hp
1965-1968	200	110	121	4-cyl gas, 104 hp
1965-1968	200D	110	OM621	4-cyl diesel, 60 hp

Driving Impressions: Fin-Backs

In a fin-back car, the first feature that may strike you is the large pad in the center of the steering wheel. Next, you'll spot the unique vertical ribbon speedometer. Exterior visibility is excellent, thanks to the huge window area.

The sixes love to rev, and you'd better take advantage of that. These cars are slow off the mark, but once you get them rolling, they'll stay at high speeds. The 300s have more torque, so you need not downshift as much. These big cars are heavy, and their aging suspension and brakes may not live up to their power. Still, disc brakes are a big improvement over the 1950s drums.

The automatic transmissions are hard-shifting, and they sap power. A manual gearbox is smoother and more fun. Heating, cooling, and fresh air ventilation are generations behind 1990s cars.

Little sisters of the six-cylinder 220 were the four-cylinder 190 and 190D. *Mercedes-Benz Sales*

cars. In relation to the tens of thousands built, few remain in daily use. Most are now well worn and no longer suitable for much but short drives. Their low power and pragmatic nature appeal to few.

The 190c, appearing in 1961, used a fin-back body, but was shorter than the 220Sb and SEb and had single instead of dual stacked headlights. The 200, another four-cylinder version, got two carburetors and higher compression, making 105 horsepower SAE. Diesels are described in Chapter 18.

220S and 220SE Sedans 1960–1965 ★★

The new-for-1960 111 chassis dual-carbureted 220, 220S, and fuel-injected 220SE used the six-cylinder engine of the 1950s cars. The 220 used dual Solex carburetors throughout its model run. The 220S had dual Solexes until mid-1963, when Zeniths appeared. The SE ("E" signifying *Einspritzer*) had mechanical, two-plunger, port injection. These models also brought automatic transmissions to the mid-range.

The fin-back even enjoyed a rally career. Factory 220SEs placed one-two-three in the 1960 Monte Carlo Rally and did well in other European, African, and South American events. Factory drivers won the 1960 and 1962 European Rally Championships.

One feature that gives grief are the Zenith 35/40 INAAT downdraft carburetors on some 1963 to 1972 models. Even new, these were difficult to keep working properly. As they wear, and as the bodies warp, allowing air and vacuum leaks, they refuse to be tuned. Service experts are scarce, but after the leaks are patiently found and eradicated, the carburetors can work well. Some owners convert to Weber or Holley 32/36 DGEV downdrafts, but even these demand proper jetting and adjustment, especially with automatic transmissions (which use engine vacuum for shifting). Fuel injection is more reliable, but its pump is subject to wear and is not inexpensive to overhaul.

The 220S and 220SE fin-backs were the first mass-market models to provide factory or dealer-installed air conditioning. It's not very effective now, but you're not buying a 1960s car because it has a great air conditioner. Another first (apart from the 300SL) was the appearance of disc brakes in April 1962, albeit only at the front; the 190s switched from drums in August 1963. Dual-circuit brakes were first fitted in 1963.

230 and 230S Sedans 1965–1968 ★★

The final iteration of the fin-back came in the slightly larger engined 230 and 230S. If you must have a fin-back, these (or a 220SE) are probably your best bet. The 230s are easy to find and economical. Except for the Zenith carburetors, they are dead simple. They exude an innocent charm,

Visibility was much improved, and the fin-back was the first Mercedes-Benz (and probably the first production car) to be thoroughly crash-tested. *DBAG*

but even better, they are cheap. A few years ago a friend advertised his near-perfect 230S. After a few wary nibbles, the price eroded until it was shamefully low, $1,500.

Like the other small-displacement "finnies," both 230 models are slow, especially with the optional automatic transmission, a clunky affair. Try for a nice one with a floorshift manual transmission and a sunroof.

In February 1968, the factory gate finally closed behind the last fin-back. No matter what comments you hear about the styling of these cars, their charm grows on you, especially in these days of characterless cars.

300SE and 300SE Long Sedans 1961–1967★★★

The rarest and most desirable fin-back sedans are the top-of-the line 300SE and 300SE Long

sedans, practically limousines. Their 3.0-liter, alloy, inline sixes pushed out up to 185 horsepower SAE, but the chassis was lumbered with an early version of air suspension and an automatic transmission. The SE Long rides on a 100-millimeter (3.9-inch)-longer wheelbase, with the extra space in the back seat area.

Both 300s had four disc brakes, with a dual-circuit system after 1963. Starting in January 1964, their two-plunger fuel injection pump was replaced by a six-plunger unit, boosting power by about 10 horsepower. Compression ratio was nudged from 8.7:1 to 8.8:1 at the same time. Virtually all used four-speed automatic transmissions, although a four-speed manual was optional in Europe.

Underappreciated and rarely seen today, these fin-back flagships embody every styling concept of early 1960s Euro-chic. There is plenty of chrome, medium-wide whitewalls, a "300SE" logo cast into

Chassis and Engine Prefix Numbers

Years	Model	Chassis Prefix	Engine Prefix	Description
1965–1968	230	110	180	6-cyl gas, 118 hp
1965–1968	230S	111/1A	180	6-cyl gas, 135 hp
1961–1965	300SE	112/3	189	6-cyl gas, 185-195 hp
1963–1965	300SE Long	112/3	189	6-cyl gas, 185-195 hp

Technical Specifications

Model	220S	220SE	300SE
Years	1960–1965	1960–1965	1961–1965
Engine			
Type	Inline ohc six (all)		
Engine No. prefix	180V	127III	189
Displacement	2,195 cc (133.9 ci)	2,195 cc (133.9 ci)	2,996 cc (182.8 ci)
Bore x stroke	80x72.8 mm	80x72.8 mm	85x88 mm
Compression ratio	8.7:1	8.7:1	8.8:1
DIN horsepower	110 hp @ 5,000 rpm	120 hp @ 4,800 rpm	160-170 hp @ 5,400 rpm
Torque	17.5 mkg @ 3,500 rpm	19.3 mkg @ 3,900 rpm	25.4 mkg @ 4,000 rpm
Fuel system	2 Solex 34 PAJTA (Zenith 35/40 INAT after July 1963)	Bosch mechanical fuel injection	
Fuel required	Premium (all)		
Chassis			
Type	Unibody; steel (all)		
Chassis No. prefix	111/2	111/3	112/3
Transmission	4-speed manual (all) (4-speed auto optional)		
Rear-axle ratio	4.10:1	4.10:1	3.92 or 3.69:1
Rear suspension	Swing-axle, coil springs (all)		
Front suspension			
Wheels	Steel, 5x13 in.	5x13 in.	6x14 in.
Tires	7.25x13 in.	7.25x13 in.	7.35x14 in. or 185H14
Brakes	F disc, R drum	F disc, R drum	4-wheel disc
Fuel capacity	17.2 gal	17.2 gal	21.7 gal
Weight	2,976 lb	3,042 lb	3,649 lb
Performance			
0–60 mph	15 sec	14 sec	12 sec
Top speed	103 mph	107 mph	115–120 mph
Fuel consumption	16–18 mpg	16–18 mpg	14–17 mpg

Note: Earlier 300SE Coupes and Convertibles had less power, 5x13-in. wheels, different rear-axle ratios, and so forth.

the C-pillar trim (on the 300SE only, not on the Long version), even two-tone paint. They are easily spotted via the trim in the side body crease. A black 300SE Long is *très elegant*, but a two-tone blue or green example is nostalgia on wheels.

DBAG's first high-volume application of air suspension and power steering can leak via fittings, pump seals, and old hoses. The air suspension pump is coupled to the power steering pump, and air must be carefully bled out of the steering lines. Because the self-leveling air suspension is expensive to repair, some cars have been converted to coil springs. European fin-backs used a streamlined one-piece headlight housing; American cars used separate headlights and parking lights. Both 300 fin-back sedans were last built for the 1965 model year.

The 300s were among the world's fastest and strongest sedans. Led by driver Eugen Böhringer, factory 300SE sedans were successful in racing and rallying. A 300SE makes a fun vintage racer.

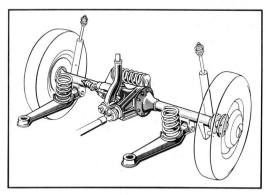

Rear swing-axle is fixed to the chassis at the center; coil springs at each wheel are supplemented by a load-compensating coil spring at the center. *DBAG*

Compared to the 300SE Coupe and Convertible, the 300 sedans are bargains. In fact, nice four-doors are far more rare, though plenty of run-down examples are quietly rotting away out there.

What to Look For

Condition is everything. No total restoration can be economically justified, so find the best original example. Rust likes to eat around the headlight buckets, along the edges of the wheelwells, and in the doors and rocker panels. Condition of trim is important because replacement pieces are hard to find. Bumpers seem especially vulnerable to dents; those can be fixed and replated, but you'll have to completely replace a rusty bumper.

Notice how a Zenith-equipped six starts and idles. Smooth drivability depends on the condition of the carburetors. The fuel-injected engines are smoother and more flexible. Since the automatic transmission is controlled by vacuum, shifts are subject to carburetor condition. Old motor mounts sag but aren't tough to replace. The preferred manual transmission's column shift should work smoothly and precisely; floorshifts were optional on some models.

If it has had any care at all, a 1960s interior should be excellent. MB-tex (vinyl) can't be killed, and most models had rubber floor mats. Sun-dam-

The 300SE Convertible is distinguished by the thin chrome trim in the side body crease, not present on 220, 250, 280, or 280SE 3.5 versions. Even on these luxury four-seaters, the top was still manually operated. *DBAG*

Last of the fin-backs was the 230S, seen here autocrossing. *FDB*

The 300SE was the finest and the fanciest, with plenty of chrome trim and ample rear legroom backed up by a four-speed automatic transmission, air suspension, and power steering. A four-speed manual gearbox was an option, and even a few five-speeds were fitted. *DBAG*

Interior of the 300SE could be swathed in leather or cloth, with select woods and wool carpets. With the demise of the 300d, this and the similar 300SE Long were the top Mercedes-Benz sedans until the 600 appeared. *DBAG*

For 1970, the Coupe and Convertible grilles were lowered and widened; early version on left, 1970 and later version on right. Both of these cars have European headlights. Empty space between headlight and grille contained turn signals on U.S. cars. *DBAG*

Driving Impressions: 220 and 280 Coupes and Convertibles

The 220 and 280 Coupes and Convertibles are more luxurious than the sedans, frequently including reclining bucket seats and, in later cars, power windows. A round speedometer and an equal-sized tachometer lie in an attractive wood binnacle. Air conditioning was not universal, but underdash Kuhlmeister units are found.

Performance is directly related to engine displacement. If performance is important, go for the 280SE, 300SE, or 280SE 3.5. Fuel injection means a much smoother, more responsive engine than the carbureted power units. The four-wheel disc brakes are powerful and easy to maintain. The automatic transmission usually doesn't match the sophistication of the rest of the car. Convertible tops on these models are manually operated, but simple to raise and lower.

Thanks to air suspension, the 300SE stays level in corners. Power steering can be vague. These cars sometimes suffer vapor lock in hot weather, partly because the high-pressure injection lines wrap around the front of the engine. Spraying cold water on the pump and lines gets you going, but switching gasoline brands and applying insulation can help.

aged wood is common; finding good replacement wood may cost less than professional refinishing. Amateur refinishing usually ends in a mess because the wood is just a thin veneer. As soon as sandpaper hits it, the thin veneer is gone, so a typical amateur just refinishes the base wood.

Restoration

Fin-backs were built in huge numbers, so used parts are plentiful. Sold as economy cars, they are uncomplicated and inexpensive to operate, maintain, and restore. Because few seek them, they can be stunning bargains.

If possible, stick to the fuel-injected models. The Solex and Zenith carburetors were poor in performance, durability, and fuel consumption, and they are expensive to replace or repair.

Professional wood restoration is expensive but best. A pro can match the existing color and grain (to see what it should be, see the inside of the glovebox lid) and make it last.

Good original fin-backs can be bought for less than the cost of a simple restoration. Resist an inexpensive project car. A truly cheap show car may be just around the corner. Even if you already own a fin-back,

try to resist the urge to restore it. Unless it's rare—a 300SE, SE Long, or a Coupe or Convertible—better sell it and find another in better condition.

Summary

None of the 190s and 220s are widely considered to be collector cars, but they provide useful and economical transport. Because they are the newest and have the most powerful engines, the 230 and 230S are good for low-budget collectors. The best fin-backs are beginning to be preserved, but restoration cost is far more than the cost of a better car.

The big 300SE and SEL sedans are rare; in fact, good sedans are rarer than Coupes and Convertibles. Most desirable are the ornate ones in full two-tone and whitewall plumage.

220SE to 280SE 3.5 Coupes and Convertibles ★★

Early 1960s Coupes and Convertibles were mechanically similar to the contemporary sedans, but eschewed fins in favor of more subtly rounded rear fenders. A finely shaped roofline plus stylish C-pillars gave the Coupe an elegant look.

From the 220, the Coupes and Convertibles continued into the 250, 280, and 300 versions. As you can guess from those numbers, the biggest differences lie under the hood. The 220 Coupe and Convertible have the smallest engine; later models were somewhat better equipped and developed, too.

220SEb 1960–1965 ★★

Designed as a true 2+2, the 220SEb (the b sets it apart from the late 1950s round-body Coupe) was the first of a line of similar Coupes stretching into the early 1970s. The engine was the fuel-injected six, but its 134 horsepower SAE has its work cut out shifting the 3,200-pound body.

Because they are outwardly similar to the more desirable 300SE Coupes and Convertibles, many 220SEs are overpriced. Lacking only air suspension and some luxury touches, they cost nearly the same to restore. Mechanically, they lack the 300's rear disc brakes, but as a bonus they were often equipped with manual transmissions. Wheels and tires were 13 inch, tough to find now, but later 14-inch wheels fit.

The 280SE 3.5 Coupe is perhaps the prettiest Mercedes-Benz of the era. Its high-compression V-8 made 230 horsepower SAE.

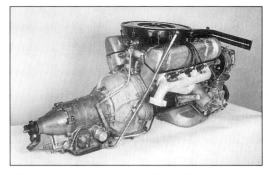

The M116 engine had a redline of 6,050 rpm. An automatic transmission was normally fitted, but a four-speed manual was offered. *DBAG*

A V-8 was a natural for the wide engine compartment of the 111 Coupe body; Bosch electronic injection was employed. *Dennis Adler*

Technical Specifications			
Model	220SE Coupe/Conv.	220SE Coupe/Conv.	280SE 3.5 Coupe/Conv.
Years	1965-1967	1968-1971	1970-1971
Engine			
Type	Inline sohc six	Inline sohc six	Sohc V-8
Engine No. prefix	129.980	130.980	116.980
Displacement	2,496 cc (152.3 ci)	2,778 cc (169.5 ci)	3,499 cc (213.5 ci)
Bore x stroke	82x78.8 mm	86.5x78.8 mm	92x65.8 mm
Compression ratio	9.5:1 (all)		
DIN horsepower	150 hp @ 5,500 rpm	160 hp @ 5,500 rpm	200 hp @ 5,800 rpm
Torque	22.0 mkg @ 4,200 rpm	24.5 mkg @ 4,250 rpm	29.2 mkg @ 4,000 rpm
Fuel system	Mechanical fuel injection	Mechanical fuel injection	Electronic fuel injection
Fuel required	Premium (all)		
Chassis			
Type	Unibody; steel (all)		
Chassis No. prefix	111.021 (Coupe)	111.024 (Coupe)	111.026 (Coupe)
	111.023 (Conv.)	111.025 (Conv.)	111.027 (Conv.)
Transmission	4-speed auto or	4-speed auto	4-speed auto
	4-speed manual		
Rear-axle ratio	3.92:1	3.92:1	3.69:1
Rear suspension	Swing-axle, coil springs (all)		
Front suspension	Unequal-length A-arms (all)		
Wheels	6x14 in. (all)		
Tires	185HR14	185HR14	185VR14
Brakes	4-wheel disc (all)		
Fuel capacity	21.7 gal (all)		
Weight	3,285 lb	3,570 lb	3,770 lb
Performance			
0–60 mph	12 sec	11 sec	10 sec
Top speed	117–120 mph	117–120 mph	130 mph
Fuel consumption	14–16 mpg	14–16 mpg	12–14 mpg

300SE 1961–1967 ★★★

This model seems out of order because it came along right after the 220, in 1962. Set apart by a horizontal side trim strip and chrome-plated wheelwell moldings, a 300SE is the ultimate 1960s Coupe or Convertible. Its broad-shouldered M189 single-overhead-cam six shrugs off the 3,500–3,700-pound weight. Performance is excellent, especially with the optional manual transmission (controlled by either a column-shifter or a floorshift). Top speed is 115–125 miles per hour, depending on final drive ratio (3.75 or 3.92:1 could be specified) and transmission. Tires were 13 inch through 1965, 14 inch thereafter.

These Coupes and Convertibles were built until 1967, so the later the better. Like the 300 sedans, they were air-suspended and had four-wheel disc brakes. Standard equipment included reclining seats and leather upholstery. Options varied annually but included cloth upholstery,

power windows, bucket seats, and fitted luggage. These Coupes and Convertibles were rare when new, and today a good one is a keeper.

250SE 1966–1967 ★★

The 250SE Coupe and Convertible, built alongside the 300s as 1966 and 1967 models, enlivened the 220SE with a 300-cc displacement increase and a boost in compression to 9.3:1, bumping power to 170 horsepower. Wheel diameter went to 14 inches, sprung via coil springs with a hydro-pneumatic compensating unit on the rear axle. Brakes were uprated to four-wheel discs.

280SE 1968–1972 ★★

For the 1968 model year, the 280SE replaced the previous 250SE and 300SE. Its 2,778-cc single-overhead-cam M130 six makes 180 horsepower SAE and gets the big Coupe up to about 115 miles per hour. Other benefits of the new engine were improved cooling and seven main bearings. The 2.2- to 3.0-liter sixes can be expected to cover 100,000 miles without overhaul. Smoke usually appears first from worn valve guides; overheating indicates water pump, radiator, or head gasket problems.

In 1970, when the 3.5-liter V-8 was made available in this chassis, the hood and grille were lowered and reshaped to a more contemporary style. For 1970 and 1971, about 680 six-cylinder 280SE Coupes and Convertibles also used this low grille and hood.

The next best thing to a 300SE, the 280SE sixes are usually priced much lower, so bargains exist.

280SE 3.5 1969–1971 ★★★

The 280SE 3.5 Convertible is among the most collectible models of its era. When Mercedes-Benz developed its 3.5-liter V-8, the high-end Coupes and Convertibles were a natural home for it. The resulting five-passenger 280SE 3.5 Convertible is luxurious, powerful, and exclusive. Its folding top created an instant classic.

Introduced in 1969 as a 1970 model, the 280SE 3.5 was also available as a sedan and a Coupe (note that, bargain hunters). Its M116 V-8 powerplant used the new Bosch D-Jetronic electronic fuel injection, a transistorized ignition, and a 9.5:1 compression ratio to deliver 230 horsepower SAE, more than 1 horsepower per cubic inch. Most cars had four-speed automatic transmissions, but a few were built with a four-speed manual gearbox.

Rather than air suspension, the 280SE 3.5 used standard coil springs at each corner, so there's less concern about suspension maintenance. Four-wheel disc brakes were standard, and a limited-slip differential was optional. The Convertible's top is easily lowered and raised by hand. The interior is clad in leather, wood, and chrome; amenities include power windows, air conditioning, and reclining seats with center armrests. Fitted luggage was an option, of course.

The grille and hood of the 280SE 3.5 Coupe and Convertible were lowered, giving them an entirely new look from the more upright earlier models. As many as 1,232 280SE 3.5 Convertibles were manufactured for the 1970 and 1971 model years. Many more sedans (about 12,000) and Coupes (about 3,270) were built. The Convertible was the last four- or five-seat Mercedes-Benz Convertible until the 300CE Cabriolet of 1993.

What to Look For

Make sure the Convertible boot (top cover) is with the car. Check power window operation, too. Because of the demand for Convertibles, some 1960s W111 Coupes have been made into Convertibles, sometimes to sell them at a higher price disguised as genuine Convertibles. If you're looking at a Convertible that had a Coupe equivalent, especially a 280SE 3.5, be sure that it is an original, factory-built Convertible. Verify the chassis number. The 1970 280SE Coupe numbers begin with 111.024, Convertible numbers with 111.025. The 1971 280SE Coupe numbers begin with 111.026, Convertibles with 111.027.

Check beyond the ID plate on the radiator support, which can be switched. If you buy a Convertible that turns out to be a phony, you could lose tens of thousands of dollars. An honest seller will tell you about a conversion; less scrupulous people may conveniently forget.

Safety is also a factor. To substitute for the steel top's rigidity, the original Convertible chassis was reinforced based on factory engineering and tests. Most conversions are done with little regard for structural integrity and safety. Since older cars are involved, often well-used examples, the basic structure can be lacking.

Restoration

These cars are young enough so that excellent original examples can still be found. Unless you plan to show the car, you are better off buying a clean original than obligating yourself to a huge restoration.

These are not small cars, so there's more to restore. Their low-production volume means that some parts are hard to find, but because of the cars' value, more parts can be expected to be reproduced. A Convertible is always more expensive to restore than an equivalent Coupe and often is in worse shape to begin with. Water and sun damage not only the top but often the leather. Mechanically there's no problem; the Coupe and Convertible use parts from the common sedans.

If you're farming out your restoration, find a shop that has done several, then examine their work. If you want yours restored properly, experience counts. These cars are usually restored well, so if you plan to sell yours later, it will have to be restored properly to match the competition. Collectors expect these cars to be right, so short-cuts really show. Unless you already own a clean original example, buy a well-restored car rather than trying to rescue a poor one.

Summary

All 1960s Mercedes-Benz Coupes and Convertibles are elegant and interesting cars that can still be driven anywhere and maintained without fuss. The later and bigger-engined examples are preferred. If you can live without a folding top, the 280SE 3.5 Coupe is the best bargain. For perhaps a quarter of the price of the 280SE 3.5 Convertible, you get nearly the same car.

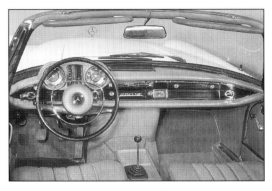

This 280SE 3.5 Convertible is unusual in that it has no air conditioning (usually hung below the dash), no radio (note the blanking plate with the "280SE" designation), and a floorshift four-speed manual transmission. *DBAG*

The 280SE 3.5 Convertible has great potential as a future collector car, but the Coupe version is much under-rated. *DBAG*

Chapter 12

The 1960s V-8s

Mercedes-Benz engineers built their first production V-8 engine for a flagrantly luxurious limousine series, the 600. Then, using this and other V-8s, they created an upscale series headed by the amazing 300SEL 6.3, then the world's fastest production sedan.

600 1963–1981 ★★★

By 1962 the 1950s six-cylinder 300 luxury sedan and four-door Convertible had grown long in the tooth. As a replacement, DBAG planned a new luxury model that may remain forever unsurpassed in elegance, comfort, quality, engineering, and performance—the 600. For all of that, though, this car engenders a love-hate relationship among collectors: it's wonderful to own, painful to restore.

Introduced at the 1963 Frankfurt auto show, the 600 was built until 1981 as a four-door "short wheelbase" (ahem) sedan, the most popular model; Pullmans (also known as Seven Passenger Limousines) with four or six doors; and—rarely—as a Pullman-Landaulet with a folding rear top section. The short Sedan version is often called the SWB, for short wheelbase. Pullmans and Landaulets stood on

In five-passenger sedan form, this is the shortest (or least lengthy?) 600 model. *MBNA*

The 600 Pullman was also available in six-door form. This car and the regular 600 on page 105 have U.S. headlights. *MBNA*

For occasions of state, may we present the ultimate 600, the Pullman-Landaulet, with folding rear top, perhaps for tossing flower petals to the peasants. *DBAG*

a 700-millimeter (27.6-inch) longer wheelbase, allowing additional rear seats and, in some cases, 3 doors per side. At least one 600 Coupe was built, as chief engineer Fritz Nallinger's retirement gift.

Custom touches were the norm for 600s, so defining factory options is difficult, but apart from leather or velour upholstery, the most popular were a sunroof, a divider window, refrigerated bars, and, of course, flag mounts for the front fenders. All four seats plus windows, sunroof, trunk lid, and doors (on early models) were hydraulically power-assisted via a complicated system with pressures of up to 3,000 psi. Even the cowl vent is power-operated.

Remote-control exterior rearview mirrors and vacuum-operated central locking were both firsts. Heating and air conditioning systems were integrated, with separate controls for driver and passengers. Radio controls were duplicated for back-seat passengers, who also had an intercom to speak with their driver (it sim-

Driving Impressions: 600

Just opening and closing the door of a 600 is different. Its hydraulic door assists inspired those of the 1992–on 600SEL. The steering wheel can be adjusted in and out, and the parking brake releases automatically as you shift the column-mounted lever into gear.

A driver must become accustomed to the car's length and breadth, but once you do, driving a 600 is easy. You might expect such a luxury car to handle like the *Queen Mary*, but the 600 is surpassingly competent. Body roll is low, and once the car takes a set in a hard corner, it hangs on tenaciously. Great fun, even without a chandelier in the back.

Be aware of vibrations, possibly from the three-section driveshaft. The brakes should work evenly; if not, the calipers may have corroded, especially if the car has been driven rarely. A 600 deteriorates from lack of use. Test the suspension firmness adjustment. Fuel mileage? If you care, it's under 15 miles per gallon, depending on bodystyle and mechanical state.

Even 30 years later in a world jaded by stretched Lincolns, a 600 has more pure presence than any other luxury vehicle. You're going to be looked at in this car.

ply wouldn't do to shout from way back there). The 600 was tantalizingly close to outrageous, a no-holds-barred example of luxury, power, and elegance taken almost—but not quite—to excess.

The 600 was the first production Mercedes-Benz car to be powered by a V-8 engine. The gigantic 6,330-cc mechanically fuel-injected motor looks as if it were winched out of a U-boat, with huge dual air intake tubes in the center and a cam atop each cylinder bank, splayed apart at a generous 90 degrees. This virtually bulletproof engine went on to power the 300SEL 6.3 and in different form, the 450SEL 6.9. Despite the weight of the 600s, which varied from about 5,300 pounds to over 6,000 pounds, and their huge frontal area, this motor's giant torque and power could push them to 125–130 miles per hour.

Hauling them down again required unusual dual-caliper front disc brakes plus normal discs at the rear. Brakes are boosted by compressed air from the self-leveling suspension system, which uses air bags and A-arms at the front and a low-pivot swing-axle with antibrake force arms at the rear. Shock absorbers are driver-adjustable, and the 9.00x15-inch radial tires (equivalent of today's 235-70R15) fit on steel wheels with painted and plated hubcaps rather than alloy wheels. Five to seven vee-belts drive two alternators, the air conditioning compressor, the hydraulic pump, the cooling fan, and the air compressor.

Virtually every part was built solely for the 600 in small volume. All systems are complex, and interchangeability with other models is low except for the engine. Restoration is outrageously expensive. A 600 is even expensive to drive—highway fuel mileage hovered around 10 miles per gallon. Even undriven, the car consumes an inordinate amount of space.

We must add the obligatory mention that 600s were owned by such incomparables as King Hussein, Mao Tse-Tung, Queen Elizabeth II, the Shah of Iran, Hugh Hefner, Marshal Tito, Prince Rainier, the Beetles, and President Ceasescu of Romania. Of course, the Pope had one, a special-bodied Landaulet with a raised roofline. What most people don't mention is that 600s were also owned by scalawags who thought they could use them to impress someone. It worked, too!

The 2,677th and final 600 was built in June 1981. The 600's 18-year life span remains the longest of any Mercedes-Benz model.

What to Look For

Apart from the normal points, be curious about the power-assisted systems, especially seats, windows, and air suspension. If they don't function properly, count on major expense and effort. The suspension is most likely to let you down, pun intended. (See the section on the 300SEL 6.3 in this chapter.) Neither end of the car should sag. Good air suspension should maintain the proper level even when parked for weeks.

Check the air conditioning and heating systems, and if the car has a divider window, make sure it works. The 6.3-liter V-8 is dependable, but some ancillary bits (water pump, alternators, fuel injection pump, exhaust system) bear watching.

Before you buy, make sure the 600 will fit your garage. The short-wheelbase sedan is 18 feet, 2 inches long, the Pullman covers 20 feet, 6 inches, and the Landaulet simply requires a hangar.

No 600 was immune to rust or accident damage, just because it's a great car. Everyone who sees your 600 will sight down those long, flat flanks and see every single door ding and ripple.

Restoration

With complicated engineering to match its imposing appearance, a 600 is full of hydraulics, sophisticated mechanisms, and expensive and rare

trim. For instance, while a 1960s 220SE Coupe or Convertible has only 12 pieces of wood to restore, the average 600 has nearly 50.

A 600 can be restored, but any sane person will try to avoid the experience. Buy the best you can find and afford. Low-volume, practically hand-built parts are extremely expensive, and these cars shouldn't be turned over to just any restorer. You'll need a real expert. The volume of parts and labor needed for a 600 restoration is bad enough, and the complex nature of the car only worsens the prospect.

108 and 109 Squareback Sedans 1965–1972 ★★

In 1965, Mercedes-Benz revealed the successor to the fin-back sedans, the New Generation. Sometimes called "squarebacks" because their trunk and rear fenders are squared-off, these cars are roomier than their predecessors, but they are also bigger, heavier, and more complex. Their W108 and W109 chassis are the same except for suspension; the 108 use coil springs, the 109 uses air. (Some think that the difference is the wheelbase, but that's not so; some long-wheelbase SEL sedans—the 280SEL 4.5, for instance—have 108 chassis numbers.) For more rear legroom, all 4 inches of extra length are in the back-seat area. These roomy, conservatively styled bodies still appear elegant.

Various models were powered by six-and eight-cylinder fuel-injected gasoline engines. First came the sixes: the 250S for the 1966 model year, followed by the 280SE, 280SEL, 300SE, and 300SEL. Both 280s use a 180 horsepower single-overhead-cam six-cylinder engine similar to that of the 280SL, with decent performance. The 300's 185 horsepower six was only slightly bigger but offered more torque.

The eight-cylinder models were DBAG's first mass-market V-8s, and most were sold in the United States, the 4.5-liter versions being the most common. The 3.5-liter is obviously smaller in displacement, but it shouldn't be overlooked. Thanks to higher compression and less restrictive smog gear, its 230 horsepower superseded the output of subsequent 4.5s, especially 1973 and later. Engines are thirsty by today's standards, consuming a gallon every 11 to 15 miles.

Options include factory air conditioning (no longer dealer-installed), an electric sunroof, and vacuum door locks. Coil-spring suspension was fitted except for the 109 chassis 300SEL, 300SEL 3.5, 300SEL 4.5, and 300SEL 6.3, which used air suspension.

Technical Specifications

Model	600	300SEL 6.3
Years	1964-1981	1968-1972
Engine		
Type	90-degree sohc V-8 (all)	
Engine No. prefix	100.980	100.981
Displacement	6,329 cc (386.2 ci) (all)	
Bore x stroke	103x95 mm (all)	
DIN horsepower	250 hp (300 hp SAE) @ 4,000 rpm (all)	
Torque	369 lb-ft @ 2,800 rpm DIN	434 lb-ft @ 3,000 rpm SAE
Fuel system	Mechanical fuel injected (all)	
Fuel required	Premium (all)	
Coolant capacity	24.3 qt	19.0 qt
Chassis		
Type	Unibody; steel (all)	
Chassis No. prefix	100. (varies)	109.018
Transmission	4-speed automatic (all)	
Rear-axle ratio	3.23:1 (limited-slip)	2.85:1 (limited-slip)
Rear suspension	Air, low-pivot swing-axle (self-leveling) (all)	
Front suspension	Air, unequal-length A-arms (self-leveling) (all)	
Wheels	6.5x15 in.	6.5x14 in.
Tires	9.00x15 in.	195x14 in.
Brakes	4-wheel disc, dual front calipers, air-assisted	4-wheel disc, vacuum-assisted
Fuel capacity	29.6 gal	27.7 gal
Weight	5,732 lb (SWB); 6,107 lb (Pullman)	4,034 lb
Performance		
0–60 mph	10 sec (SWB); 12 sec (Pullman)	7 sec
Top speed	115–129 mph	137 mph
Fuel consumption	9–12 mpg	11–15 mpg
Production and Model	**Production**	
600	2,190	
600 Pullman	428	
600 Landaulet	59	
300SEL 6.3	6,526	

The Landaulet with top up for potentate protection; note the European lights. *DBAG*

Rear axles on some coil-sprung cars used a transverse spring above the differential as a self-leveling device. Called a compensating spring, it can compress with age, resulting in excess negative camber, even with no load. Others used a hydro-pneumatic compensating unit; the hydraulic replacement is expensive, so the spring is sometimes substituted.

All 108- and 109-bodied cars used sliding heater and defroster controls with plastic levers, which break with age. Replacement with original levers is difficult, but an aftermarket lever replacement kit takes minutes to install. The heater cables may corrode, along with the coolant flow valves they control, making their action stiff. The remedy is to clean the valves and exercise the levers.

The 600's engine compartment was filled with this mighty 6.3-liter, 300-horsepower SAE powerplant, the first Mercedes-Benz passenger car V-8. *DBAG*

What to Look For

Rust is your main enemy. Most sedans are not worth spending a lot to restore, so find a rust-free example. If you'll use the car as a driver, you can tolerate a little rust in noncritical areas if the price is right. Check the front radiator support cross-member, around the headlights (for a better look, remove the headlight units from their buckets), and in the fenders behind the wheels. At the rear, rust eats at the wheel opening lip. Remove the trunk mat and check the side and rear edges of the trunk floor.

Used regularly, mechanical fuel injection is reliable. Nonuse typically causes dried-up seals, corrosion in the injection pump, and more. A common operation problem, vapor lock, can be fixed by modifying the system so that the cold-start injector squirts gasoline not only when the engine is cold (as designed), but also when it's hot. Some people do this with a switch under the dash, but Mercedes-Benz sells a factory relay and cable for the job.

The Bosch fuel injection pump usually lasts at least 100,000 miles before needing overhaul, which is best left to specialists. Keep yours away from anyone without proper equipment and experience.

Check for burned-smelling automatic transmission fluid, slow gear engagement, and leaks. Worn motor mounts allow the engine to sag and move under acceleration.

Restoration

Avoid it. You can buy a perfectly good example for half the cost of restoration.

Working in the engine bay of the V-8 cars is more time- and knuckle-consuming than on the sixes because more stuff is crammed in. Everything takes longer and costs more. Heater controls and

Chassis and Engine Prefix Numbers

Years	Model	Chassis Prefix	Engine Prefix	Description
1965–1969	250S	108.012	108.920	6-cyl. gas, 146 hp
1965–1968	250SE	108.014	129.980	6-cyl. gas, 170 hp
1966–1967	300SE	108.015	189.989	6-cyl. gas, 195 hp
1966–1967	300SEL	109.015	189.988	6-cyl. gas, 195 hp
1968–1972	280S	108.016	130.920	6-cyl. gas, 157 hp
1968–1972	280SE	108.018	130.980	6-cyl. gas, 180 hp
1968–1971	280SEL	108.01	130.980	6-cyl. gas, 180 hp
1968–1970	300SEL	109.016	130.908 (2.8)	6-cyl. gas, 180 hp
1970–1972	300SEL 3.5	109.056	116.981	8-cyl. gas, 230 hp
1971–1972	280SE 3.5	108.018	116.980	8-cyl. gas, 230 hp
1971–1972	280SEL 3.5	108.019	116.980	8-cyl. gas, 230 hp (rare)
1971–1972	280SE 4.5	108.067	117.984	8-cyl. gas, 230 hp
1971–1972	280SEL 4.5	108.068	117.984	8-cyl. gas, 230 hp
1971–1972	300SEL 4.5	109.057	117.981	8-cyl. gas, 230 hp
1968–1972	300SEL 6.3	109.018	100.981	8-cyl. gas, 300 hp

This typical 600 Pullman interior contains the first Mercedes-Benz power seats which were hydraulically operated. A wide variety of options and custom features could be ordered. *DBAG*

The 300SEL 6.3 in original form. Bullet turn signals were later replaced by larger lamps resembling fog lights. Original hubcaps and wheels are often replaced by factory alloy wheels. *MBNA*

blowers are especially tough to work on. Heater blower motors and windshield wiper motors are tough to reach, so make sure they work.

For an air-suspended car, air valves are expensive, so if the car shows any sign of sinking to its knees, proceed with caution. Unless the rest of the car is in exemplary condition, a 300 with air suspension problems is a car to be avoided for the normal restorer (or is that a contradiction?).

300SEL 6.3 1968–1972 ★★★

Looking at the 600's huge V-8, DBAG engineers Erich Waxenberger and Rudolf Uhlenhaut couldn't resist creating this factory hot rod. For 1968, they squeezed the V-8 into the 109 chassis, and thousands still thank them for the resulting 300SEL 6.3. This huge two-ton, four-door sedan managed 0–60 miles per hour in under 7 seconds and topped out at about 135 miles per hour, impressive for an aerodynamic brick.

The M100 engine used a cast-iron block and aluminum alloy heads with a 9:1 compression ratio that demands today's highest octane premium fuel.

By 1960s Mercedes-Benz standards, the 6.3 has a luxurious interior, but today it seems stark. Wood trim is minimal. Leather was standard on U.S. cars, as was central locking, but the seats are manually adjusted, and a sunroof was optional. The 1968–1969 cars had power window controls on the doors plus a central wooden tray behind the shifter. For 1970–1971, the window switches moved to the console, replacing the tray. The 1968–1969 cars has small, bullet-shaped front turn signals, while 1970–1971 cars had larger, flatter orange lights shaped like driving lights.

Technical Specifications

Model	250SE Sedan	280SE Sedan	280SEL 4.5 Sedan
Years	1965–1968	1968–1972	1971–1972
Engine			
Type	Inline sohc six	Inline sohc six	V-8
Engine No. prefix	129.980	130.980	117.984
Displacement	2496 cc	2778 cc	4520 cc (276 ci)
Bore x stroke	82x78.8 mm	86.5x78.8 mm	92x85 mm
Compression ratio	9.3:1	9.5:1	8:1
SAE horsepower	170 hp	180 hp	230 hp
Torque	22.0 mkg	26.7 mkg	38.5 mkg (279 lb-ft)
Fuel system	Mechanical fuel injection	Electronic FI	Electronic FI
Fuel required	Premium (all)		
Chassis			
Type	Unibody; steel (all)		
Chassis No. prefix	108.014	108.018	108.068
Transmission	4-speed-auto	4-speed-auto	3-speed auto
Rear-axle ratio	3.92:1	4.08:1	3.23:1
Rear suspension	Swing-axle, coil springs		
Front suspension	Unequal-length A-arms (all)		
Wheels	6x14 in. (all)		
Tires	185x14 in. (all)		
Brakes	4-wheel disc (all)		
Fuel capacity	21.7 gal (all)		
Weight	3,329 lb	3,439 lb	3,775 lb
Performance			
0-60 mph	12 sec	11 sec	12 sec
Top speed	118 mph (all)		
Fuel consumption	15 mph	15 mpg	14-16 mpg

Driving Impressions: 300SEL 6.3

On hot days, the 300SEL 6.3's fuel injection may suffer from vapor lock during hot-start attempts, but once you get it going, the engine should keep running. If you're stuck, let the engine cool. Turning the ignition key on and off for a few seconds at a time briefly activates the electric pump, moving cooler fuel from tank to engine. If you're in a hurry, spray the injection system with cold water. A simple factory fix for this problem is a relay (time switch, Part Number 001 545 16 24) and cable harness rack next to the other electrical relays that turns the cold-start injector on, even when the engine is hot.

A 6.3 is not much fun to drive at low speeds, but on the highway it comes into its own. Enjoying a good 6.3 on the open road will make you grin until your cheeks ache, but a bad one can make you cry. Low-speed ride is sharp over bumps, but speed up, and the car takes a set in a hard corner and goes around quickly in a surprisingly flat mode. If the steering wheel has a lot of play and the car wanders, the steering box mounting bolts may have loosened, and the chassis around them may have cracked.

The four-speed automatic transmission is typical of the era, with hard shifts the norm and a reluctance to downshift. The limited-slip differential is a liability in snow; low-rpm torque spins both wheels and may cause the entire rear of the car to slide sideways. On the track, the limited-slip gets you out of slow corners without spinning and frying the inside tire. During sharp turns at low speeds you'll hear groaning from the differential; that's normal. You may also hear gear whine, also normal; the differential mounts to the chassis, which transmits the sound.

Listen for noise from the power steering pump. Driveline vibrations indicate worn flex discs at each end of the driveshaft. You'll probably hear wind noise around the front vent windows, and by today's standards, the air conditioning and heating is mediocre. Engine vibration can signify a seizing air conditioning compressor.

The central locking may not work. Fixing it is usually a matter of discovering which door lock has the broken actuator diaphragm, involving more time than parts cost.

A good 6.3 will make at least 15 miles per gallon at highway speeds; around town you don't want to know. But no one buys these cars for fuel efficiency. Anyone who has driven one will tell you that.

The rarest 600 is this two-door Coupe, one of possibly two built. *FDB*

Proper tires are a common question. Originally the 6.3 wore special 195x14-inch radials, but that size went out of production. Many now have 205/70R14s, but Mercedes-Benz warns against that size; this is a heavy car, so load-carrying capacity is a factor. The best replacement size is 215/70VR14. Until the tires were found wanting when it came to handling its speed and weight, the 6.3 was headed for a racing career. DBAG built several with roll cages, racing seats, fender flares, and engine output bumped to around 350 horsepower. The 6.3 originally had aluminum/steel wheels and hubcaps, but many have been retrofitted with factory alloy wheels.

The 6.3 was a hit on the autobahns and in the United States, then in the throes of the musclecar era. Rudolf Uhlenhaut himself drove demonstration laps on the Laguna Seca track during the U.S. introduction, and contemporary journalists had plenty of fun with the car, there and later. The 6.3 is a classic sleeper. You can pull up next to a Corvette at a light and act innocent. When the light turns green, you stay just far enough ahead to get the 'Vette driver to try harder . . . and harder . . . and harder!

The 6.3 engine compartment is nowhere for the novice mechanic to practice, but the engine is extremely reliable and durable. *FDB*

What to Look For

Refer to the previous section dealing with potential rust areas in 108 and 109 bodies. That apart, maintenance records are important with 6.3s because they can be expensive to repair properly. Good, experienced, factory-trained mechanics are growing harder to find, and previous owners some-

This 280SE sedan has the larger front turn signals. Painted door frames are common to the 108 body, and the air-suspended 109 bodies used chrome-plated door trim. *FDB*

times attempt to fix things cheaply. Problem areas include the air suspension, the transmission, and the differential. If the expensive jobs have been done properly before you buy the car, that's good; most are once-in-a-lifetime procedures.

Some are wary of air suspension, but the system is simple. A compressor feeds air into a reservoir, then through tubes to an air bag at each wheel. Four valves control airflow—one master valve, one level control valve at each front wheel, and one at the rear axle. Problems involve corrosion in the valves and air lines or deteriorated air bags. A control knob is used to raise the car or lock the suspension (for jacking).

Alcohol in the reservoir behind the radiator is intended to dry the compressed air in the system, reducing condensation. Most owners let the reservoir run dry—finding any alcohol in it is a good sign. The metal air lines rust from the inside, but used ones can be found. Some control valves remain available now at stunning cost. Old ones can be rebuilt.

The air reservoir, ahead of the left front wheel, has a drain valve in the wheelwell. Push sideways on the drain tube, and you'll be rewarded with a slimy ejaculation of a revolting mixture of oil, condensation, and God knows what else. Seeing and smelling this (and cleaning it off your hand) is all the more reason to keep after the air suspension.

Each wheel's rubber air bag ages due to heat and ozone, so with the car on a lift, check to see how badly cracked or hardened they are. Replacement is simple, but do it now rather than later. When an air bag fails, the suspension bottoms out, a nuisance if you're far from help. Emergency metal supports were provided for insertion into the suspension to hold it up; look inside the spare wheel. If the car is on its knees, the owner has obviously not taken care of it. Properly maintained air suspension should allow an undriven car to stay up almost indefinitely.

Forces on the steering box may crack the steel chassis. The cure is to remove the steering box, weld reinforcing plates to the chassis, and remount the box. With the car stationary and the engine running, watch the steering box for movement as the wheels are turned in each direction.

The differential can be a trouble spot, but they all make noise, so don't replace it until it literally screams at you. Check the lubricant level in the differential. The limited-slip unit uses special fluid, available at dealers. Make sure the axle and suspension mounts are solid and rust-free, especially where the trailing arms connect to the chassis.

A 6.3 engine (and other early V-8s) may leak oil from an oil passage near the rear of the heads, demanding a new head gasket. Easier to fix, warped valve covers also cause oil leaks. Overheating can warp the aluminum heads, but they can be straightened and/or machined.

When you turn on the radio, the automatic electric Hirschmann antenna should rise fully, lowering again when you switch it off.

Restoration

A 300SEL 6.3 can be neither as easy nor as hard to restore as it might seem. Bargains exist, but here more than ever, avoiding them in favor of a better car can avoid a nightmare restoration. Buy a cheap 6.3, and you will end up using it as a parts car.

Rust thrives in rocker panels, lower doors, around headlights and fender openings, in the trunk, and in the closing panels behind the front wheels. Even a car that looks great can have plenty of rust under its shiny new paint. With many Mercedes-Benz restorations, the tendency is to dazzle the viewer with slick paint, but neglect the basics and the details. These big cars have a lot of glass and exterior trim, and a good restoration is often spoiled by poor metalwork or failure to replace pitted glass or scratched trim.

Luckily, most body parts and trim on a 6.3 are shared with 108- and other 109-bodied cars. A good informal network of 6.3 owners and suppliers has evolved, so you are never alone.

Summary

Best bang for the buck is how we'll sum up these V-8s. You can enjoy their high performance, but it's in a cruder form than today's smoother cars. And be prepared to pay for it at the pump. Still, the big maintenance jobs are done only once per 100,000 miles, so long-term ownership can be reasonable.

The sixes and small V-8s are economical to buy and not expensive to maintain. A 600 or a 300SEL 6.3 is demanding to own, maintain, and restore, but it is sure to grow in value, kept in good condition. Few other old Mercedes-Benz cars are more fun to drive.

This interior happens to be a 280SE, but apart from the column-mounted shifter, it is similar to that of all contemporary 280 and 300 models. Air conditioning was now integral with the dash. *FDB*

The 280SE engine is similar to that of the 280SL. Six-cylinder cars mounted the air conditioning compressor high instead of below the engine as in V-8 cars. *FDB*

The 300SEL 3.5 is quite rare, but with 230 horsepower, it is a surprisingly strong performer. *DBAG*

Chapter 13

350SL, 380SL, 450SL, 500SL, and 560SL 1970–1989

The W107 chassis of the 350, 380, 450, 500, and 560SLs was one of Daimler-Benz AG's longest-running production bodies. With a variety of six- and eight-cylinder engines, it bridged the considerable gap between the 1971 280SL and the 1990s SL models. Between April 1971 and August 1989, more than 237,000 W107 SLs were built; about two-thirds were sold new in the United States.

The 1971 350SL was completely different from the 1960s 230, 250, and 280SLs. that it replaced. The only recognizable carryover styling trait is the dip and the trim strips crossing the pagoda-shaped hardtop roof. Below that, everything was new.

Here was the first SL with a V-8, the 3.5-liter powerhouse that had made its debut in the 280SE 3.5. In the late 1960s, Daimler-Benz foresaw the conflict of performance and environmental controls. While customers craved power, the American government demanded lower emissions and proffered new rules about crashworthy bumpers. Meeting these conflicting demands meant bigger engines, heavier cars, and more fuel.

The new SL was not only faster and safer than the 1960s 280SL but also bigger, heavier, costlier, and thirstier. Like the old SLs, the new ones softened as the years passed, becoming mere boulevardiers, and most owners used only a fraction of the car's performance. Thanks to gentle treatment and popularity, thousands survive in excellent condition.

350SL 1971–1980 and 450SL 1972–1980 ★★★

Confusion exists about engine displacement in the 350SL, sometimes called the 350SL 4.5. The new SL was introduced in Europe as a 1971 350SL with a 3.5-liter, iron-block M116 V-8. The first U.S. 350SL, for 1972, actually had a low-compression 4.5-liter engine and bore the chassis number prefix 107.044. European 3.5-liter 350SL engine numbers (see rear of the block) start with 116.982 (high-compression) or 116.992(low-compression). All 4.5-liter engine numbers start with 117. According to one veteran mechanic, "In 1972, when those cars came into the dealerships for their first service, we would remove the '350SL' emblem and replace it with a '450SL' emblem."

All 1971–1980 SLs sold in America had three-speed automatics. The 350SL (and later European SLs) had manual climate controls allowing driver and passenger to adjust heat or cooling separately, but the U.S. 450SL soon got the complex Automatic Climate Control (ACC) system. With painted hubcaps and hand-cranked windows, a 1971 350SL sold for $11,059; its descendant, the 1989 560SL, cost $64,230.

The pre-1974 350SL and 450SL have the graceful original-design bumpers rather than the clumsy crash bumpers fitted to 1974 and later cars. Early-style bumpers continued on European cars and can be fitted to most U.S. SLs. Alloy wheels became optional equipment for 1976 and standard for 1980; by now, most SLs have had them retrofitted.

The 450SL had excellent performance, but early emission controls strangled the engine. Performance, drivability, and fuel efficiency suffered, and vapor lock caused hot-start problems. The 1972–1974 U.S. models could use leaded or unleaded gasoline, but 1975 and 1976 models had the most vapor lock problems because their catalytic converters were in the engine compartment, where airflow was restricted by the tight-fitting engine

The first and last of two decades: the 350SL, above, and the 560SL, below. Besides the obvious powerplant changes, many other more subtle improvements were made. *MBNA*

Technical Specifications			
Model	450SL	380SL	560SL
Years	1972-1980	1981-1985	1986-1989
Engine			
Type	Sohc V-8 (all)		
Engine No. prefix	M117.982	M116.962	M117.967
Displacement	4,520 cc (275.8 ci)	3,839 cc (234.3 ci)	5,547 cc(338.5 ci)
Bore x stroke	92x85 mm	88x78.9 mm	96.5x94.8 mm
Compression ratio	8.0:1 (1980)	8.3:1	9.0:1
SAE horsepower	180 hp @ 4,750 rpm (to 1979) 160 hp @ 4,200 rpm (1980)	155 hp @ 4,750 rpm	227 hp @ 4,750 rpm
Torque	230 lb-ft @ 2,500 rpm (to 1979)	196 lb-ft @ 2,750 rpm	279 lb-ft @ 3,250 rpm
Fuel system	Bosch D or K-Jetronic fuel injection	K-Jetronic fuel injection	KE-Jetronic fuel injection
Fuel required	Unleaded, 91 octane		Unleaded, 92 octane
Chassis			
Type	Unibody; steel with aluminum		
Chassis No. prefix	107.044	107.045	107.048
Transmission	3-speed auto	4-speed auto	4-speed auto
Rear-axle ratio	3.07:1 (to 1979) 2.65:1 (1980)	2.47:1	2.47:1
Rear suspension	Semi-trailing arm, coil springs (all)		
Front suspension	Unequal length A-arms, coil springs (all)		
Wheels	6.5x14 in.	6.5x14 in.	7x15 in.
Tires	205/70VR14	205/70HR14	205/65VR15
Brakes	4-wheel disc, power-assisted (all)		
Fuel capacity	23.8 gal	22.5 gal	22.5 gal
Weight	3,615 lb (+hardtop)	3,495 lb (+hardtop)	3,670 lb
Performance			
0-60 mph	11.5 sec (1980) 10.7 sec (to 1979)	11.5 sec	7.5 sec
Top speed	112 mph (1980)	110 mph	130 mph
Fuel consumption	12-19 mpg (to 1979) 16-22 mpg (1980)	16-22 mpg	15-17 mpg

Note: The 450SL figures are for a 1980 model; 380SL figures are for a 1985 model.

hood. For 1977, the catalytic converters were moved back beneath the floor.

For 1976, CIS fuel injection replaced the earlier electronic injection, accompanied by hydraulic valve lifters and breakerless electronic ignition. Some years ago Mercedes-Benz recalled all 450SLs and SLCs to weld a reinforcing bracket to the lower control arm mounting of the front suspension.

To avoid camshaft wear, all 4.5-liter V-8s require frequent oil changes and top-quality oil. The right-side camshaft usually wears first. If you're having a mechanic check the car, ask him to remove the valve covers and look at the cam lobes.

For the 1978 model year, the 450SL (and SLC) were fitted with automatic climate control, never known for durability. Problems involve the electronic controls, the servo that directs coolant flow, and the vacuum-operated air flaps. A good Mercedes-Benz mechanic will be familiar enough with the system to fix it, but the work can require extensive diagnosis and labor.

To improve fuel economy, the 1980 450SL's engine was detuned from 180 to 160 horsepower SAE and a higher (lower numerically) rear axle was fitted, which cut performance. To help prevent vapor lock, for 1980, the air conditioner was used to cool fuel being fed to the engine. Earlier cars can be fitted with a switch to run the electric fuel pump and circulate cooler fuel from the tank before starting. It helps to keep the tank as full as possible. If vapor lock occurs, try turning the ignition switch on and off rapidly. This starts the fuel pump and may move cooler fuel into the injection system. Another way to do this is to disconnect the plug on the airflow sensor plate safety switch and let the fuel pump run with the key on to flush the system. If all else fails, pour cold water on the injection system.

Between 1971 and 1980, a total of 66,298 450SLs were produced, making it by far the most numerous SL. Next most popular was the 380SL, with 53,000 built from 1980 through 1985.

380SL 1981–1985 ★★★

Thanks to the new-for-1981 380SL's 3.8-liter V-8, some carefully added lightness, and a new four-speed automatic transmission, performance of the smaller engine was adequate, and the SL continued as a sales success in the United States despite its aging design.

The M116 aluminum-block V-8 was designed to work well with emission controls. Apart from the engine saving about 110 pounds, the 380SL was also lightened by its aluminum engine hood. Again, leather upholstery was an option. None of the U.S. 450SLs or 380SLs had factory alarm systems or power seats, not to mention air bags or ABS brakes.

The 1981–1983 380SL had a mechanical quirk—it used a single-row cam chain instead of the usual dual-row chain. If the oil wasn't changed, friction under load could cause the chain to wear and stretch. If a single-row chain jumped a tooth on its sprockets, the valves could hit the pistons, with expensive consequences. For the 1984 model year, DBAG went to a duplex (double-row) chain that can be retrofitted to any older 380SL. If your car has a single-row chain, check the tension every 10,000 miles; at the first sign of wear, convert to the dual-row chain. MBNA no longer sells the old single-row

The 350SL with soft top up, European headlights, short bumpers. Michelin XWX tires were standard equipment, and even today they look just right on a restored car. *DBAG.*

chain, and no good mechanic would install one. You must convert to the double-row chain. Conversion won't be cheap, but it will cost far less than an engine overhaul, improve reliability, and enhance the car's value. If you're looking at a 1981–1983 SL, check the records to see if the conversion was made, or ask the owner if you can have a mechanic pull a valve cover to see.

The 380SL was the least powerful of these U.S. sports roadsters. For that reason, and because some still have the single-row timing chain, their values are lower than they might be. The 380SL's last model year was 1985.

Although the 500SL was popular in Europe, it was never sold as a U.S. model. Early 1980s gray market importers fed American desires for a more powerful SL, and hundreds of 500SLs were "unoffi-

This early 350SLC four-seater clearly shows the added length and louvered rear windows. See how good this car looks with the original bumper design? *DBAG*

cially" imported. (For more on gray market cars, see Chapter 2). Watching these private imports sell thousands of European SLs, Mercedes-Benz of North America acted . . .

560SL 1986–1989 ★★★

For 1986, DBAG cured the 380SL's modest power and skewered the gray market by sending America the much stronger 560SL. The power and torque of its 47 percent larger engine better suited the big Roadster's personality, especially around town. This final iteration of the W107 chassis SL was sold only in North America.

The 560SLŌs 227-horsepower M117 V-8 gave it a tremendous performance boost over the 380SL, 450SL, and even the U.S. 500SL. With a new double-wishbone rear suspension, a front air dam, and new-styled 7x15-inch alloy wheels, the 560SL did 0–60 miles per hour in 8 seconds, down dramatically from the 11.5 seconds of the 500SL. Top speed

leapt from the 380SL's 115 to 13 7 miles per hour. A third brake light was first required in 1986, so it was stuck onto the trunk lid in a blister-like enclosure. More importantly, the 560SL also had a limited-slip differential, leather upholstery, ABS brakes, and an alarm. To reduce rear-end squat and lift, a torque compensation arm braced the rear axle. Tire width stayed at 205 millimeters, but wheels went from 6.5x14 to 7x15. The seats were still hand-adjusted, but a driver's side air bag was standard fare.

Given that it was the most powerful and best developed, the 560SL is the most desirable 1980s SL. The sole disappointment was that Mercedes-Benz never did heal those ugly bumpers.

The SLC ★★★

The four-seater SLC differs from the SL in having two habitable rear seats, a 14.2-inch longer wheelbase, and a slightly higher fixed steel top. First sold in America for 1972 as the 350SLC, this 2 +2 SL added the extra length right behind the door. To fill the longer quarter window, a unique set of vertical louvers was positioned to maintain visibility.

Air conditioning, power windows, central locking, a leather interior, and an automatic transmission were standard on the American SLC. An electric sunroof was optional, along with a heated rear window, and more.

As in the American 350SL, the 350SLC designation was a misnomer. Both had the M117 4.5-liter V-8, and in 1973 they officially became the 450SL and 450SLC. This engine first made about 195 horsepower, but emissions controls cut the

Chassis and Engine Prefix Numbers

Years	Model	Chassis Prefix	Engine Prefix	Description
1971–1980	350SL	107.043	116	8-cyl 190 hp SAE
1972–1980	350SLC	107.023	116	8-cyl 190 hp SAE
1970–1980	450SL (includes U.S. 350SL 4.5)	107.044	117.982 or .985	8-cyl 160–230 hp SAE
1970–1980	450SLC	107.024	117.982 or .985	8-cyl 160–230 hp SAE
1974–1985	280SL	R107 E 28	110	6-cyl gas, 117-185 hp DIN
1974–1981	280SLC	C107 E 28	110	6-cyl gas, 185 hp DIN
1978–1980	450SLC 5.0	C107 E 50	117	8-cyl gas, 240 hp DIN
1980–1985	380SL	107.045	116.960 or .962	8-cyl gas, 115 hp (U.S.)
1980–1981	380SLC	107.025	116.960 or .962	8-cyl gas, 115 hp (U.S.)
1985–1989	300SL	R107 E 30	103 E 30	6-cyl gas, 180–188 hp DIN
1985–1989	450SL	R107 E 42	116 E 42	8-cyl gas, 204–218 hp DIN
1980–1985	500SL	107.	117	8-cyl gas, 240 hp DIN
1980–1981	500SLC	C107 E 50	117	8-cyl gas, 240 hp DIN
1986–1989	560SL	107.048	117.967	8-cyl gas, 227 hp (U.S.)

Note: Models listed with DIN horsepower ratings were not officially imported to the United States, but are listed here because many arrived via the gray market.

The SLC's U.S. version grew 5-mile per hour crash bumpers for the 1974 model year, and alloy wheels became standard equipment for 1977. *MBNA*

450SLC's output to about 160 horsepower by 1980, the model's last year before being replaced by the 380SL and the rare 380SLC. The SLC's last model year in any form was 1981. The most popular SLC was the 450, with 31,739 made from 1972 to 1980. Only 3,789 380SLCs were built.

European Variations

Between 1967 and 1990, U.S. and European safety and emission regulations at first diverged, then practically merged. At first, European cars got all the good stuff. Their headlights were more aerodynamic and attractive than the sealed-beams of U.S. models. Their early bumpers were lighter and cleaner. Unburdened by emission control, European engines generated far more power. But by the late 1980s, even German SLs had catalytic converters.

European SLs could be bought with six-cylinder engines (the 280SL) and a four- or five-speed manual transmission. Thousands of 107 chassis 280SLs and 500SLs were imported as gray market cars. Even a 420SL was made, and from 1985, a 300SL used the 188-horsepower M103 inline six of the 300E. These cars may offer excellent performance, but their low U.S. prices now are a result of their low trade-in value and the potential difficulties of a gray market car.

As the U.S. 380SL grew more expensive, the European 500SL became popular on the gray market. With 240 horsepower and a wide range of options (ABS brakes, velour interiors, manual climate control, limited-slip differential, rear spoiler, wider wheels, and so on) combined with lower

This rare 450SLC 5.0 has rocker panels of contrasting color and a small rear spoiler atop the trunk lid. *DBAG*

prices, these 500SLs were attractive to Americans. But improper conversions and the reluctance of some U.S. Mercedes-Benz dealers to even service gray market cars limited their popularity and hastened depreciation.

An exception is the 450SLC 5.0 built as a 1978–1980 European model. A small rubber rear spoiler and a different front spoiler make the 450SLC 5.0 easy to spot. Its aluminum engine lid and trunk lid saved about 125 pounds, and the new M117 aluminum-block 5,025-cc engine was about 95 pounds lighter. Power went up to 240 DIN horsepower, torque was 297 lb-ft, and top speed was about 140 miles per hour. Compression ratio was 8.8:1.

The 1978–79 450SLC 5.0, a homologation special for the factory rally team, was a European model. Lighter and more powerful than the 450SLC, it was superseded by the 1980-81 500SLC, upgraded with a four-speed automatic instead of the previous three-

European SLs such as this 450SLC 5.0 continued with the original short bumpers. *FDB*

speed. With aluminum engine hoods, trunk lids, and rear valances, both 5-liter SLCs are relatively rare.

What to Look For

Rust is a relatively minor problem with these cars, but look for it anyway. Besides the normal places under the fenders and around the headlights and wheelwells, open the metal tonneau cover and check the top well. The front valence may show damage from concrete curbs. Look for water and sun damage to upholstery, wood, and carpets. Lift the front and rear floor mats to look for water-soaked foam padding. Water also collects in the front frame members on the left and right side of the radiator mounts. If you find significant rust or much accident damage, find a better car. So many good examples exist that there's no savings in buying and restoring a heap.

To avoid having to repair cam wear on the 450SL, pull the right-side (or both) valve covers and look closely at every cam lobe. Rotate the engine (using a wrench on the crankshaft) and look for pitting at the top of each lobe.

On a 1981–1983 380SL, check the cam chain to see whether it is the original single-row type or the desirable double-row replacement. If the car doesn't have a double chain, figure on substantial cost to install it (about $3,500 in 1998). All 1984 and later 380SLs originally came with double-row chains, so there's no need to check them. All other things being equal, this is one reason to buy a 1984 or later car.

Despite the durability problems of some automakers' aluminum blocks, the better-designed Mercedes-Benz blocks are at least as durable as their cast-iron equivalents. An SL is generally one of the most durable Mercedes-Benz cars.

Smooth-faced European lights lent themselves to fitting headlight wipers. *FDB*

In 1985, MBNA warned owners of the 350SL, 350SLC, 450SL, and 450SLC to have their cars inspected for cracks in the lower rear control arm mountings of the front suspension. Reinforcement brackets can be welded in. The 380SL and 560SL were unaffected.

Older cars are somewhat prone to overheating and vapor lock, particularly with today's fuels and because the 450SL's catalytic converters were up front, under the tight-fitting engine hood. Hot start problems are a sign of vapor lock; the engine will restart immediately when hot and when cold, but left standing for a few minutes while hot, it will not fire.

Another similar problem can exist in pre-1980 models. While difficult hot starts may seem to signal vapor lock, the real cause may be worn valve seats. When a hot engine fails to start, improperly seating valves allow combustion pressure back into the intake manifold. When the fuel injection system's manifold pressure sensor reads this surge, the computer leans the

Whatever grace an SL has is severely compromised by these U.S. bumpers. *FDB*

fuel mixture so much that the engine won't start. A valve job cures the problem. More immediate cures include waiting for the engine to cool or spraying water on it. The 1980 and later CIS fuel injection helped, too.

Examining the service records not only assures you that the proper service was done, but also that it was performed by a qualified mechanic. Look for mechanics' comments on invoices, particularly such phases as "Customer declines . . ."

As a driver and a collector car, we suggest either the earliest or the latest—either a 1972 350SL (definitely collectible, with the small bumpers and perhaps a manual transmission) or a late-model 560SL. As a second choice we'd suggest a late 450SL, perhaps 1979 (before the 1980 power decrease) so that you get as many improvements as possible. A 380SL may be the least desirable, but it can make a fine daily driver, with better fuel mileage than the 450SL or the 560SL. As a high performance rarity, try the

The 450SLC 5.0 did surprisingly well in long-distance international rallies; here Andrew Cowan approaches the finish of a 30,000-kilometer event in South America in 1978. *DBAG*

450SLC or 500SLC, but make sure this frequently abused European model hasn't been ridden hard and put away wet.

One final caution. If you're looking at a 560SL at a price within, say, 20 percent of that of an equally good 1990 or later 300SL or 500SL, consider buying the newer car, especially if you'll drive it a lot. The newer car is more agile, spacious, safe, and enjoyable—but it is also much more complex.

Restoration

Since thousands of excellent original examples still exist, restoration of these SLs has been limited. A new top is logical, but fighting rust, incorrectly repaired damage, or big mechanical problems makes little sense. Even if you already own the car, you're likely far better off finding a cleaner, original example.

Because they were more complex, bigger, and heavier than the 1960s 280SLs, these cars cost more to restore properly. Later models have more complicated

systems, especially the climate controls, but a 350SL is relatively simple. About the only W107 SLs that justify expensive restoration now are the 450SLC 5.0 and 500SLC, because of their rarity and performance.

Operation of these cars will not be inexpensive, and neither will parts and repairs; you'll likely have to rely on a professional mechanic to maintain these sophisticated cars. Since they are too new to qualify for classic car coverage, insurance will be costly, too, and you'll need a garage to protect your investment. Check licensing and insurance costs before you commit.

Summary

As the earliest W107 SLs began to be considered collectible, the latest are still in the early or middle stages of depreciation. Dating from the 1960s, their design may be ancient, but these SL models have served reliably. The 380SLs are good buys, and the 560 is the most fun for those who like to drive quickly, but none of these cars will disappoint you.

American racer Neal DeAtley entered an SL, driven by Loren St. Lawrence, in the Trans-Am series in 1981-1982, tuning the engine to around 450 horsepower and paring weight to 2,400 pounds. *DeAtley*

The 227-horsepower 560SL, sold only in the United States, gained a new front air dam and ABS brakes. By then, leather upholstery and the hardtop were standard equipment. *MBNA*

Chapter 14

Sedans and Coupes 1968–1980

Safety and emissions assumed new importance in the late 1960s. As the flagship for the 1970s, the 450SE and SEL addressed these concerns and was regarded as the best sedan in the world. The new midrange models joining it were equally successful.

Between 1967 and 1973, DBAG put almost every engine into almost every chassis, and some models were short-lived. Apart from the 1968–1973 V-8s described in Chapter 12, let's look at the other sedans.

450SE and 450SEL 1973–1980 ★★

In 1973, the world standard for luxury cars was reestablished by the new 450SE, soon followed by the 450SEL with a 3.9-inch longer wheelbase and more rear legroom. Although the W116 used practically the same V-8 engine as the preceding 1971–1973 4.5s, it was a completely different chassis.

For the S-Class, Daimler-Benz finally abandoned the rear swing-axles in favor of trailing arms, which kept the rear wheels more upright throughout the range of suspension travel. Less drastic camber change improved stability, even in a straight line, by limiting rear toe-in and toe-out. The entire body was stronger, with additional interior padding and improved seatbelts. The 450SE and SEL strongly resemble a Mercedes-Benz safety car unveiled in 1971. The structure was designed to meet the new impact requirements.

Between 1973 and 1980, the 450SE and SEL were the world's best overall cars, combining the highest levels in safety, interior space, handling, performance, and ride.

The 1973 model was the only U.S. 450 sedan to have the original, slim, European-style bumpers. Later U.S. versions are protected by federally

In its first U.S. model year, the 1973 450SE came with hubcaps (instead of alloy wheels) and short, European style bumpers. *MBNA*

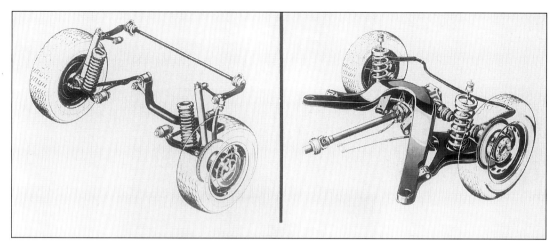

The 450SE had new suspension at each end. The front uses a MacPherson strut with separate coil springs and shock absorbers; the rear gave up on the swing-axle in favor of semi-trailing arms. *DBAG*

mandated 5-mile-per-hour battering rams that don't harmonize with the lines of the car. Mercedes-Benz left them that way for the life of the model.

The 450SE and SEL arrived just as the emission and fuel crises struck, and both harmed the cars. Emissions technology was in its infancy, so drivability sometimes suffered. Fuel mileage rarely bettered the mid-teens. As the cars age, problems such as vapor lock, aging wiring, and fuel consumption worsen. The 1973–1975 450SEs and SELs used an early version of electronic fuel injec-

tion, but 1976 and later cars had the more reliable Bosch CIS injection, also called K-Jetronic. Quantity is matched to the amount of intake air, and fuel is injected continuously, hence the name Continuous Injection System.

The 4.5 V-8 was a great engine with one weak point: Its camshafts were susceptible to premature wear. Camshafts are difficult parts of any engine to lubricate. The oil lines to the camshafts were held by plastic clips, which become brittle and break. When you have a valve cover off, make sure these

Driving Impression: 450SE, 450SEL, and 450SEL 6.9

Because it lacks the smog clutter, an early 450SE or SEL is a good performer. The shorter wheelbase makes the SE more nimble than the SEL, which is more spacious for back-seat passengers. These are long-legged cars, about the earliest models that you can drive hard for a thousand miles without collapsing at day's end.

The 6.9 feels like driving your living room down the road at 130 miles per hour. The car is quiet, smooth, and astonishingly fast, yet is totally unfussy. It demands only that you feed it massive quantities of fuel and maintain it in the manner to which it has become accustomed. Despite having power windows (controlled by switches awkwardly mounted on the console), the 6.9 had manually adjusted seats.

Comparisons with the 300SEL 6.3 are inevitable. The earlier car is less sophisticated and not as quiet and smooth, yet it's more fun. Most acknowledge that the 6.3 accelerates more quickly but that the 6.9 is better handling, more comfortable, and easier to drive fast. A good 6.3 will get slightly better gas mileage, and maintenance cost is probably a toss-up.

The 6.9 is a generation better than the 6.3. Its controls and transmission are smoother, and the steering is more precise. Besides having better heating and air conditioning, a 6.9 is safer, too. Even little things such as the windshield wipers work better.

Short of a 500E, the driver of 450SEL 6.9 will find that it is still one of the best sedans of all time.

Even the SE is a big car, so the SEL's extra rear legroom is not absolutely necessary. The SE is only slightly lighter than the SEL, so there's no real performance benefit; few can feel the slight handling difference due to the longer wheelbase. A good 1973 450SE is a joy to drive. It tracks down the road straight, smooth, and true, and you feel like Superman behind the wheel.

In its time, the W116 chassis was the best-driving sedan in the world. Credit for this goes to its suspension, especially the semi-trailing arms in the rear, which gave it great stability.

125

The loss suffered from the 450SEL's transition to U.S. government-mandated bumpers was somewhat offset by the appearance boost of alloy wheels. *MBNA*

clips are in place, and check the peaks of the cam lobes for wear.

Another problem can exist in pre-1980 models. While difficult hot starts may seem to indicate vapor lock, the real cause is often worn valve seats. When a hot engine fails to start, improperly seating valves may be allowing combustion pressure back into the intake manifold. When the fuel injection system's manifold pressure sensor reads this surge, it signals the computer to lean the fuel mixture so much that the engine won't start. A valve job cures the problem. More immediate cures include waiting for the engine to cool or spraying water on it. The 1980 and later CIS fuel injection helped, too.

Other common problems include the automatic climate control servo (1976–1979) and the water pump. The 450SE and SEL were the first Mercedes-Benz models to use an automatic climate control; you set the desired temperature on a wheel, set the mode, and the system maintains the temperature. Before operating this system, read the owners manual. A seeming failure may be simply due to incorrect setting.

This system had weak spots. Chief of these was the electrically operated servo valve controlling coolant flow through the heating system, the same ex-Chrysler unit used in W123 (300D, 300TD, and so on) bodies. Replacement servos and electronic controllers are available.

The three-speed automatic transmissions in these cars were noted for their durability.

These cars are so enjoyable that their owners never know when to stop driving them. Today it's hard to find a 450 with fewer than 100,000 miles behind it. The 1976 model year was the 450SE's last in the United States; from then until the end of the 1980 model year, only the 450SEL was available. Between 1972 and 1980, 41,604 450SEs and 59,578 450SELs were made.

450SEL 6.9 ★★★

Not until 1975 did DBAG get around to replacing the 300SEL 6.3—with the 450SEL 6.9. Its M100 engine was developed from the 6.3-liter unit but appeared only in this car; the 600 continued with the 6.3-liter. The 6.9's main advantages over the 450SEL included better performance, more advanced suspension, and slightly more luxury.

The 6.9's engine improvements included dry-sump lubrication and K-Jetronic fuel injection. A more sophisticated valve clearance method using oil to support the rocker arm fulcrum eliminated the need for mechanical valve adjustment and quieted the valvetrain. The oil tank is alongside the engine.

The 450SEL 6.9 was sold in Europe starting in 1975. Of 7,380 built, 1,816 were 1977–1979 U.S. models (often called the 6.9, without the 450SEL prefix). To meet emission laws, the U.S. version had a tad less power, with minimal effect. A European version may have ABS brakes. Quite a few found their way to the United States unofficially, but your typical Serious German Motoring Enthusiast back then bought the newest, biggest, fastest car and drove the living tar out of it. When the car would no longer pass the rigid German TUV safety inspection, he or she found a ready market among U.S. enthusiasts. Hence, *caveat emptor* (let the buyer beware) when looking at any European 6.9.

Lead, follow, or get the hell out of the way—this 6.9-liter 450SEL means business! Bumper faces are all-black; tires are huge Michelin XWX's. *MBNA/John Lamm*

The 6.9's interior had a little more wood than the garden-variety 450SEL, but manual seats remained the only choice on this $50,000 car.

Besides the chassis numbers, the easiest way to tell a European 6.9 is by its smaller bumpers, metric instruments, and possibly a cloth interior. European power was 286 DIN horsepower with 405 lb-ft of torque. U.S. emission controls included air injection and a catalytic converter, cutting power to 250 horsepower and torque to 360 lb-ft. In U.S. form, the 4,400-pound car could reach 60 miles per hour in just over 8 seconds, topping out at about 137 miles per hour.

Built before the days of traction control, a 6.9 (or a 6.3) can be kicked sideways by heavy throttle on a slick street. You could also outrun just about any production car from a standing start, looking relaxed and comfy doing so. Part of the fun of owning these cars is that they may be the ultimate "sleeper."

The 6.9 is more comfortable than the 6.3 (and even the 450SE) because it has a sophisticated hydropneumatic suspension. Instead of the 6.3's air system or the 450SE's coil springs, the 6.9 uses nitrogen gas and hydraulic oil with a spherical pressure reservoir at each wheel. This provides better low-speed ride than the air system and responds

European captains of industry could buy a 450SEL 6.9 with small bumpers, flush headlights, and headlight wipers. *DBAG*

better to changing suspension loads. Instead of the 6.3's rear swing-axle, the 6.9 uses semi-trailing arms, which better control camber change.

In a 6.9, the transmission handles a lot more torque than in the 450SE or SEL. Tires should be 215/70VR14 on 6.5x14-inch alloy wheels; the original Michelin XWXs are expensive and short-lived. Standard features on U.S. 6.9s included leather upholstery, central locking, four headrests, rear reading lamps, fog lights, a fully carpeted trunk, and a tachometer. Options were an electric sunroof, velour seats, orthopedic and/or heated seats, and metallic paint. European 6.9s have a switch to increase ride height about 1.6 inches. The same switch is used to lock the suspension into place for jacking. U.S. cars have the high-ride position blocked.

The market for 6.9s is unusual. American models sold new for $40,000–$50,000, a fortune at the time. Some cherry examples "meticulously maintained" (the Mercedes-Benz seller's favorite term) by original owners with delusions of great value top today's price scale, but others with obscure histories and lots of miles can be had for a fraction of the higher prices. Aim for the midrange and be patient. Every time a 6.9 owner pays for service, he or she considers selling it. Time your offer accordingly!

The massive W116 body could still mix it up with the best of them; witness this modified 450SEL at a club driving event. *FDB*

What to Look For

Rusty 450SE and SEL sedans are uncommon. These cars, now growing old, are more likely to have suffered from improper maintenance. Some second or third owners can't afford to keep them up properly, so they postpone repairs or try a cheap patch job. The cars grow ever more tired and unkempt. Maintenance records mean a lot with these cars.

Because these cars are often owned by nonenthusiasts, they are more likely to be shabby. Be suspicious of fresh paint and undercoating. One clear indication of whether an owner cares about his car is its tires. Are they the right size and speed rating, or are they cheap substitutes for the genuine item?

Test every system, especially the heating and air conditioning and the instruments, power windows, power antenna, windshield wipers, and locks. The automatic climate control servo is notorious for failure, usually involving a cracked valve body. Left unattended, this can lead to coolant loss, with the usual serious consequences. Original equipment plastic servos are available from Mercedes-Benz dealers, and aftermarket suppliers offer aluminum servo bodies. Look for coolant seepage around the water pump, which is expensive to replace.

On the 6.9, check the suspension thoroughly. First, make sure it works properly. On a European 6.9, use the level control to adjust the ride height. On all 6.9s, invite a couple of people into the trunk to make sure the self-leveling does so. The trunk should contain four rubber blocks—two front and two rear—to support the car if the suspension fails. Should the car drop to its knees, you jack it up, take off each wheel, insert the block, and tie it in place with an attached wire. Often missing, these blocks are hard to find. A harsh ride indicates the needs for new nitrogen spheres; the suspension should not leak fluid.

Since the 6.9 has a dry-sump oil system, its oil level is checked with the engine idling at normal operating temperature.

Technical Specifications			
Model	280S/SE	450SE/SEL	450SEL 6.9
Years	1972–1980	1973–1980	1977–1979 (U.S.)
Engine			
Type	Inline dohc six	V-8	V-8
Engine No. prefix	110.922/110.985	116.983, 116.985	100.985
Displacement	2,746 cc (168 ci)	4,520 cc 276 ci)	6,834 cc (417 ci)
Bore x stroke	86x78.8 mm	92x85 mm	107x95 mm
Compression ratio	8:1 (all)		
SAE horsepower	120 hp (U.S.)	190 hp (1973 U.S.)	240 hp (U.S.)
Torque	143 lb-ft	240 lb-ft	360 lb-ft
Fuel system	Solex 4-bbl carb (to 1976)	Electronic fuel injection(1973–75)	K-Jetronic fuel
	K-Jetronic fuel injection (1977–80)	K- Jetronic fuel injection(1976–80)	injection
Fuel required	Unleaded	Regular (1973)	Unleaded
Chassis			
Type	Unibody; steel (all)		
Chassis No. prefix	116.020	116.032/116.033	116.036
Transmission	4-speed auto	3-speed auto	3-speed auto
Rear-axle ratio	3.69:1	3.07:1	2.65:1
Rear suspension	Semi-trailing arms, coil springs	Semi-trailing arms, coil springs	Hydro-pneumatic
Front suspension	Lower A-arms, lateral links, coil springs		
Wheels	6.5x14in (all)		
Tires	185HR14	205/70VR14	215/70VR14
Brakes	4-wheel disc (all)		
Fuel capacity	25.4 gal (all)		
Weight	3,890 lb	4,030 lb	4,300 lb
Performance			
0-60 mph	17 sec	11 sec	8 sec
Top speed	103 mph	125 mph	140 mph
Fuel consumption	15 mpg	12-15 mpg	11–15 mpg

Restoration

Few of these cars have been restored much beyond a paint job. It's still simpler to sell your old one and find a fresher one. These are large and fairly complex cars, so they cost a lot in parts and labor to refurbish (or even to furbish, for that matter).

The early electronic fuel injection was susceptible to bad wiring connections, especially with age. You might be able to make the car run better by methodically cleaning connections; otherwise, a new fuel injection wiring harness may help. Apart from the cam lubrication problem, engines routinely last well beyond 200,000 miles before overhaul or replacement. If you decide to overhaul the engine, check out the replacement engines offered by Mercedes-Benz and other rebuilders.

Restoring a 6.9 is exceeded in cost only by restoring a 600 or prewar classic. If you have to ask how much, forget it. Classified ad sections are full of owners who are financially buried in their 6.9s, and you needn't join them

Because the W116 bodied cars are so numerous, the choice of a restorer is not as critical as it can be with a rare model. Most foreign car body shops have already seen plenty of these cars and have built up experience. All you need do is judge their previous work and communicate what you expect. Right.

280S and 280SE: A Six-Cylinder Variant

A twin-cam 2.8-liter six in the big W116 sedan chassis created the 280S/SE models. In Germany, the fuel-injected 280SE engine sang unfettered at around 185 horsepower, but in the United States, limited to 120 horsepower by emission laws, the carbureted 280S sedans could barely get out of their own way. A four-speed automatic (instead of the 450's three-speed) helped, but the four-barrel Solex carburetor didn't. Gas mileage was disappointing.

For 1977, with fuel injection, the model became the 280SE, but Americans weren't used to revving an engine to redline, so first impressions caused many U.S. sales prospects to think, "Gee, I could have a V-8." Few 280SEs were sold in the United States.

The 114 and 115 sedans (here in European form) were faithful daily drivers for hundreds of thousands of Mercedes-Benz owners. *DBAG*

Technical Specifications

Model	220 Sedan	250 Sedan	280 Sedan
Years	1968-1973	1969	1971-1976
Engine			
Type	Inline four	Inline sohc six	Inline dohc six
Engine No. prefix	115.920	130.923 or 114.920	110.921
Displacement	2,197 cc (134 ci)	2,778 cc (169 ci)	2,746 cc (168 ci)
Bore x stroke	87.0x92.4 mm	86.5x78.8 mm	86x78.8 mm
Compression ratio	9:1	9:1	8:1
SAE horsepower	116 hp	157 hp	120-160 hp
Torque	19.7 mkg (143 lb-ft)	25.1 mkg (182 lb-ft)	23.0 mkg (166 lb-ft)
Fuel system	Solex or Stromberg (U.S.) carbs	Dual Zenith carbs	Dual Solex carbs
Fuel required	Premium	Premium	Premium or unleaded
Chassis			
Type	Unibody; steel (all)		
Chassis No. prefix	115.010	114.010	114.060
Transmission	4-speed, automatic or manual	4-speed automatic	4-speed automatic
Rear-axle ratio	4.08:1	3.92:1	3.69:1
Rear suspension	Semi-trailing arms, springs (all)		
Front suspension	Unequal-length A-arms (all)		
Wheels	5.5x14	5.5x14	6x14
Tires	175x14 in.	175x14 in.	185x14 in.
Brakes	4-wheel disc (all)		
Fuel capacity	17.2 gal (all)		
Weight	2,890 lb	3,179 lb	3,200 lb
Performance			
0–60 mph	14 sec	12 sec	13 sec
Top speed	100 mph	118 mph	118 mph
Fuel consumption	18-22 mpg	14-18 mpg	14-18 mph

Summary

The 450SE and SEL's bang-for-the-buck factor is right up there, but if you drive in town much, your gas bills may be higher than your car payments. Find a good one to start with; if and when you wear it out, find another.

The 450SE and SEL hold scant interest for collectors, but they can make great drivers. The 6.9 is incredible, but buy one only if you can afford to keep it properly. Best bets for future collector interest are the 6.9 and the 1973 450SE.

Chassis and Engine Prefix Numbers

Years	Model	Chassis Prefix	Engine Prefix	Description
1968–1976	200	115.015	115.923	4-cyl gas, 105 hp
1968–1976	200DD	115.115	OM615.912	4-cyl diesel, 61 hp
1968–1973	220	115.010	115.920	4-cyl gas, 116 hp
1968–1976	220D	115.110	OM615.912	4-cyl diesel, 65 hp
1968–1976	230	114.015	180.954	6-cyl gas, 135 hp
1972–1976	230/4	115.017	115.951	4-cyl gas, 85–95 hp
1973–1976	240D	115.117	OM616.916	4-cyl diesel, 62 hp
1974–1976	300D	115.114	OM617.910	5-cyl diesel, 77 hp
1968–1972	250	114.010	114.920	6-cyl gas, 146 hp
1970–1976	250 (2.8)	114.011	130.923	6-cyl gas, 157 hp
1972–1976	280	114.060	110.921	6-cyl gas, 120–180 hp
1969–1972	250C	114.023	114.920	6-cyl gas, 130 hp DIN
1969–1976	250C	114.023	130.923	6-cyl gas, 150 hp DIN (2.8 liter)
1969–1972	250CE	114	130	6-cyl gas, 157 hp (fuel-injected)
1972–1976	280C	114.073	110.921	6-cyl gas, 120–180 hp
1972–1976	280CE	114	110	6-cyl gas, 195 hp DIN (fuel-injected)

The squared-off grille of the W114 and W115 nicely matches its U.S. headlight units. *MBNA*

114 and 115 Sedans Fours and Sixes ★★

For 1968, a new sedan chassis was introduced for the four- and six-cylinder economy models. Many of these faithful workhorses were diesel-powered (see Chapter 18). We'll cover the gasoline models here, but only the most unusual and pristine examples even begin to approach collectible status.

Besides the new body, the biggest chassis improvement was the semi-trailing arm rear suspension. Most powerplants were identical to those of the earlier fin-back models, but several U.S. gasoline models used Stromberg carburetors. A four-speed manual transmission was standard; the optional automatic is best avoided on smaller-engined or diesel models.

The 250 ran from model year 1968 through 1972, and the 280 from 1973 through 1976. The 250 used the proven single overhead cam M130 six, but the 280 was fitted with the new M110 twin-cam six. Power output of U.S. models was strangled by emission controls.

The 114 and 115 chassis look nearly identical; the 114 chassis (powered by six-cylinder gaso-line engines) had spot welds every 25 millimeters, but the 115 chassis (which usually carried four or five-cylinder diesel or four-cylinder gasoline engines) had them every 10 millimeters. Incidentally, the designation "/8" (as in 230/8 or 250/8), indicates the 114 or 115 chassis, introduced for 1968. All of these sedans were popular as daily drivers, with many still going after hundreds of thousands of miles.

The most common of these cars is the 200D, followed by the 1973–1976 240D. The smaller-engined gasoline models are slow but durable, and the 2.8-liter sixes are faster but shorter-lived. Parts are inexpensive and easy to find. Rust and poor carburetion are the main faults.

114 and 115 Coupes ★★

Early coupe versions of the 114 and 115 chassis provided alternatives to the expensive 280SE 3.5 Coupe. All had gasoline engines, and convertibles were never offered, but a sunroof was optional. If any 114 or 115 model offers collector interest, it's these Coupes.

By 1975, the 280 Coupe had crash bumpers and was available with two-tone paint. Power came via a dohc six. *MBNA*

The squared-off W114 Coupe was first sold in the United States as the 1969 250C. Its proportions resemble those of a 300SEL 6.3 show car built by Pininfarina, but mechanically the Coupes are identical to their sedan brethren. Four-speed manual transmissions were available, but most U.S. cars have automatics.

U.S. models have the M130 2.8-liter engines. Again, because of the peculiarities of carburetors designed to stifle emissions, the electronic fuel injection models, designated CE, are your best bet. U.S. models from 1974 onward had the unattractive extended bumpers, but in compensation these Coupes look quite attractive with alloy wheels, which by then had found their way down from the SL models.

W123 Midrange Models ★★

The midrange W114 and W115 sedans were replaced by the S123. These were mostly fitted with diesel engines (see Chapter 18), but gasoline models included sedans, wagons, and Coupes.

This list includes only the most popular models; some utilitarian models sold only in Europe aren't shown. Few made it to the United States as gray market imports, also the case with the 280, 230C and CE, and 280C. Because MBNA offered no gasoline-powered wagon at the time, the 280TE wagon was a popular gray market car.

The twin-cam six was a much better match to the 123 chassis than it was to the 300-pound-heavier 116 chassis. K-Jetronic injection boosted power to 142 horsepower, except in the California version, where a catalytic converter held it to 137 horsepower. Zero to 60 miles per hour took 11.5 seconds; top speed was about 110. U.S. cars got four-speed automatics, but European versions offered five-speed manuals. Expect 16–20 miles per gallon with an automatic; a manual can do much better.

Because they were relatively expensive and a V-8 450SE and SEL could be had for little more, these sixes are almost rare. If you can find one, it can be a good buy today. Body and chassis were identical to those of the popular W123 diesels, so parts are easy to find.

Summary

Although numerous, the 1970s sedans are growing old, and some have been subjected to shoddy maintenance. Gas mileage is not their forte (even the sixes), but these cars are spacious and safe, and the V-8s can be quite rapid.

Prices are reasonable, and the parts supply is excellent, but restoration usually isn't warranted financially. Most collectors are interested only in the short-bumper 1973 450SE and SEL and the 450SEL 6.9, although any excellent example is worth preserving.

The gasoline-powered 1979 280CE Coupe was followed by a similar diesel version, the 300CD. *MBNA*

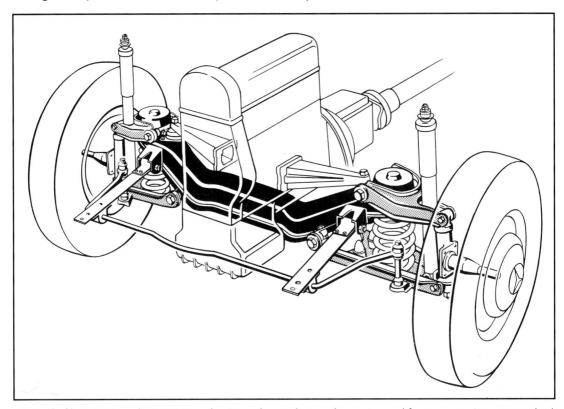

Typical of late 1950s and 1960s Mercedes-Benz chassis design, the engine and front suspension are attached to a subframe and thus can be removed as a unit (110, 111, 112, 113-chassis here).

Chapter 15

Sedans and Coupes 1980–1991

The 1980s saw huge progress in safety, emission controls, suspension, and performance. Mercedes-Benz also introduced new midrange cars that some believe outshone even the S-Class.

During the 1980s, Mercedes-Benz made tremendous advances in design and construction. For instance, 1960s and even 1970s cars rust, but if there's even one rusty 300E out there, it's well hidden. Safety improvements involved air bags and seatbelts that tighten on impact (the Supplemental Restraint System). When you have an accident, you'll want the protection that these cars offer.

ABS brakes stop you no shorter, but they do let you steer under maximum braking. If you're buying a family car, it's worth saving up for. Electronic traction control systems also appeared on these cars.

Drivability improved incredibly during the 1980s and early 1990s. Engines start and run well in all temperatures. More refined automatic transmissions allowed smoother shifting. Electronic glitches did appear occasionally, but the refinement provided by microprocessors was worth the price.

The S-Class: 380 to 560

An S-Class Mercedes-Benz says that you've arrived. If that doesn't matter to you, they are still one hell of a car. From 1981 through 1991, the W126 chassis came with a variety of diesels

The W126 chassis was the basis for all S-Class cars through the 1991 model year. Apart from its inset U.S. headlights, early alloy wheels, and ribbed side moldings, this U.S. 1981 380SEL could pass for a 1991 560SEL. *MBNA*

For 1982, the United States got a new four-seater Coupe, the 380SEC, meant to replace the SLC. *MBNA*

(300SD, 300SDL), plus six-cylinder and eight-cylinder gasoline engines (380SE and SEL, 450SEL, 500SEL, 560SEL).

380 to 560SEL Sedans ★★

Sleeker than the old 450SE and SEL, the W126 body premiered in the United States as the flagship 1981 380SEL, with the 3.8-liter V-8 supplying a reasonable, if not exorbitant, 155 horsepower with good fuel economy. The latter was also aided by added lightness and better aerodynamics, with the side effect of back-seat space that was practically decadent in the long-wheelbase SEL. The electrically powered seats were the first in a Mercedes-Benz (the 600's were hydraulic), and ingenious seat-shaped switches made adjustment intuitive.

Technical Specifications			
Model	380SE/SEL	500SEL	560SEL
Years	1981-1985	1984-1985	1986-1991
Engine			
Type	Sohc V-8 (all)		
Displacement	3,839 cc	4,973 cc	5,547 cc (338.5 ci)
Bore x stroke	88x78.9 mm	96.5x85 mm	96.5x94.8 mm
Compression ratio	8.3:1	8.0:1	
SAE horsepower	155 hp @4,750 rpm	185 hp @ 4,500 rpm	238 hp @ 4,800 rpm
Torque	196 lb-ft @ 2,750 rpm	247 lb-ft @ 2,000 rpm	287 lb-ft @ 3,500 rpm
Fuel system	Electronic fuel injection (all)		
Fuel required	Unleaded regular	Premium	Premium
Chassis			
Type	Unibody; steel (all)		
Chassis No. prefix	126.032	126.037	126.039
Transmission	4-speed, automatic (all)		
Rear-axle ratio	2.47:1 (all)		
Rear suspension	Semi-trailing arms, coil springs (all)		
Front suspension	Damper strut, coil springs (all)		
Wheels	6.5x14 in.	6.5x14 in.	7x15 in.
Tires	205/70HR14	205/70HR14	205/65VR15
Brakes	4-wheel disc (all)		
Fuel capacity	23.8 (all)		
Weight	3,815 lb	3,900 lb	4,125 lb
Performance			
0-60 mph	10.5 sec	9.0 sec	7.4 sec
Top speed	115 mph	135 mph	140 mph (est.)
Fuel consumption	16-19 mpg	14-18 mpg	13-17 mpg

Because it was available in Europe several years before it came to the United States, the 500 was a popular gray market model; this is a European 500SEC engine. *FDB*

To allow occupants easier access to seatbelts, the SEC used an automatic seatbelt arm, which presents the belt when the engine is started. *DBAG*

Given regular oil changes, these V-8s are reliable. Given less, they are subject to camshaft wear. The 1981–1983 380 engines used a single-row timing chain. With age and neglected oil changes, the chain may wear and stretch. As noted in the preceding chapter, if it jumps on the sprocket, the valves can hit the pistons, with expensive results. For 1984, a double-row chain appeared, and it can be retrofitted. Mercedes-Benz recommends that timing chains be inspected regularly. Most good mechanics replace them every 60–100,000 miles. If related work is needed, the single-row chain must be replaced with a double-row unit.

After customers requested more power, and as the gray market in European 500SEL sedans grew, Mercedes-Benz of North America responded with the 500SEL as a 1984 U.S. model, relegating the 380 engine to the shorter-wheelbase 380SE for 1984 and 1985. With 184 horsepower, the U.S. 500 was faster than the 380 but not as hot as the European 500, so in 1986 the United States got the 238 horsepower 560SEL, the final W126 sedan.

The 1986 and 1987 S-Class cars had 7x15-inch alloy wheels. For a smoother ride, rim width was decreased to 6.5 inches for 1988–1991; tire sizes remained the same. Electronic traction control (ASR) was first made available on 1991 S-Class models.

The 420SEL, using a 201 horsepower, 4.2-liter version of the M116 engine, was built as a 1986–1991 model. With 17 more horsepower than the U.S. 500, it topped out at 135 miles per hour and reached 60 miles per hour in 9 seconds. A six-cylinder 300SEL, using the 300E's 177-

Driving Impressions: S-Class

An S-Class model gives you that King of the Road feeling, and your passengers will be equally comfortable and impressed. As with all 1980s Mercedes-Benz models, their controls are instantly familiar. Even the transmission shift-gate design dates back to the early 1960s, but it makes it easy to manually override the automatic transmission.

Rear passengers can play with a power back seat on some sedans, and an SEL provides limousine legroom. The 560 has a huge power advantage over the 380 and the U.S. 500 that you can feel instantly on the road. The car sometimes feels as if it's going 20 miles per hour slower than it really is. Thanks to 200 pounds less weight and slightly better aerodynamics, the Coupes are a bit quicker and less thirsty than the sedans.

Go for the car with ABS, but traction control isn't a necessity. Fuel mileage is nothing to write home about, but that's the price of all this space, luxury, and safety. The forte of these V-8s is their ability to effortlessly cruise the interstates at any safe speed.

horsepower engine in the S-Class body, was sold as a 1988–1991 model, accompanied by the virtually identical but 5.5-inch shorter 300SE.

From 1986 through 1991, the 560SEL topped the line. Its catalyst-equipped 238-horsepower V-8 was the final development of the alloy M117 engine. A 56-horsepower boost from the 500SEL and SEC chopped 0–60 times to 7.5 seconds, fully 2.5 seconds faster than the U.S. 500. Bosch's electronically controlled fuel injection had matured into the KE-III, a blend of electronic and mechanical systems with a "limp home" mode, should the electrons

The SEC could form the basis for a personalized hot rod. Wider tires and European headlights were popular. *FDB*

cease. The headlights were made flush, like the 300's, and flatter alloy wheels (similar to those on the 190) appeared. Interior options included a suede-like synthetic called Amaretta, and a memory for the driver's seat and steering wheel position.

The 560SEL was the ultimate 1980s "businessman's express." For 1992, it was replaced by the all-new W140 S-Class.

380–560SEC Coupes ★★

These grand touring Coupes filled the void left by the demise of the SLC. The 380SEC was first built for the 1981 model year (1982 in the United States). Mechanically it was identical to the equivalent sedan. Inside, a pair of electrically driven seatbelts automatically offered themselves to driver and passenger after the doors were closed.

For 1984, the 380SEC became the 500SEC, gaining 29 horsepower; for 1986, it became the 560SEC with 238 horsepower. Production was low, so if kept in excellent condition, collector potential is excellent, especially for the higher-powered versions.

Many still serve their original owners, occasionally becoming available as used cars at reasonable prices.

What to Look For

Problem areas on the 380, 500, and 560SEL and SEC include the radio, air conditioning, and power windows. The 1981–1983 380s with single-row timing chains have already been discussed; the fix is expensive, but it's a one-time deal.

The 1981–1991 S-Class models are almost bulletproof except for the radio and automatic climate control. Listen for rear-axle whine, but even if you hear it, chances are that everything is OK; even with the differential rubber-mounted on the subframe, noise travels readily.

If you're looking at a pre-1984 500 sedan or Coupe in the United States, it's a gray market car. Be wary of silly spoilers, deeply tinted windows, and elaborate audio systems or alarms. The best buys are the original cars, whose conservative owners gave them the best care and modest use. Plenty are out there, so take your time.

Summary

The 560SEL is the finest and the final 1980s S-Class car. The 380 and 500 engined cars were less expensive and will remain so. Collectors don't find much of interest here, but they may aim for low-production models such as the late S-Class Coupes. Great bang for the buck here if you can afford the admission fee.

300 Midrange Models

For most people, a 300E or one of its derivatives is the best car in the world. A clean, used 300E is your best buy in a luxury sedan. Its ABS, air bag(s), and advanced rear suspension are complemented by a willing yet economical six-cylinder engine. The car is unostentatious, nimble, safe, reasonably fast, durable, and fun to drive.

300E 1986–1993 ★★★

Introduced for 1986 in the United States, the midrange 300E's W124 chassis replaced the venerable but bluff W123. Its new body incorporated safety features developed with decades of experi- ence. A five-link rear suspension (similar to that of the 190) provided stability and excellent handling under any load. The single-arm windshield wiper works well, and the interior has almost everything except a cupholder.

The 300E came to the United States with the new M103 3.0-liter, single-cam six making 177 horsepower. A four-speed automatic transmission or a five-speed manual could be ordered, but few had the latter, and only in 1986 and 1988. Fifth gear was really an overdrive (0.80:1). The lower four gears are in an H-pattern with fifth and reverse off to the right. Automatic transmission in 1986 through 1990 cars started in second gear, but in 1991 this was changed to a first-gear start with a higher-ratio rear end (2.87:1 vs. the previous 3.27:1).

The 1986 300E outperformed the 380 and 500 engined S-Class cars plus the contemporary Porsche 944 and IROC Z28 Camaro. Top speed was 140 miles per hour, with 60 miles per hour reached in about 8 seconds. Even so, highway fuel

Technical Specifications			
Model	300E	300E 2.8	300E
Years	1986–1992	1993	1993–1995
Engine			
Type	Inline sohc six	Inline dohc six	Inline dohc six
Engine No. prefix	103.983	104.942	104.992
Displacement	2,962 cc (180.8 ci)	2,794 cc (170.5 ci)	3,199 cc (195.2 ci)
Bore x stroke	88.5x80.3 mm	89.9x73.4 mm	89.9x84.8 mm
Compression ratio	9.2:1	10:1	10:1
SAE horsepower	117 hp @5,700 rpm	194 hp @ 5,500 rpm	217 hp @ 5,500 rpm
Torque	188 lb-ft @ 4,400 rpm	199 lb-ft @ 3,750 rpm	229 lb-ft @ 3,750 rpm
Fuel system	Electronic fuel injection (all)		
Fuel required	Premium (all)		
Chassis			
Type	Unibody; steel (all)		
Chassis No. prefix	124.030	124.028	124.032
Transmission	4-speed, automatic (all) 5-speed manual option		
Rear-axle ratio	3.07:1	2.65:1	2.65:1
Rear suspension	Multilink, coil springs (all)		
Front suspension	Damper strut, coil springs (all)		
Wheels	6.5x15 in. (all)		
Tires	195/65VR15 (all)		
Brakes	4-wheel disc (all)		
Fuel capacity	18.5 gal (all)		
Weight	3,295 lb	3,460 lb	3,525 lb
Performance			
0–60 mph	7.8 sec	8.8 sec	8.0 sec
Top speed	140 mph (manual) 137 mph (auto)	125 mph	140 mph (est.)
Fuel consumption	19–25 mpg (all)		

mileage could easily reach the mid-twenties, and 30 miles per gallon was possible.

The 300E's biggest weakness is the automatic climate control system. Effective and reliable heating and air conditioning systems have long eluded Mercedes-Benz, costing thousands of repeat sales in America. The complicated system is ridden with potential failures. The switch pad on the console can fail. Vacuum-operated air flaps fail. Air conditioning compressors fail. Climate control problems apply to all Mercedes-Benz cars, but don't let that put you off. It's just part of the price for the excellence of the rest of the car.

The 300E evolved quietly. A passenger-side air bag was offered for 1989. For 1990, the sedan and wagon got new lower body cladding and a less austere interior. Better sound systems arrived for 1991,

---

Driving Impressions: 300 Series

The modest 300E hides its capabilities. The 300s offer much more space than the 190s. They are as fast as an S-Class car with an equivalent engine, practically as luxurious, and just as durable.

Pre-1992 automatic transmissions start in second, so they feel sluggish off the line. Press down your right foot, and they downshift to first. The 1991 and later 300s start in first and shift more smoothly. The five-speed manual transmission is fun, but has a rubbery wind-up under hard acceleration. Fifth is tall—60 miles per hour yields only 2,100 rpm on the tach—so it saves fuel.

The four-valve engine, seen first in the 1990 300CE and the 1993 300E and 300TE, transforms the car. All 300Es require premium gas, but mileage is in the mid-twenties at modest highway speeds, and a heavy foot is required to earn less than 20 miles per gallon.

The 300E is among the world's best cars for the driver. Precise steering and comfortable ride make them particularly good long-distance cars. The 300CE's subtle speed makes it almost a stealth bomber.

Discussing the handling of these cars is academic. Anything that you can do to break them loose on the public road is not only irresponsible and illegal, but also highly unlikely. The only thing better than a 1986-1992 300E is the later version with the more powerful twin-cam, four-valve engine.

---

along with optional ASR traction control. For 1993, the 300E underwent other drivetrain changes that vastly improved performance; see Chapter 17 for more on those. Chapter 18 contains information on the 300 diesel models, and Chapter 17 covers the 1994 and later E320, the next step up from the early 300E.

300TD and 300TE Wagons ★★

As a replacement for the earlier W123-chassis diesel and turbo-diesel wagons, the W124-chassis 300TD turbo-diesel wagon showed up as a 1987 model. The 177-horsepower 300TE gasoline wagon replaced it for 1988. Both came only with a four-speed automatic transmission and self-leveling rear suspension. The wagon was taller than the sedan, with more headroom; empty weight was nearly 300 pounds more, so 0–60 miles per hour took about 9 seconds. For 1991 ASR traction control was optional, and for 1993, the 300TE got the four-valve 227-horsepower engine.

The wagon's most popular option was a rear-facing third seat for two passengers. The second-row seat folds flat, expanding cargo space. A 300TE has a payload of about 1,250 pounds but will easily carry more. The self-leveling rear suspension helps it to handle well even with a load. One serves as our business car, so we're biased, but if you want a "different" Mercedes-Benz that's eminently practical, a 300TE is hard to beat.

Many 300TEs were used as roadside assistance vehicles by dealers. If you need a low-priced wagon and don't mind white, these can be good buys; you'll pay a premium for a "civilian" wagon.

300CE Coupe and E320 Coupe, 1988–1995 ★★★

The subtle 300CE Coupe is underappreciated. Making its debut as a 1988 model using 300E mechanical pieces, it rides on a 3.3-inch-shorter wheelbase. In 1988, the Coupe was the first midrange model to use the plastic lower body cladding, and it has the automatic seatbelt feeders. Velour upholstery was optional; few U.S. cars had it.

For 1990, the 300CE became the first non-SL to enjoy the variable-intake valve timing and the four-valve head. These four-valve Coupes fly. Because a 300CE is lighter than a 300SL, it beat the sports car to 60 miles per hour. Like the 300E and TE, the CE got a first-gear start plus a higher rear-end ratio in 1991.

For 1994, the 300CE was renamed the E320 Coupe and shared the modest facelift of all 1994 E-Class models. Production ended in late 1995, as the much less expensive CLK coupe was on its way.

260E, 300E 2.6, and 300E 2.8 ★★★

The 260E and 300E 2.6 are one and the same. Marketed as an economical alternative to the 300E, the 260E came with the 158-horse-

Coincidence or not, the 300E appeared in the company's 100th year, 1986. *DBAG*

power six. To minimize price, it had few standard luxuries, but a long option list. The connotation of "260E" made the car hard to sell, so in 1990 its model designation changed to 300E 2.6. For one model year, 1993, the 300E 2.8 was built.

These smaller-engined cars required the same power as the 300E to maintain a given speed, so no substantial fuel savings are involved. Lower initial cost was the main advantage; trade-in value will be lower than the comparable 300E. These are cars for using, with almost no potential collector interest.

300E 4Matic and 300TE 4Matic ★★

Introduced at the 1985 Frankfurt Auto Show and appearing first in the United States on 1990 models, the 300E 4Matic sedan and 300TE 4Matic wagon were equipped with MBAG's first passenger car four-wheel-drive system. Until mid-1993, when the 4Matic system was discontinued for the United States, these were the only two models to use it. See below.

What to Look For

The 300s share the weak automatic climate control and the Becker Grand Prix radio. Read the owners manual and test the climate control system. Set the horizontal push-buttons to full automatic (hit the button with arrows up and down), set the fan to automatic, and crank the temperature wheel to Min. The air conditioning should blow cold air. Set the wheel to Max, and it should blow hot air. A gurgling noise in the dash is just coolant flow; an "antigurgle kit" is available.

Valve seals on pre-1988 cars should have been replaced with new seals of viton material. The automatic transmission can leak, usually evidenced by smoke at sustained high speed. Some leaks can be fixed with the unit in the car, but usually it must come out. The radiator's top outlet pipe is plastic and can crack if American (alkaline) coolant is used instead of (pH neutral) Mercedes-Benz-brand coolant. The original plastic thermostat housing should have already been replaced with a stronger aluminum part; this is inexpensive to do. Look for excessive oil leaks from the valve cover gasket and the timing cover at the front of the 300E engine; most seep a bit, which doesn't hurt. Make sure the accessory drive belt isn't cracked or worn; changing it is no roadside job. When looking at a 300TE, make sure the self-leveling system works.

Pay attention when shifting at full throttle or on high-speed curves. Age and use can harden and wear driveshaft flex disks plus the bushings in the rear suspension, causing loose handling under high torque and loads. At idle, shift the transmission back and forth between Reverse and Drive; if you notice a clunk, the flex disks are probably worn.

To test the ABS, find a road with no traffic, and punch the brakes hard. Don't squeeze them, punch them! You should feel a slight pulsing in the pedal, and the car should stop in a straight line. Get used to the feeling—when ABS engages, some people think something is wrong and lift off the brakes.

Summary

Mercedes-Benz has always built terrific inline sixes, and this one is their best. If you can't find what you want in this 3.0-liter gasoline sedan, try

The 300CE, foreground, soon joined the 300E sedan. Mechanically, the two were virtually identical until 1990, when the coupe got the four-valve engine.

one of its variations: diesel, wagon, Coupe, Convertible, four-wheel drive. The market has an excellent supply of well-maintained 300 models at a good discount from their original prices. A 300E is your best overall buy in a used Mercedes-Benz. Period. End of discussion.

Traction Control Systems

Three traction control systems were developed by Mercedes-Benz during the 1980s. One (ASD) is a simple mechanical/electronic system, the second (ASR) uses more sophisticated electronics and is more effective, and the third (4Matic) was excellent but too much for the market. By maintaining traction, these systems improve stability, helping to prevent skids.

All three traction control systems share hardware with ABS brakes, which preceded them. If an individual brake begins to lock, ABS automatically "pumps" it, preventing the tire from skidding and allowing you to steer the car. ABS is most useful on

slick pavement. If you're wondering, ABS can't be retrofitted practically.

Mercedes-Benz began fitting ABS in 1976, but it didn't appear on its U.S. cars until the 1985 model year. By 1986, it was standard on all but the 190E 2.3 and the 190D 2.2, where it was a popular option. Since 1989, ABS has been standard on all U.S. models. To determine whether a car has ABS, look for the small circular red ABS warning light or symbol below the instruments or the hydraulic valve marked "ABS" under the hood.

ASD

The Automatic Locking Differential (ASD) was the simplest of MBAG's traction control systems. Using the ABS wheel sensors to detect rear wheelspin at speeds under 21 miles per hour, a microprocessor signals hydraulically actuated clutches to lock the differential, so that both rear wheels turn at the same speed. A light in the speedometer indicates that the system is working.

The 300TE wagon has a slightly higher roof than the sedan, self-leveling rear suspension, and an optional third, rear-facing seat. This 300TD Turbo is a diesel version. *DBAG*

Traction regained, ASD disengages when the car reaches 22 miles per hour. The simple system has similar limits to a mechanically locking differential—if traction is equally bad at both rear wheels, both may spin. ASD saw only brief use as a U.S. option on the 190E 2.3, 190E 2.6, turbo-diesels, and the 300SL. It was superseded by ASR, which took matters beyond the differential.

ASR

Acceleration Skid Control (ASR) is more sophisticated and effective than ASD, especially at improving stability, and was more widely used. Instead of locking the differential, ASR uses the brake to slow a spinning wheel. If two wheels spin, ASR brakes them both and reduces engine torque. Even with the throttle mashed to the floor, ASR prevents wheelspin. As the system engages, an indicator light comes on in the speedometer face.

Put two wheels in mud or snow, and ASR allows steady acceleration without swerves. Turning and applying heavy power may also engage ASR. In snow, ASR gives you some of the advantages of four-wheel drive without the drawbacks. In the United States, ASR first appeared as an option for the 1991 model year on six- and eight-cylinder gasoline-engined models.

A criticism of ASR is that on models through 1994 it can't be switched off, as might be desirable under some winter conditions or by enthusiasts who use power to provoke oversteer. A dash switch allows the wheelspin rate to increase to accommodate tire chains or snow clumps on the tires.

4Matic

4Matic means automatic four-wheel drive. In two-wheel-drive mode, this automatic system senses wheelspin via the wheel sensors, then goes through three stages. First, front-wheel drive is engaged, with rear, center, and front differentials left disengaged. If wheelspin continues, the center differential is engaged. If that's not enough to stop wheelspin, the rear differential locks. Disengagement also occurs in stages unless the brakes are applied, whereupon 4Matic uncouples so that ABS can work.

The process is automatic, beyond control of the driver, who sees only the 4Matic indicator light, a safety feature in itself, telling unwitting drivers that they are entering low-traction conditions. The system senses steering angle and engages 4Matic sooner if the car is turning. All four tires should be the same type and size, but 4Matic accommodates wear by compensating for slight differences in diameter.

143

Four-valve head boosted power from 177 to 217 horsepower in the 1990 300CE, but the 300E sedan and the 300TE wagon had to wait until 1993. *FDB*

Although heavy (300 pounds), expensive (over $6,500 new), and complicated, 4Matic was judged the best of contemporary four-wheel-drive traction control systems. Whether you need it depends on where and how you drive. In ski country it's useful. In Los Angeles, it's not. 4Matic was discontinued during the 1993 model year. Even though the system was effective, cost made many buyers think twice, especially when ASR functioned almost as well. As the system ages, the risk of expensive repairs only increases.

Becker Grand Prix Radio

The most common failure in 1980s models involves the Becker Grand Prix Electronic radio. The tiny controls are complicated and difficult to operate, reliability is poor, and sensitivity and sound quality are inferior. Even the automatic antenna can fail.

The radio was once a popular target for thieves, so an antitheft feature was added, but it could backfire. If power to the radio was cut off with the alarm system on, the radio scrambled its controls, requiring at least a trip to the dealer to have it descrambled.

In 1986–1987 models, a supplementary lithium battery maintains power to the radio, but if the standby battery fails, the radio may scramble. The batteries weren't used in 1988–1989 models, and 1990–onward models provide the owner with a code to punch in to reactivate the radio. Descrambling a pre-1990 radio can be arranged through dealers or through Becker North America. The radio scrambling device can be disabled.

The Grand Prix radio's sensitivity was low, so it wouldn't pick up many stations, and sound quality was only fair. The tape deck and controls were subject to failure. Many Grand Prix radios were replaced. If the car you're considering has a Sony or an Alpine, that's probably a plus.

The 300CE inspired turners such as AMG to create high-performance alternatives, this one with a 32-valve, 6.0-liter V-8. *AMG*

Chapter 16

The 190 1983–1993

As an entry-level model for the 1980s, Mercedes-Benz developed its first new compact sedan in three decades, the 190. This series successfully encompassed uses from taxicab to racer. It had been nearly 30 years since Mercedes-Benz had built a small car, so the new one was designed entirely from scratch.

In 1983, the 190 appeared in Europe with a 2.0–liter gasoline engine, not sold in the United States. For 1984, two entry-level four-cylinder sedans, the diesel 190D 2.2 and the gasoline 190E 2.3, came to the United States. Both were well-equipped but could have used more torque. Later displacement increases met this need, and more standard equipment and options appeared. The 201 chassis was built only as a four-door sedan. Its potential was best realized in the 190D 2.5, the 190D 2.5 Turbo, the 190E 2.6, and the 190E 2.3–16 sports sedan.

Handling improvements came with the 190's totally fresh rear suspension. The computer-designed five-link system better controlled track width, toe-in, and rear wheel camber, providing more stable handling under a variety of loads and while accelerating or braking. Front suspension is by MacPherson strut; coil springs are fitted all around, as are disc brakes. The 190 introduced the "new-style" flatter-faced alloy wheel, which is easier to clean than the more intricately shaped earlier alloy wheel.

The 190E 2.3 and 190D 2.2 in original U.S. form had new alloy wheels (easier to clean) and inset headlights. *MBNA*

146

The four-valve Cosworth cylinder head of the 190E 2.3–16 makes it the choice for an enthusiast driver. Note the front air dam, modest fender flares, aerodynamic lower body molding, and rear spoiler. *FDB*

The 190's limitations are low power, shortage of rear legroom, and a few early build quality snags. Advantages include low price, light weight, high fuel efficiency, a choice of manual or automatic transmission, and nimble yet stable handling. Over a million 190s were built before the C220 and C280 replaced them for the 1994 model year.

190E 2.3 ★★

The gasoline-powered 190E 2.3 combined light weight with 113 horsepower, increased to 121 horsepower for 1985. At 2,500 pounds, the 2.3 was the lightest Mercedes-Benz sedan since the 1930s. Drag coefficient was 0.33, compared to the 0.36 of the contemporary S-Class sedans. Four-speed automatic and five-speed manual transmissions were offered. In the lower four gears, the latter's shift pattern forms an H; fifth and reverse are off to the right.

The 190s introduced the single-arm windshield wiper, which sweeps 86 percent of the glass area. A few problems occurred with climate control systems and power windows. Even though the auto-matic climate controls appear similar, 190s used a completely different system than did earlier models. Still, they had similar problems—with controls, compressor, and so forth—but nothing that an experienced Mercedes-Benz mechanic can't handle.

A 1991 factory service bulletin covered a parking brake modification to prevent accidental release; the parts can be retrofitted to 1984–mid-1988 190s. The 1984 and 1985 190s used 14-inch alloy wheels; later models used 15-inch wheels. Steel wheels were sold in Europe but not in the United States.

Driver's side air bags were optional on 1984 and later 190s. ABS braking became an option for 1985 and was made standard for 1989. Other options were an alarm system, power seats, sunroof, metallic paint, and more.

For the 1987 model year, all 190s (gasoline and diesel) were fitted with better headlights and a slightly revised climate control system; when the difference between inside and outside air temperatures exceeded a certain level, the system switched to recirculate air. The 1987 190E 2.3 had a power boost to 130 horsepower. For 1989, the 190s got

Technical Specifications

Model	190E 2.3	190E 2.3-16	190E 2.6
Years	1984-1988 1991-1993	1986-1987	1987-1993
Engine			
Type	Inline sohc four	Inline dohc four, 4 valves/cyl	Inline sohc six
Engine No. prefix	102.961 or 985	102.983	103.942
Displacement	2,299 cc (140.3 ci)	2,299 cc (140.3 ci)	2,599 cc (158.6 ci)
Compression ratio	8.0:1	9.7:1	9.2:1
SAE horsepower	121 hp @ 5,000 rpm	167 hp @ 5,800 rpm	158 hp @ 5,800 rpm
Torque	136 lb-ft @ 3,500 rpm	162 lb-ft @ 4,750 rpm	162 lb-ft @ 4,600 rpm
Fuel system	Electronic fuel injection (all)		
Fuel required	Premium unleaded (all)		
Chassis			
Type	Unibody sedan; steel (all)		
Chassis No. prefix	201.024	201.034	201.029
Transmission	4-speed auto or 4-speed auto	5-speed manual or 4-speed auto	4-speed auto or 5-speed manual
Rear-axle ratio	3.23:1	3.27:1	3.27:1
Rear suspension	Multilink, coil springs (all)		
Front suspension	Damper strut, coil springs (all)		
Wheels	6x15 in.	7x15 in.	6x15 in.
Tires	185/65x15	205/55VR15	185/65VR15
Brakes	4-wheel disc (all)		
Fuel capacity	14.5 gal + 1.8 (reserve)	18.7 gal + 2.3	14.5 gal + 1.8
Weight	2,745 lb	3,030 lb	2,880 lb
Performance			
0–60 mph	10.0 sec	8.6 sec (auto) 8.3 sec (manual)	9.5 sec (auto) 9.1 sec (manual)
Top speed	121 mph	134 mph (auto) 137 mph (manual)	126 mph (auto) 129 mph (manual)
Fuel consumption	22–30+ mpg	20–30 mpg (est.)	22–30+ mph (est.)

Note: Specifications for the 190E 2.3 are for the 1985 model year; those for the 190E 2.3-16 are for U.S. models.

new lower body cladding, plus new front and rear valances. Starting with the 1990 model year, an Alpine radio replaced the trouble-prone Becker Grand Prix Electronic unit.

In 1991, after two model years when only the 190E 2.6 came to the United States, the 190E 2.3 returned with a new head and improved fuel injection. The 190E's final American fling was as the 1993 Limited Edition 190E 2.3 and 2.6. The 2.3 came only in metallic green with creme beige leather and burl walnut; the 2.6 was black with black and red leather interior and cross-hatch pattern trim. The package also included a power sunroof, headlight washers and wipers, and rear seat headrests. Eight-hole alloy wheels were fitted, and the trunk lid carried no model identification. The 2.6 is interesting to enthusiasts because it has stiffer shocks, shorter springs, larger wheels and tires, a faster steering ratio, and a smaller steering wheel. About 700 of each were built exclusively for the U.S. market.

With long-lived engines and rust-free bodies, a well-kept four-cylinder 190E 2.3 can be a bargain today. Still, if you can stretch your budget a bit, you'll like the six-cylinder 190E 2.6, introduced as a 1987 model, even better. And then there's the high-performance 190E 2.3–16.

190E 2.3–16 ★★★

The most collectible 190 is this four-door pocket rocket. Sold in the United States only for 1986 and 1987, the 190E 2.3–16 was a sporting version of the 190E 2.3. The four-valve head by Cosworth in England improved gas flow, so power jumped to 185 horsepower in Europe. With a compression ratio of 9.7:1 instead of the European car's 10.5:1, American cars had 167 horsepower, but a lower rear-axle ratio compensates. Redline is 6,800 rpm, up 600 over the 190E 2.3, and an external engine oil cooler was added. Suspension improvements, wider wheels and tires, supportive

The rear spoiler of the 190E 2.3–16 also accommodates the high-mounted brake light. *DBAG*

leather seats, bigger (vented) brakes, and a Getrag five-speed manual transmission make this car a joy to drive.

American "16-valves" were available in two colors, smoke silver and black pearl, both with black leather upholstery. In Europe the model was sold only with a close-ratio five-speed manual transmission, but about half of U.S. cars came with a four-speed automatic. All had hydropneumatic self-leveling and a mechanical limited-slip differential.

DBAG took several slightly modified 190E 2.3–16 cars to the high-speed Nardo test track in Italy in 1983 and set 15 world speed records. The highest was 154.06 miles per hour for 50,000 kilometers, just over 31,000 miles. A taller rear-axle ratio allowed this; European production cars top out at 140, American versions hit 135 or so.

The car was a hit among Mercedes-Benz performance fans, who used them successfully in club driving events. A squadron of 190E 2.3–16s, piloted by renowned race drivers, christened the new Nürburgring in 1985. The factory entered several teams in the German Touring Car Championship races. In the United States, Rick Hurst Racing ran a tuned 190E 2.3–16 in IMSA's International Sedan Series. A stock 190E 2.3–16 could whip any other Mercedes-Benz on an autocross course.

European 190E 2.3–16 models quickly appeared on the U.S. gray market. MBNA first brought the car over for 1986, but it became clear that it would sell in limited numbers in America. It was expensive (over $40,000), and conservative Mercedes-Benz buyers were put off by its spoilers and air dams. Although Mercedes-Benz performance models were renowned in Europe, Americans had been taught to consider them as luxury cars instead.

After 1987, the 190E 2.3–16 was dropped as a U.S. model, fewer than 2,000 having been imported officially. In Europe, though, spurred by the burgeoning German Touring Car Championship, the 2.3-liter version grew into the 190E 2.5–16 and eventually the limited-production, high-winged Evolution II, neither of which came to the United States. The 197-horsepower 190E 2.5–16 made 60 miles per hour in 7.5 (manual) or 7.8 seconds (automatic) and could hit 146 miles per hour.

Few changes occurred during 190E 2.3–16 production. A 1987 version differs from a 1986 car only in its more aerodynamic headlights (with

Driving Impressions: 190 Series

The compact, nimble, and economical 190s make good city cars. With the front seats occupied, back seat legroom is less than spacious, but it's sufficient for kids.

The normally aspirated diesels are slow, but the 190D 2.5 Turbo can be fun. The 190E, which brought the words "sports sedan" back to Mercedes-Benz, is excellent in 2.6-liter form. A five-speed 190E 2.6 is practically the equivalent of the 190E 2.3-16. Enthusiasts should avoid the automatic transmission, which can have a mind of its own. The 1992 and later 190E models with the Sportline option are even closer to a 190E 2.3-16.

Agility is the 190E 2.3-16's most enjoyable attribute. Relatively light weight, great suspension, and good tires make it respond instantly. Braking is excellent, and ABS keeps you out of trouble. The limited-slip differential (mechanical, not the ASD or ASR electronic traction control that couldn't be switched off) lets you get the power down early and smoothly in tight corners without melting the inside tire. Supportive seats hold you firmly in place during all this fun.

The five-speed's shift pattern has first doglegged to the left, below reverse, so the four top gears are in an H-pattern, best suited to high-speed driving. (Other five-speeds put reverse to the right, leaving the lower four gears in an H, easier in town.)

All 190Es need lead-free premium gasoline. Highway fuel mileage of the 190E 2.3 could exceed 40 miles per gallon at 55 miles per hour and is unlikely to drop below 22. A 190D 2.2 normally gets 35-40 miles per gallon on the open road. In a 190E 2.3-16, you just don't care.

Sportline-equipped 1992–1993 190E 2.6 stands lower, had wider wheels and tires, logo behind front wheels, and other features. All 1987 and later U.S. 190s had these improved headlights; the lower body molding first appeared on 1989 models.

standard washers and wipers) and the revised air conditioning. The engine eschews hydraulic valve adjustment in favor of mechanical shims requiring cam removal for adjustment. Fuel capacity increased to 18.7 gallons plus a 2.3-gallon reserve, up from the 14.5 and 1.8 of the 190E 2.3.

The 190E 2.3–16 is an exceptional value for an enthusiast. The time to buy a recent collector car is just as depreciation ends and appreciation begins, when prices dip their lowest. The 190E 2.3–16 is now a prime candidate. Because of their low volume and high performance, the 190E 2.3–16, the European 190E 2.5–16, and the Evolution II are the only 190s generating collector interest.

190E 2.6 ★

The biggest-engined 190E was the 190E 2.6, which appeared for 1987 with 159 horsepower inline six; either a four-speed automatic or a five-speed manual transmission, ABS brakes, and a revised front air dam. Much less expensive than the 190E 2.3–16 but with only slightly less power, it became quite popular. Increased torque made the car easier to drive.

Rear seat legroom grew a bit in 1989, when the front seatbacks were re-shaped. For 1992, the fac-

The 190E 2.3–16 engine made 167 horsepower in U.S. form; higher-compression European version made 185 horsepower. *FDB*

tory's Sportline option became available, bringing the 190E 2.6 even closer to its 16-valve brother. With Sportline and the right tires, a good driver can at least equal the times of a 190E 2.3–16.

190D 2.2 ★

At 72 horsepower, the 1984–1986 190D 2.2, especially with an automatic transmission, is only for the devoted diesel fan. Even though it starts in

A factory team of modified 190E 2.3–16 sedans set several world speed records at Nardo, Italy, in 1983. *DBAG*

first gear, acceleration is sluggish. Entering a freeway via a short, uphill ramp can be tense. The 5-speed manual transmission allows slightly better performance. On the plus side, fuel mileage often exceeds 40 miles per gallon, and these cars are affordable. The 190D 2.2 was the first Mercedes-Benz to employ an engine encapsulation system to decrease interior and exterior engine noise.

Displacement was boosted to 2.5 liters in the 93 horsepower 1986–1987 190D 2.5 (automatic only), and for 1987 a turbocharger was added, creating the sprightly, 123-horsepower 190D 2.5 Turbo. For more on diesel 190s, see Chapter 18.

Sportline ★★★

Mercedes-Benz has a strong performance image in Europe but not yet in the United States. For the 1992 model year, MBNA's new option, Sportline, made the cars more appealing to enthusiasts. To the 190E 2.6 (and the 300E and 300CE), Sportline brought stiffer springs and shock absorbers, wider eight-hole alloy wheels, wider tires, a quicker steering ratio, more supportive seats, and a smaller-diameter steering wheel. For models without leather seats, Sportline added them, too. No changes were made in the engine or transmission. Cars with Sportline stand slightly

lower and bear a blue and silver logo on their front fenders and their shift knobs.

Without sacrificing comfort, Sportline brings out these cars' inherent handling abilities, and we highly recommend it. Few cars were sold with Sportline, and because it was an expensive and desirable option, it can be expected to increase the value of a used car.

Apart from the factory-installed gear, AMG spoilers and wheels for SLs, 190s, and 300 class models became available through U.S. Mercedes-Benz dealers in 1993.

What to Look For

As with any recent model, service records are critical. Some early 190s experienced high oil consumption, traced to valve seals, which were replaced under warranty. In 1985, because of possible cracking, MBNA issued a recall on 14-inch alloy wheels with date codes between 3583 and 4983.

The most likely snag will be in the automatic climate control, so read the owners manual and test the ACC at all settings. The power windows weren't the most reliable, so make sure they all work smoothly; try the sunroof, antenna, and power seats, too. Manual transmissions should make no bearing noise; look for leaks from auto-

With the latest eight-hole wheels, the 1993 Limited Edition 190E 2.3 and 190E 2.6 were the final U.S. versions; the 2.6 has wider wheels and stiffer springs. *MBNA*

matics. Check to see that the ABS works correctly. If the Becker Grand Prix Electronic radio has been replaced, you're one step ahead, but late models have better sound systems.

That's about it. The basic car is sound, and we've yet to see a rusty 190. For a completely new design, the 190 got off to an excellent start. Today a used 190 is the most affordable "modern" Mercedes-Benz sedan available. Still, these were the company's least expensive models, and as they age over the miles and years, they easily show interior or mechanical wear. (In the 190E 2.3–16, timing chain wear can be cured by improving lubrication sprayed through the front bearing cap of the exhaust camshaft.) If you buy any 190, budget appropriately for repair or restoration work.

The high-winged Evolution 190E 2.5–16 proved extremely successful in the German Touring Car Championship. *DBAG*

The interior of a 1993 Limited Edition 190E 2.3, laid out similarly to other models. *MBNA*

Chapter 17

The Latest: C-, E-, S-Class and SL 1994–1998

Current models are entering the used car market, and although few are inexpensive, these are the best Mercedes-Benz cars ever. Several are already collectible.

During the early 1990s, competition proved strong, and U.S. luxury and gas guzzler taxes didn't help sales, so Mercedes-Benz broadened its range with niche models appealing to special buyers; 20 years hence these will be collector cars.

Mercedes-Benz competed at the low end, too. The C-Class cars were more than a refinement of the preceding 190s. For 1994, just as the C-Class was introduced, Mercedes-Benz simplified its model designations. The new names were based on three classes: C (Compact), E (Executive), and S ('Spensive?), plus engine displacements—220 (2.2-liter), 320 (3.2-liter), and so on.

400E 1992–1993 and E420 1993–1995 ★★★

For 1992, Mercedes-Benz offered a new mid-range sedan as a Lexus-fighter for the United States, the V-8-powered 400E. For not much more than the

1993 Models	1994 Models
190E 2.3	C220
190E 2.6	C280
300E 2.8	—
300E	E320
300TE	E320 Wagon
300CE	E320 Coupe
300CE Cabriolet	E320 Cabriolet
300D 2.5 Turbo	—
—	E300 Diesel
400E	E420
500E	E500
300SD	S350 Turbodiesel
300SE	S300
400SE	S420
500SEL	S500
600SEL	S600
500SEC	S500 Coupe
600SEC	S600 Coupe
300SL	SL300
500SL	SL500
600SL	SL600

The E320 is a refined 300E. This 1994 model has the updated grille and headlights, eight-hole wheels, lower body cladding, and a 217-horsepower four-valve engine. *MBNA*

cost of a 300E, Americans could enjoy more power and torque. With an improved transmission, the 4.0 V-8 gives strong performance.

The 400E actually has a 4.2-liter engine. Peak power from the 32 valver is 268 horsepower, about 90 more than the original 300E and about 50 more than the 3.2-liter 300E. Suspension and brake improvements accompanied this extra power, but tire size stayed the same as the 300E at 195/65VR15. (Given the 400E's potential, they could have been wider.) Variable intake cam timing spread torque over a wider rpm range; the car feels strong whenever you punch it. A leather interior is standard, ASR traction control optional.

This 1993 300CE Cabriolet, which actually displaces 3.2 liters, is similar to the 1994 E320 Cabriolet, which had a slightly updated grille, engine hood, and headlights. The screen behind the seats folds up to prevent air turbulence; the rear headrests serve as an automatic roll bar. Top on U.S. version is power-operated. *MBAG*

Since 60 miles per hour came up in 7 seconds and its speed ran to 149 miles per hour, the 400E approached 500E performance at a savings of more than $20,000. This is what the 300E should have been all along! A slightly restyled body (new grille, headlights, engine hood) came in the 1994 model year.

The big change came for 1997, when the E420 got the totally new W210 chassis; for that model year it kept the M119 V-8. Popular with drivers who wanted a sporting yet subtle sedan, the E420 was replaced for 1998 by the E430 with the new modular M113 V-8 and a five-speed automatic. Power (275 horsepower) and torque (295 ft-lb) were the same for both engines, but the E430 ran from 0 to 60 miles per hour in 6.4 seconds vs. the E420's 6.7, and it got better mileage to boot.

Like the E420, many E430s were fitted with the Sport option package, which upgraded suspension, wheels, and trim but provided no additional power. Xenon headlights (low beam only) are an option worth having; although expensive, they last longer, have tougher lenses, and are far brighter than the standard quartz-halogen lights. Leather upholstery, burl walnut trim, and a Bose sound system were standard on the E430.

Combining quality, safety, and stunning performance, the E500 was one heck of a car, but the E430—at little more than half its new price, yet boasting an updated chassis and practically equal performance—is especially tempting for the enthusiast.

500E 1992–1993 and E500 1994 ★★★★

Once a decade, Mercedes-Benz builds the world's fastest and finest sedan. In the 1960s, it was the 300SEL 6.3. In the 1970s, it was the 450SEL 6.9. In the 1980s—well, we had to wait until 1992, for the astonishing 500E.

Anybody can plunk a big, powerful engine into a small chassis, but MBAG created a well-integrated, tractable, and safe super-sedan by redesigning and strengthening the W124 chassis and suspension, improving the brakes, fitting wider wheels and tires, and upgrading the seats. AMG had tried this earlier with their Hammer, but at $150,000 a copy, few were sold. The far more refined 500E was available at your local Mercedes-Benz dealer for around $80,000, and it could be serviced there, too.

A lowered and strengthened body shell was designed and assembled with Porsche's help. The 5.0-liter 32-valve V-8 produced 322 horsepower and 354 ft-lb of torque, exceeded only by the V-12. All U.S. 500Es had ASR traction control (optional on European versions) and self-leveling rear suspension. Tires were 225/55ZR16 front and rear. The 3,750-pound sedan reached 60 miles per hour in under 6 seconds, with a governed top end of 155 miles per hour. Ungoverned, a 500E would be capable of at least 165 miles per hour.

This pre-1996 E420 interior is typical of the 1990s cars with dual air bags, center console. *MBAG*

Driving Impressions: 300E, 400E, and 500E

In a sedan, a 300E or E320 is your best buy. This car will last nearly forever and remain fun to drive. The 1986-1992 300Es are good, but if you can, pick the more refined 3.2-liter, four-valve (1993 and later) version. The better-shifting transmission is worth a lot, but even the older version performs well if you shift by hand, made easy by the excellent shift gate.

Mercedes-Benz has stuck to recirculating ball steering, which you might guess would be less precise than rack and pinion, but given good tires that's not so. The 300E goes exactly where you point it, every time.

The new E-Class chassis for 1996 finally brought rack-and-pinion steering, along with fantastic xenon headlights (low beams only, but get them if you can). The lighter, more fuel-efficient V-6 that powers 1997 and later E320s provides much more low-end torque, so the car gets off the line much more quickly. You'll also find the driver-adaptive five-speed transmission to be the smoothest and most enjoyable automatic that Daimler-Benz has ever built. Its sideways 4-5 shift is especially handy, and a Summer/Winter switch allows you to start in either first or second gear.

The 400E adds power, and the 500E is the driver's instant favorite. Buying either V-8 is a no-brainer. If you can afford it, just do it and be happy. These cars will cover more miles in a day than you can, but we give the edge to the 500E for its better seats and its stunning performance. The new Bose sound system is far better than the old Becker rig. The other attraction of these cars is their highway stealth capability.

Between 500 and 600 cars reportedly came to the United States as 1992 models, and although sales slowed, the model continued through 1994. The 500E is the prime Mercedes-Benz collector car of the early 1990s.

300CE Cabriolet 1993 and E320 Cabriolet 1994–on ★★★★

If you had bought a new 280SE 3.5 Convertible in 1971 and kept it, today it would be worth many times its original price, and meanwhile you'd have enjoyed a great car. Well, our advice is to find yourself a 1993 300CE Cabriolet or the equivalent 1994–95 E320 Cabriolet, and do just that.

Like the 1993 300E, the Cabriolet incorporates all the modern amenities, with the power soft top as a bonus. It's a safe Convertible—thanks to pop-up rear headrests, side door beams, and engineers who design for real-world crash requirements rather than government standards.

The four-valve, 3.2-liter, 217-horsepower six pushes the Cabriolet to 60 in 8.6 seconds, slower than other 300s because it is 500 pounds heavier than a 300CE Coupe. Chassis reinforcements avoid body twist and vibration, also discouraged by rubber and lead dampers in the windshield header, on the left front shock tower, and in the trunk.

This car is a low-production luxury model with a folding top, so as a future classic, it's a no-brainer. Cash in that sluggish mutual fund. You're not getting any younger.

300E 1993 and E320 1994–on ★★★

We said good things about the original 300E, but for 1993, Mercedes-Benz made the car even better. Displacement was nudged from 3.0 to 3.2 liters, and a new four-valve head utilized variable intake cam timing. Power jumped from 177 horsepower to 217. Peak torque increased, and variable cam timing provided a flatter and fatter torque curve. The four-speed automatic transmission, which had previously started in second gear, was altered to start in first gear, improving take off. The transmission is electronically linked to the ignition system so that timing is momentarily adjusted to smoothen shifts.

These changes make a 1993 300E or later E320 more enjoyable. Given some right foot, the car steps out smartly. Keep your foot down, and at redline the transmission powershifts silkily into the next gear. Downshifts are far quicker than in older models. This transmission works just the way you think an automatic transmission should work. For the enthusiast, the Sportline option provided wider wheels and tires, shorter and stiffer springs, supportive seats, and more.

For 1994, the 3.2-liter 300E got a truer name, E320, and styling was updated with a grille

The 1992–93 500E (shown here) got a facelift for 1994 and became the E500, but the two models are essentially identical otherwise and are definitely future collector cars.

resembling the S-Class. Other changes included new headlights, taillights, and trunk lid center panel.

For model year 1996, an entirely new E-Class chassis (W210) was introduced, featuring distinctive ovoid headlights, rack-and-pinion steering, and hundreds of other improvements. This was the last hurrah for the venerable inline six-cylinder engine, a Mercedes-Benz hallmark, and the four-speed automatic transmission, but performance was improved, and a 1996 E320 will out-drag a BMW 540i, a Lexus LS400, or a Jaguar XJ6. An all-new innovative and lighter V-6 powered the 1997 E320, feeding power through an even better driver-adaptive five-speed automatic, standard throughout the line.

The equivalent E-Class wagon came out for 1998 with the V-6 as the E320 in the United States, but it was also available with the V-8 as the E430 in Germany. At the same time, a new all-wheel-drive system, 4ETS—similar to that of the M-Class but without its low-range—became a reasonably priced option on the E-Class sedan and wagon. Instead of the previous 4Matic's locking differentials, this simpler yet more effective system used the brakes to direct torque to the wheels with traction (for a complete description, see Chapter 19).

E300 Diesel 1994–on ★★

So that its new diesels could again be sold in highly regulated states, Mercedes-Benz reverted to a non-turbocharged, 3.0-liter diesel for the 1994 E300 Diesel. See the next chapter for details.

300SL and 500SL 1990–on, and 600SL, 1993–on ★★★

Introduced for 1990, the R129 SL was a revolutionary step beyond the aging 560SL. Its totally fresh chassis was powered by a 3.0-liter, 228-horsepower inline six, in the 300SL, or a 5.0-liter, four-valve 322-horsepower V-8, in the 500SL. For 1993, these were joined by the 6.0-liter V-12 600SL.

For 1994, all model designations changed, and these cars were renamed the SL320, SL500, and SL600. In 1997, when most sedans switched to the new V-6, the SL320 kept the old inline six.

All three SLs shared significant advances including an automatic power top (the first on any SL) and the world's first automatic roll bar. Automatically adjusting shock absorbers (ADS) and electronic traction control (ASR) were options on the 1991 500SL, standard on the 600SL. All SLs had self-leveling rear suspension, dual air bags, remote locking, an electrostatic air filter

Technical Specifications

Model	300E/E320	400E/E420	500E/E500
Years	1993, 1994–1995	1992–1995	1992–1994
Engine			
Type	Inline dohc six	Dohc V-8	Dohc V-8
Engine No. prefix	104.992	119.975	119.974
Displacement	3,199 cc (195 ci)	4,196 cc (256 ci)	4,973 cc (303 ci)
Compression ratio	10:1	11:1	10:1
SAE horsepower	217 hp @ ,5500 rpm	275 hp @ 5,700 rpm	322 hp @ 5,700 rpm
Torque	229 lb-ft @ 3,750 rpm	295 lb-ft @ 3,900 rpm	354 lb-ft @ 3,900 rpm
Fuel system	Electronic fuel injection (all)		
Fuel required	Premium (all)		
Chassis			
Type	Unibody; steel (all)		
Chassis No. prefix	124.032	124.034	124.036
Transmission	4-speed automatic (all)		
Rear-axle ratio	2.65:1	2.24:1	2.82:1
Rear suspension	Multilink, coil springs (all)		
Front suspension	Damper strut, coil springs (all)		
Wheels	6.5x15 in.	6.5x15 in.	8x16 in.
Tires	195/65VRx15	195/65VR15	225/55ZR16
Brakes	4-wheel disc (all)		
Fuel capacity	18.5 gal	18.5 gal	23.8 gal
Weight	3,525 lb	3,745 lb	3,855 lb
Performance			
0–60 mph	8.0 sec	7.1 sec	6.3 sec
Top speed	140 mph	149 mph	155 mph (governed)
Fuel consumption	19–25 mpg	18–24 mpg	16–19 mph

Model	E320	E430
Years	1997–	1998–
Engine		
Type	Sohc V-6	Sohc V-8
Engine No. prefix	112.941	113.940
Displacement	3,199 cc (195.2 ci)	4,266 cc/260.3 ci
Bore x stroke	89.9x84/3.54x3.30 in (all)	
Compression ratio	10.0:1	11.0:1
Horsepower	221 @ 5,500 rpm	275 @ 5,750 rpm
Torque	232 lb-ft @ 3,000–4,800 rpm	295 lb-ft @ 3,000–4,000 rpm
Intake system	3-valve, fuel-injection (all)	
Chassis		
Type		
Chassis No. prefix	210.065 (sedan)	210.070
Transmission	5-speed automatic (all)	
Axle ratio	3.07:1	2.82:1
Front suspension	Double wishbone, coil springs (all)	
Rear suspension	Multilink, coil springs (all)	
Wheels	7.5x16 in. (17 in. w/Sport package)	
Tires	215/55 (235/45ZR17 w/Sport package)	
Brakes	4-wheel disc (all)	
Fuel capacity	21.1 gal (18.5 wagon)	21.1 gal
Weight	3,460 lb	3,640 lb
Performance		
0–60 mph	7.1 sec	6.4 sec
Top speed	130 (gov.) (all)	
Fuel consumption	21 city/29 hwy	19 city, 26 hwy

Note: E320 wagon weighs 3,670 pounds, gets about 3 miles per gallon less, does 0-60 in 7.5 seconds. In E320 sedan or wagon, add 198 pounds for AWD.

Technical Specifications			
Model	300SL	500SL	600SL
Years	1990–	1990–	1993–
Engine			
Type	Inline dohc six	Dohc V-8	Dohc V-12
Engine No. prefix	104.981	119.960	120.981
Displacement	2,962 cc (180.6 ci)	4,973 cc (303.5 ci)	5,987 cc (365.4 ci)
Bore x stroke	88.5x80.25 mm	96.5x85 mm	89x80.2 mm
Compression ratio	10:1 (all)		
Horsepower	228 hp @ 6,300 rpm	322–315 hp @ 5,600 rpm	389 hp @ 5,200 rpm
Torque	201 lb-ft @ 4,600 rpm	347–332 lb-ft @ 3,900 rpm	420 lb-ft @ 3,800 rpm
Fuel system	Electronic fuel injection (all)		
Fuel required	Premium unleaded (all)		
Chassis			
Type	Monocoque, power soft top, automatic roll bar		
Chassis No. prefix	129.061	129.067	129.076
Transmission	5-speed auto	4-speed auto	4-speed auto
	5-speed manual (option)		
Rear-axle ratio	3.69:1 (auto)	2.65:1	
	3.46:1 (manual)		
Rear suspension	Multilink, coil springs (all)		
Front suspension	Damper strut, coil springs (all)		
Wheels	8x16 in. (all)		
Tires	225/55ZR16 (all)		
Brakes	4-wheel disc, ABS (all)		
Fuel capacity	21.2 gal (all)		
Weight	4,035 lb	4,165 lb	4,555 lb
Performance			
0–60 mph	8.3 sec (auto)	6.4 sec	5.9 sec
Top speed	149 mph	149 mph	155 mph (governed)
Fuel consumption	15–22 mpg	16–20 mpg	13–18 mpg

to capture smog and dust particles, and more. Leather upholstery is standard on U.S. models.

Although other convertibles had used them for years, the first power top for a Mercedes-Benz was impressive. No fiddling with latches or panels. Just rock the switch, and the top goes up or down in about 30 seconds, automatically, including latching and unlatching at the windshield header. This engineering tour de force uses 15 hydraulic cylinders, 11 solenoids, and 17 proximity switches.

While the 300SL offered the world's first five-speed automatic transmission, the torque of the 500SL and 600SL allowed them to use four speeds instead. For the first time in two decades, an SL offered a manual transmission in America. The early 300SL's manual five-speed was delightful, but since Americans were inured to automatics in previous SLs, it is rare.

Both 500SL and 300SL had automatic intake valve timing for better power and torque over a wider rpm range. Zero to 60 times were 8.3 seconds for the 300SL, 6.3 seconds for the 500. The V-12 600SL cut this to 5.9 seconds.

One styling feature of the SL took a while to catch on. The plastic lower body molding, including front and rear bumpers, was painted a color slightly different from the body color. The red combination wasn't well received, so MBAG began painting the moldings on red cars in body color.

For model year 1996, the SL's styling was softened with a more rounded grille and bumpers, new lower body cladding, and 12-hole alloy wheels. The new panorama see-through glass hardtop became a 1997 option and can be retrofitted to 1992 and later SLs. As of early 1998, three special edition SLs had been built for America, the 1996 U.S. 500 edition, the 1997 Anniversary Edition (celebrating the SL's 40th year), and the 1997 La Costa (golf) edition.

ADS first became available on the 1991 300SL and 500SL. The adaptive damping system allows a comfortable ride, yet maintains maximum tire contact with the road. Judging a road's bumpiness (through vertical wheel acceleration sensors), driving speed, steering wheel

In 1993, AMG's links with Mercedes-Benz strengthened, so more cars were originally fitted with wider wheels and tires, aerodynamic aids, and similar features. *MBAG*

Model	Engine Type	Engine No. Prefix
300SL	3.5-liter six (diesel), 148 hp	OM603.971
300SE	3.0-liter six, 228 hp	M104.990
400SE	4.2-liter V-8, 282 hp	M119.971
500SEL	5.0-liter V-8, 322 hp	M119.970
600SEL	6.0-liter V-12, 402 hp	M120.980

For 1993, the 400SE was replaced with the longer-wheelbase 400SEL. For 1994, model designations changed as previously shown.

angle, and load, ADS adjusts individual shock absorber damping between taut, normal, soft, and comfort settings.

How do you spot a V-12 600SL? Besides the model number on the trunk, a V-12 emblem adorns each front fender vent. Because of its longer engine, the 600SL's front bumper projects 2 inches farther forward than those of the 300 and 500SL. The V-12 has a few deluxe interior trim touches, including a leather and wood shift knob and a wood-trimmed shift gate panel. A cellular telephone and a CD changer are standard equipment, as is ASR traction control.

S-Class Sedans 1992–on ★★

The first new S-Class sedan in more than a decade, the W140 S-Class appeared at the 1991 Geneva show. Normal and long-wheelbase versions were powered by gasoline engines from a 3.2-liter inline six to a 6.0-liter V-12 or a turbo-diesel. U.S. 1992 S-Class models included:

These interstate cruisers offer unparalleled space, safety, and comfort for four. Elbow, head, and legroom seem limitless, with your personal environment enhanced by individual climate controls and an elaborate air filtering system. Innovations include double-paned side windows to reduce heat transfer

159

Introduced for 1990, the 315-horsepower, V-8-powered 500SL is a twin to the 228-horsepower, six-cylinder 300SL. *MBAG*

and noise, self-latching doors, reverse-sighting rods (on early cars), and even a retracting trunk lid handle to keep your fingers clean. The W140 used computers to control everything from ignition timing to rear brake bias. It introduced a new Bose sound system far better than anything previously fitted. It was the first car to substitute nonpolluting R134a for the old freon (R12) air conditioning medium.

The 1992 S-Class sedans often suffered from a front-end vibration related to their weight, suspension, and tires. The official Mercedes-Benz remedy—new suspension parts, different tires—was not always totally effective, so check maintenance records and beware of a shimmy or vibration, especially on cold tires.

These S-Class sedans are more daily drivers than collector cars, but the 600SEL may be an exception. Production of the V-12 sedan was low (1,000 in 1993 worldwide, 600 for the United States), and price was high. Look for the V-12 emblem on the rear pillar. It's no coincidence that this car bears the famous 600 number.

You can buy a cheaper car, but if and when you and your family have The Big One, what would you rather be in? Just take the time to buckle your seatbelt.

For model year 1995, the S-Class was restyled slightly with new lower body moldings and bumper trim giving it a lighter look. Finally, too, the Germans caved in and gave Americans what they demanded

---

Driving Impressions: 300SL, 500SL, and 600SL

A 300SL, 500SL, or 600SL will allow the enthusiast to explore his or her full driving ability. They'll go faster than you can—or should—drive on any public road. These cars all offer seamless competence. Far more contemporary than the old 560SL, they offer the latest in ergonomics and safety.

The best buy is the 300SL with the excellent five-speed manual gearbox. Even the automatics are more enjoyable than older versions, shifting more smoothly and more quickly. The most responsive six-cylinder SL is the 1994 SL320 with the 3.2-liter engine.

The 500SL has ample power for far less money than the 600SL, but being rarer, the latter is a sure collector's item. The 600SL's huge helpings of smooth torque make speed effortless. When new, it was the fastest Mercedes-Benz to 60 miles per hour at 5.9 seconds.

More sporting and aggressive than previous SLs, these cars accelerate, handle, and stop two generations better. Some new 300SL owners, accustomed to lazy V-8s, felt it sluggish. It isn't. Rather than being lugged like an old V-8, to realize its performance a 300SL must be revved to redline.

most—giant cupholders! The excellent Electronic Stability Program (ESP) was phased into S-Class production during the 1995 model year.

500SEC and 600SEC Coupes 1993–on ★★

The V-8 500SEC and V-12 600SEC Coupes introduced for 1993 are blessed with 315 and 389 horsepower, respectively, with unique headlight and taillight treatments. Mechanically they are similar to their sedan counterparts, with slight power differences due to exhaust system changes.

Standard equipment includes ASR traction control. The ADS adaptive damping system is standard on the 600SEC, optional on the 500SEC. Both have pneumatically self-closing doors. The V-12's sculpted intake manifold makes opening the hood a pleasure. The performance produced by the engine is elegantly amazing. The 5,075-pound 600SEC can reach 60 miles per hour in 6.3 seconds, and both cars are governed to a top speed of 155 miles per hour.

The 500SEC and 600SEC, renamed the S500 Coupe and S600 Coupe for model year 1994, then CL500 and CL600 for 1996, may be the last big luxury coupes from Mercedes-Benz. Priced at $98,900

Driving Impressions: S-Class

The S-Class was criticized for its size and weight, but the cars feel more at home in the open spaces of America than in crowded European streets. With four seats filled, an S-Class sedan offers your family or business the most comfortable, safe, efficient, and rapid long-distance motoring. And frankly, if you're going to be in an accident, this is the car to be in. These are the best long-distance cars of all time, and it is unlikely that they will be surpassed for a very long time.

and $132,000, their obvious luxury tested the political correctness then in vogue. Fewer than 1,000 of each came to the United States in 1993. Ever since the first 380SEC, owner loyalty has been excellent for luxury coupes. These newest versions are sure to be collectible cars.

Sportline ★★

For 1992, a new option, Sportline, appealed to the enthusiast. On the 300E, 300CE, and 190E 2.6, Sportline brought stiffer springs and shocks, wider eight-hole alloys, wider tires, quicker steering, more

Technical Specifications			
Model	500SEL	600SEL	600SEC
Years	1992–	1992–	1993–
Engine			
Type	Dohc V-8	Dohc V-12	Dohc V-12
Engine No. prefix	119.970	120.980	120.980
Displacement	4,973 cc (303 ci)	5,897 cc (365.4 ci)	5,987 cc (365.4 ci)
Bore x stroke	96.5x85 mm	89x80.2 mm	89x80.2 mm
Compression ratio	10:1 (all)		
Horsepower	322–315 hp @ 5,600 rpm	402–389 hp @ 5,200 rpm	389 hp @ 5,200 rpm
Torque	354–347 lb-ft @ 3,900 rpm	428–420 lb-ft @ 3,800 rpm	420 lb-ft @ 3,800 rpm
Fuel system	Electronic fuel injection (all)		
Fuel required	Premium unleaded (all)		
Chassis			
Type	Monocoque (all)		
Chassis No. prefix	140.051	140.057	140.076
Transmission	4-speed automatic (all)		
Rear-axle ratio	2.64:1 (all)		
Rear suspension	Multilink (all)		
Front suspension	Double wishbone, coil springs (all)		
Wheels	7.5x16 in. (all)		
Tires	235/60ZR16 (all)		
Brakes	4-wheel disc, ABS (all)		
Fuel capacity	26.4 gal (all)		
Weight	4,830 lb	5,095 lb	5,075 lb
Performance			
0-60 mph	7.2 sec	6.3 sec	6.3 sec
Top speed	155 mph (governed) (all)		
Fuel consumption	13-17 mpg	12-16 mpg	12-16 mpg

Technical Specifications			
Model	C220	C280	C280
Years	1994–	1994–	1998–
Engine			
Type	Inline dohc four	Inline dohc six	Sohc V-6
Engine No. prefix	111.961	104.941	112.920
Displacement	2,198 cc (134.1 ci)	2,798 cc (170.7 ci)	2,799 cc (170.8 ci)
Bore x stroke	89.9x86.6 mm	89.9x73.5 mm	89.9x73.5 mm
Compression ratio	10:1 (all)		
SAE horsepower	147 hp @ 5,500 rpm	194 hp @ 5,500 rpm	194 hp @ 5,800 rpm
Torque	155 lb-ft @ 4,000 rpm	199 lb-ft @ 3,750 rpm	195 lb-ft @ 3,000–4,000 rpm
Fuel system	Electronic fuel injection (all)		
Fuel required	Premium unleaded (all)		
Chassis			
Type	Unibody; steel (all)		
Chassis No. prefix	202.022	202.028	
Transmission	4-speed automatic	4-speed automatic	5-speed automatic
Rear-axle ratio	3.07:1 (all)		
Rear suspension	Multi-link (all)		
Front suspension	Upper and lower control arms, coil springs (all)		
Wheels	6.5x15 in.	6x15 in.	7x15 in.
Tires	195/65x15	195/65x15	205/60x15
Brakes	4-wheel disc, ABS (all)		
Fuel capacity	16.4 gal (all)		
Weight	3,173 lb	3,293 lb	3,316 lb
Performance			
0-60 mph	10.2 sec	8.3 sec	8.0 sec
Top speed	125 mph (est.)	130 mph (governed)	130 mph (governed)
Fuel consumption	21-28 mpg	20-26 mpg	21–27 mpg

supportive seats, and a smaller-diameter steering wheel. For models with MB-tex seats, Sportline added leather upholstery. No drivetrain changes were made. Cars with Sportline are slightly lower; a blue and silver logo appears on their front fenders and shift knobs.

Without sacrificing comfort, Sportline brings out the car's inherent handling abilities, and we recommend it. To some buyers, Sportline will increase the value of a used car. Apart from this factory-installed option, AMG spoilers and wheels for SLs, 190s, and E-Class models were sold through U.S. Mercedes-Benz dealers from 1993.

AMG-designed Sport packages spread across the U.S. product line in 1996, becoming available on the C280, the E420, and SLs. They included shorter, stiffer springs, stiffer shock absorbers, beefier wheels and tires, and slightly different interior and exterior trim but no drivetrain changes. Not only were Sport packages relatively economical when new, they were properly developed and integrated for each model. Expect to pay a bit more for a car with the Sport option.

What to Look For

The newer the car, the more important its provenance. A mid-1990s model will probably be owned by its original buyer. Service records tell you how the car was treated. Make sure that all services were carried out by an authorized dealer. Run the car by a dealership and pay them to check it thoroughly, including a leakdown test on the engine.

Make sure that all power accessories work properly, especially the automatic climate control system. The 1991–on S-Class cars use a new design, but the E-Class continues with the older system. The new S-Class cars have a good track record, but tires may suffer from flat spots when cold, and the cars are susceptible to improper front-end alignment and tire wear. The car should track properly and shouldn't wander over "ruts" worn into the asphalt.

On an SL or Cabriolet, check power top operation. Be sure that the mechanism works smoothly and that windows and seals fit tightly. A few teething troubles occurred, and this is no simple device to repair. Continually raising and lowering the top without running the car will eventually drain the battery. Try the switch raising the automatic roll bar, too.

The 500SL and 300SL were the first Mercedes-Benz models to have a power-operated convertible top and an automatic roll bar. *MBAG*

Recent models came with a factory-installed alarm, and some had factory-installed cellular telephones. Improper installation of aftermarket electronics can cause problems, so if you see evidence of rewiring, make doubly sure that every electronic system works properly.

Many of these cars were leased rather than bought, so if you seek a specific model, ask a dealer or leasing company if a good car will be coming off lease. If you're buying from a dealer, ask about MBNA's used car warranty.

A current production car may allow you to rent an example and try it out, using it the same way you'll use your new car later. This isn't cheap, but it can avoid disappointment if you discover that your dream car just isn't for you.

C-Class Sedans 1994–on ★★

For 1994, a new compact sedan series replaced the 190s. Although European versions were powered by a wide range of engines and came in four trim levels, the U.S. started with two gasoline-powered models, the four-cylinder, 147-horsepower C220 and the six-cylinder, 194-horsepower C280. Both brought big improvements in performance, space, safety, and value.

By the 1990s, Mercedes-Benz stylists had cleaned up the engine compartment, as in this 500SL. *FDB*

Key to the performance increases were the four-valve heads and variable intake cam timing on both engines, also improving fuel efficiency. The back seat is roomier, and an optional drop-down seatback allows long items to fit inside the car. Standard dual air bags and more high-strength steel offer additional protection. The rear suspension is the proven five-link system; the front's upper link design is adapted from the S-Class.

Four-valve V-12 makes around 400 horsepower and looks great doing it. *MBAG*

Standard equipment included a sunroof, wood trim, driver's side power seat, power windows, central locking, and an improved AM/FM/cassette radio with provisions for a CD unit in the trunk. A Bose sound system was standard on the C280, optional on the 220. U.S. C220s and C280s had a four-speed automatic transmission, with no manual transmission option. Climate controls are simplified, and the system uses CFC-free R134a refrigerant.

For model year 1997, the C220 was replaced by the C230 (with the same 148 horsepower but more torque), and for 1998, the C280 got the new 194 horsepower V-6 engine and restyled lower body panels. ESP became available on the C-Class for 1998, as did wider wheels and tires. Rather than comparing the C-Class to the old 190s, it is best compared to the E-Class in performance, interior space, and style.

C36 AMG, 1995-1997 ★★★★

Since the 190E 2.3-16 had been such a performance success, and to support its involvement in European touring car racing, Mercedes-Benz developed a stunningly good high-performance C-Class sedan for model year 1995, the C36 AMG. Built jointly with AMG, the 276-horsepower sedan boasted 0 to 60 mph times of 6.4 seconds and a top speed of 155 miles per hour. Beyond speed, it was a pure joy to drive—nimble and quick on a track yet safe, fuel efficient, and eminently suitable for daily use.

The C36 was a *factory developed* hot rod, a far cry from anything tossed together haphazardly by

The V-12 600SEL is distinguished by a "V-12" logo on the C-pillar, but other S-class cars look virtually identical. *MBAG*

New headlight (and taillight) styling makes the 600SEC (nee S600 Coupe) easy to identify. The similar S500 Coupe is powered by a V-8. *MBNA*

The 1994 C280 set new standards in compact car performance, comfort, and safety. *MBNA*

amateurs. Its extra power, developed with AMG's racing experience, was accompanied by an improved suspension, wider AMG wheels, and low profile, Z-rated, 17-inch tires. ASR traction control was an option, but few if any cars were delivered without it; for fun, the ASR's throttle attenuation can be turned off, but its braking feature is always on. The four-speed automatic transmission starts in first gear, and the huge brakes come from the 1,000-pound heavier V-12 SL600. More stylish trim inside and out completes the well integrated package.

Technical Specifications		
Model	C36 AMG	C43 AMG
Years	1995–97	1998–
Engine		
Type	Inline dohc six	Sohc V-8
Engine No. prefix	104.941	113.944
Displacement	3,606 cc (220 ci)	4,266 cc (260.3 ci)
Bore x stroke	90x92.4 mm (3.58x3.64 in)	89.9x84 mm (3.54x3.30 in)
Compression ratio	10.5:1	11.0:1
Horsepower	268 @ 5,750 rpm	302 @ 5,850 rpm
Torque	280 lb-ft @ 4,000 rpm	302 ft-lb @ 3,250-5,000 rpm
Intake system	4-valve, fuel-injected	3-valve, fuel-injected
Chassis		
Type		
Chassis No. prefix	201.028	202.033
Transmission	4-speed auto	5-speed adaptive auto
Rear-axle ratio	2.87:1	3.07:1
Front suspension	Double wishbone, coil springs (all)	
Rear suspension	Multilink, coil springs (all)	
Wheels	17x7.5 in. front, 17x8.5 rear	17x7.5 in. front, 17x8.5 in. rear
Tires	225/45 front, 245/40 rear	225/45 front, 245/40 rear
Brakes	4-wheel disc	4-wheel disc
Fuel capacity	16.4 gal (both)	
Weight	3,432 lb	3,461 lb
Performance		
0–60 mph	6.4 sec	5.9 sec
Top speed	155 mph	155 mph (governed)
Fuel consumption	18 mpg city, 22 mpg hwy	17 mpg city, 22 mpg hwy

The last of the high-performance Mercedes-Benz inline sixes, the C36 AMG was built in low numbers; about 1,000 of the $50,000 cars were exported to the United States, all with automatic transmissions and mostly painted silver, black, white, or red. The 1997 model has 276 horsepower (up 8 horsepower) and a lower rear-end ratio (3.07:1), so its 0–60-mile per hour time dropped to 6.4 seconds.

C43 AMG, 1998–on ★★★★

The first C-Class model to get a V-8 powerplant was the limited-production C43 AMG, which replaced the C36 AMG as a 1998 model. The basic twin-plug V-8, similar to that of the E430, CLK430 and ML430, is breathed upon by AMG to make 302 horsepower yet weighs 44 pounds less than the inline six it replaces.

Assembled in Bremen, the bodies are shipped to AMG, where the modified drivetrain is built and installed; this dual-factory, low-volume procedure is one reason for the car's original price of $52,750. Although offered as a wagon or a sedan in Europe, the C43 AMG came to North America only as the latter, and even then only in quantities of about 500

per model year. Combining subtle appearance with outstanding performance, all were fitted with the excellent five-speed, driver-adaptive automatic transmission and 17-inch wheels wrapped around huge 13-inch front brake disks.

The C43's advertised 0 to 60 miles per hour time is 5.9 seconds, and top speed (governed) is 155 miles per hour, but the car is more than just a dragstrip special. Low-profile tires, 17-inch wheels, and stiffer suspension transmit the bumps but enable this four-door sedan to out-handle most sports cars. Still, in the traditional manner of Mercedes-Benz high-performance road cars, it remains perfectly tractable and undemanding as a daily driver.

Summary

If you want the conveniences, safety, comfort, seamless performance, and the latest engineering, these are the cars for you. Their high price when new is beaten down by a few years of depreciation, so used examples can be excellent investments as well as dependable and enjoyable cars.

The S-Class may be the last new big sedan from Mercedes-Benz for decades; its replacement will be

Driving Impressions: C36 AMG and C43

With the C36 AMG, Mercedes-Benz finally had a sedan that could lure enthusiasts away from BMW. The first C-Class rocket is more sophisticated than the 190E 2.3-16 but lacks its manual transmission. Still, the author will never forget a drive from Detroit to Los Angeles in a C36 AMG. One quiet Sunday morning over the back roads of central Nebraska, we averaged 93 miles per hour for over two hours without car or driver ever breaking a sweat. We recommend turning off the throttle attenuation segment of the C36's traction control for autocross and track use.

The C43 AMG is even better. Its V-6 is 100 pounds lighter than the C36's inline six yet has a broader-shouldered torque band and 34 more horses. These and the electronic, driver-adaptive five-speed transmission cut the 0 to 60 time to 5.9 seconds, matching the SL600. The gearbox practically thinks for the driver; downshifts are faster, and on the highway you'll find the sideways 4-5 shift lever motion especially handy for passing. This transmission alone—not to mention the additional power and torque—makes the C43 a better driver's car than even the C36.

Besides the inability to completely switch off ASR and ESP to help you beat the timer's clock, our only gripe about these cars is that fuel tank capacity is insufficient to provide enough hours of fun. If you want a subtle but sporting sedan that's bound to become a collectible, either of this pair will fill the bill and entertain you mightily besides!

The E320 (top) got a new body for 1996 and new V-6 engine and five-speed automatic transmission for 1998; the E300 Diesel version is a twin in appearance. The E430 (below), here with the optional Sport package, got the new V-8 for 1998. *MBNA*

better. The 500E offers performance to take you well beyond the turn of the century in more ways than one. The C-Class is the world's most sophisticated compact car. The SLs are amazing. All of these cars will serve you seamlessly in many roles. If you want the best, Mercedes-Benz offers it.

New for 1998, the versatile E320 Wagon could be fitted with a full-time all-wheel-drive system, much simpler, lighter, and less expensive than the previous 4Matic. *DBAG*

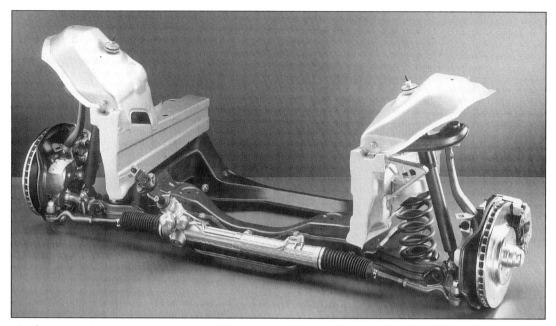

The first Mercedes-Benz production car with rack and pinion steering was the 1996 E-Class; the lower subframe, which supports the engine, helps to isolate the body from noise and vibration. *MBAG*

This 1998 SL600 is fitted with the AMG-developed Sport package and xenon gas-discharge headlights. *MBNA*

To make the capacious S-Class sedans appear more graceful, they were restyled for 1996; for 1998 these new alloy wheels appeared. *MBNA*

Last of the high-performance inline sixes (and four-speed transmissions) was the low-volume C36 AMG. *MBNA*

The first C-Class with a V-6 was the 1998 C280, but this is the first with a V-8, the 1998 C43 AMG, developed and built in conjunction with that German tuner. *MBNA*

Chapter 18

The Diesels

First to build and sell diesel-powered passenger cars, in 1936, Daimler-Benz is still the acknowledged leader in that field. In 1978, DBAG developed the first turbocharged diesel car, the 300SD. Since then it has engineered low-emission engines offering the advantages of diesel power, yet approaching the performance of its gasoline-powered models.

Mercedes-Benz diesel cars are useful, reliable, economical, luxurious, and safe, but they are not usually considered collectible, so ratings in this chapter focus on practicality and are best compared with those of similar models, not those of classics. Although few diesels even approach collector status, many enthusiastic owners become enamored with them and would never dream of owning a gasoline car.

Why own a diesel? The answer boils down to durability, performance, convenience, cost, and a few minor quirks, but improvements in newer models will affect your choice. Diesels used to be more durable than gasoline cars, but today's gaso-

Until 1979, Mercedes-Benz diesels were normally aspirated, that is, not turbocharged. In 1968, this four-cylinder 220D was the most popular diesel model. *MBNA*

Technical Specifications				
Model	220D	240D	300D	300D
Years	1968–1976	1974–1985	1975–1981	1982–85
Engine				
Type	Inline ohc four	Inline ohc four	Inline ohc five	Inline ohc five (turbo)
Engine No. prefix	615.912	616.916 or 616.912	617.910 or 617.912	617.952
Displacement	2,197 cc	2,404 cc (146.7 ci) (to 1979)	3,005 cc (183.4 ci) (to 1978)	2,998 cc (182.9 ci)
Bore x stroke	87x92.4 mm	91x92.4 mm (to 1979)	90.9x92.4 mm (to 1978)	90.9x 92.4 mm
Compression ratio	21:1	21:1+	21:1+	21.5:1
SAE horsepower	57 hp @ 4,200 rpm	62 hp @ 4,000 rpm (to 1979)	77 hp @ 4,200 rpm (to 1978)	120 hp @ 4,350 rpm
Torque	88 lb-ft @ 2,400 rpm	97 lb-ft @ 2,400 rpm	115 lb-ft @ 2,400 rpm	250 lb-ft @ 02,400 rpm
Fuel system	Mechanical injection (all)	(to 1978		
Fuel required	Diesel (all)			
Chassis				
Type	Unibody; steel (all)			
Chassis No. prefix	115.110	115.117 or 123.123	115.114 or 123.130	123.133
Transmission	4-speed auto or 4-speed manual	4-speed auto	4-speed auto	
Rear-axle ratio	3.92:1	3.69:1	3.46:1	3:07.1
Rear suspension	Semi-trailing arms, coil springs (all)			
Front suspension	Strut, coil springs (all)			
Wheels	5.5x14 in.	5.5x14 in.	5.5x14 in.	6x14 in.
Tires	175SR14	175SR14	175SR14	195/70SR14
Brakes	4-wheel discs (all)			
Fuel capacity	17.2 gal	17.2 gal	17.2 gal	21.1 gal
Weight	3,000 lb	3,164 lb	3,296 lb	3,585 lb
Performance				
0–60 mph	27 sec	25-27 sec	20-21 sec	15 sec
Top speed	83 mph	83–86 mph	90–93 mph	102 mph
Fuel consumption	25–35 mpg	24–30 mpg	20–24 mpg	27–33 mpg

line engines live longer than yesterday's. Most diesels can't match gasoline performance, but new models are narrowing the gap. Diesel fuel is harder to find than gasoline, and diesels are more susceptible to poor fuel quality. Fuel and maintenance costs once favored diesels, but these days it's a toss-up. Engine noise has been conquered in 1990s Mercedes-Benz diesels, but the fuel smells when tracked into the car. Diesels are tougher to start in winter, but in summer they produce less heat than gasoline engines. Owners who rack up a lot of miles have traditionally preferred diesels, especially for long-distance driving. Based on your needs and personal preferences, the decision is yours.

Being economical and relatively simple, diesels are popular with folks who do their own maintenance, but that's not an ownership requirement. Recent diesels under factory warranty are best maintained by Mercedes-Benz dealers, but those more than half a dozen years old can often be more economically serviced by independent mechanics and do-it-yourselfers.

After inventing the diesel car, Daimler-Benz has refined it through seven decades. The first diesel-powered passenger car, the 1936 260D, was also the first fuel-injected production car. Originally intended as commercial limousines, Mercedes-Benz diesels remain the favorite of German cabbies. Mercedes-Benz diesel longevity is legend, several having covered more than a million miles. Because diesels often cover high mileages and owners keep them longer, the quality of the basic car—chassis, body, suspension, paint, upholstery, trim—can be more important than it is for a gasoline-powered car.

Historic Diesels

Pre-World War II diesels are rare even in museums, and not until the modest 40 horsepower 170D models of the early 1950s did diesel

In 1977, the 240D switched to this roomier and more modern W123 body, which served it until the end of the model run in 1983. *MBNA*

cars start to become popular. Back then, low-priced diesel fuel made the cars attractive to high-mileage drivers, and by the late 1950s, Mercedes-Benz had developed a good export market for the uni-body 1954–62 180D and 1958–61 190D. Today these old low-powered round-body "ponton" diesel sedans are little more than a curiosity, drawing only cursory interest even among enthusiasts and collectors.

Thanks to a more advanced chassis and body, the "fin-back" diesels of the early 1960s were more refined and more popular. In America the 1961–65 190D and 1965–67 200D sedans helped Mercedes-Benz to expand its diesel foothold. Still, with just 55 horsepower pushing 3,000 pounds, these were less than rocket ships, and most people were put off by their outdated tailfins. Today they are mainly viewed as charming relics.

1970s W115 Diesels ★

These four-cylinder diesels are pretty basic cars. Although dependable and economical, they required drivers to manually activate a preglow circuit before starting, and they were sluggish per-

formers even when new. Acceleration is abysmal, but fuel efficiency is respectable. Although simpler than later diesel models and equivalent gasoline-powered models, as regular transport they are only for the serious diesel fan who doesn't mind some side effects of nostalgia.

220D 1968–1976 ★★

For 1968, a new body, the W115, appeared as the 220D, a three-box, four-door sedan replacing the fin-back body and spreading diesel desire. Visibility, comfort, handling, and safety were all improved, but performance wasn't. This is the slowest car that you should consider driving on today's highways, and even then caution is warranted. Uphill freeway ramps present a challenge, and it's easy to get into danger in fast-moving, heavy traffic. In-town and secondary road performance is more acceptable, but for heavy freeway traffic, a 300D is the minimum recommended diesel.

Of course, the 220D was dead reliable—when new. Today, unless you work on the car yourself, perhaps as a hobby, you're better off with a more modern diesel for daily use. But if you're a tinkerer and

In 1979, the five-cylinder 300D was the most popular U.S. diesel. Thousands still serve owners everywhere. *MBNA*

In 1978, the S-Class 300SD was the world's first turbodiesel production car, but its W116 chassis was soon replaced by the W126. *MBNA*

willing to accept their limitations, you can buy these cars all day long for peanuts.

Of the more than 420,000 220Ds built, one 1968 model covered more than a million miles. Used for 11 years to commute between Eugene and Portland, Oregon, it is now owned by Mercedes-Benz. Even unrestored, the car is in remarkably good condition. Still, it is second to a round-body 1957 180D, which reportedly ran for 1,184,000 miles.

1977 to 1985 Midsized (W123) Diesels

Because they arrived during the diesel's peak years in the United States, the 1977–1985 W123 midrange sedans are today's most numerous used diesels. Four-cylinder models were normally aspirated, but five-cylinder models were also offered in turbocharged form. Among the most dependable Mercedes-Benz cars, owners love them and drive them forever, so most have covered hundreds of thousands of miles. The five-cylinder engine

173

Even a diesel coupe was available; the 120-horsepower 300CD had EPA fuel mileage figures of 27 miles per gallon city, 33 miles per gallon highway. *MBNA*

Starting in 1981, the turbocharged W126-bodied 300SD led the line of diesels for almost a decade. *MBNA*

improved the diesel's performance and appeal. The 300D was easier to live with, and its more luxurious atmosphere satisfied those who had not considered earlier diesels, so it was a huge success.

While these cars have fully depreciated, making them easier to buy, they are unlikely to appreciate. That said, they are strong, roomy, and comfortable, offering such options as a sunroof, power steering, power brakes, automatic transmissions, central locking, air conditioning, power windows, and alloy wheels. Still, they never had ABS brakes and air bags. Their cruise control system—employing electrical, vacuum, and mechanical components—offers plenty of opportunity for problems, but parts and good service are still easy to find. Automatic climate control systems can also give trouble (see discussion later

in this chapter), but the basic car is as durable as an anvil.

240D 1977–1983 ★★

The proven four-cylinder OM616 (OM means *oel-motor*, oil motor) normally aspirated 2.4-liter engine helped make the 240D a reliable workhorse, and in Europe it was widely used as a taxicab. With 62 or 67 horsepower, these cars run acceptably in slow traffic, but they often struggle to merge onto busy freeways and require downshifting on hills. Fuel efficiency is high, about 30 miles per gallon. Being low powered, these are low stress cars, and their durability is among the best.

Prices are low, and 240Ds remain common, but most are well traveled by now, and you can buy a better performing 300D turbodiesel for just a little more.

300D 1977–1985 ★★★

Extremely popular, this midrange diesel on a W123 sedan chassis came with five-cylinder engines in normally aspirated (1977–81) or turbocharged (1982–85) forms. The unblown version, faster than (or not as slow as) the 240D, requires about 20 seconds to reach 60 miles per hour; the turbocharged version needs about 14 seconds and can just exceed 100 miles per hour. The latter was the first popular diesel to approach gasoline-engined performance.

U.S. cars came with air conditioning, power windows, central locking, power brakes, power steering, cruise control, and tinted glass. Options

174

One of the best midrange turbodiesels is the 1990–1993 300D 2.5 Turbo, which controlled turbo boost via computer; slots in fender are for engine air intake system. *MBNA*

usually included a sunroof, leather upholstery, power seats, heated seats, and alloy wheels. The 300D was the first Mercedes-Benz diesel to abandon the manual pre-glow knob in favor of an automatic system activated by the ignition key, making starting quicker and easier.

Durability of this chassis and its OM617 engines is legendary, but comfort-oriented options added for the U.S. market were less reliable. Typical problems center around inadequate air conditioning for America's humid heat (especially down South), climate control failures (the servo and push-button controls), and leaky vacuum lines (evidenced by inoperative central door locks). Since the Becker Grand Prix Electronic radio, a mandatory option, may have been the worst German radio ever, many owners replaced them with other, better brands. Most 300Ds had MB-tex (vinyl) upholstery, which is less expensive but more durable than leather; a 15-year-old MB-tex interior can look new. If the previous owner avoided stepping in diesel fuel at service stations, the interior shouldn't smell of diesel; if it does, replace the floor mats.

On any old diesel, check the fuel line cap on the rearmost cylinder's injector fuel leak-off fitting.

As the rubber plug ages, it will eventually blow out, so replace it as a precaution or carry a spare. The newest replacement has a metal plug in the end.

The 1985 model is the most desirable 300D, as it is turbocharged and is the best developed and best equipped. Its automatic transmission was also revised to allow downshifts to first gear while the car is moving, useful when climbing steep hills at low speeds.

300CD 1978–85 ★★★

A diesel luxury coupe? Only Daimler-Benz could pull it off! The 1978 300CD used the same body as the gasoline-fueled 280C and 280CE Coupes. A wheelbase 4.3 inches shorter than the 300D sedan's made these coupes fairly nimble. Only an automatic transmission was available, and 0–60 miles per hour took 17 seconds in the 77-horsepower nonturbo 1978–80 version or 13 seconds in the 123-horsepower 1981–85 300CD turbodiesel. The distinctively stylish coupe was more attractive than the sedan, but its price, diesel clatter, and low performance (by luxury car standards) deterred prospective high-end buyers who expected more. Sales were low.

Technical Specifications			
Model	190D 2.5	190D 2.5 Turbo	300D (Turbo)
Years	1986-1988	1987	1987
Engine			
Type	Inline ohc five	Inline ohc five	Inline ohc six
Engine No. prefix	602.911	602.961	603.960
Displacement	2,497 cc (152 ci)	2,497 cc (152 ci)	2,996 cc (183 ci)
Bore x stroke	87.0x84.0 mm	87.0x84.0 mm	87.0x84.0 mm
Compression ratio	22.0:1	22.0:1	22.0:1
SAE horsepower	93 hp @ 4,600 rpm	123 hp @ 4,600 rpm	143 hp @ 4,600 rpm
Torque	122 lb-ft @ 2,800 rpm	168 lb-ft @ 2,400 rpm	195 lb-ft @ 2,400 rpm
Fuel system	Mechanical injection (all)		
Fuel required	Diesel (all)		
Chassis			
Type	Unibody; steel		
Chassis No. prefix	201.126	201.128	124.133
Transmission	4-speed auto or 4-speed manual		4-speed auto
Rear-axle ratio	3.07:1	2.65:1	2.65:1
Rear suspension	Multilink, coil springs (all)		
Front suspension	Strut, coil springs (all)		
Wheels	6x15 in.	6x15 in.	6.5x15 in.
Tires	185/65R15	185/65R15	195/65HR15
Brakes	4-wheel disc, power-assisted (all)		
Fuel capacity	14.7 gal + 1.8 (reserve)	14.7 gal + 1.8	18.5 gal
Weight	2,845 lb	3,010 lb	3,540 lb
Performance			
0–60 mph	14.8 sec (manual) 15.2 sec (auto)	10.0 sec	10.5 sec
Top speed	107 mph (manual) 104 mph (auto)	120 mph	100 mph (est.)
Fuel consumption	25–32 mpg	22–30 mpg	22–30 mpg

300TD & 300TDT Wagon 1978–85 ★★★

In 1978, Daimler-Benz began building four-door station wagons on the W123 chassis, and these roomy, useful vehicles became popular. From the B-pillar forward the wagon is identical to the sedan, but it weighs about 300 pounds more. The 123-horsepower turbocharged 300TDT (Touring, Diesel, Turbo) is recommended over the 77-horsepower unblown 300TD.

The one-piece tailgate lifts upward; a folding, rear-facing third seat (for two children) was optional. The split seatbacks in the second row fold forward, providing ample cargo space. A full-sized spare tire is tucked inside the left rear quarter, accessed from inside the car. The self-leveling rear suspension uses nitrogen-filled spheres as shock absorbers and lifting devices to ensure normal handling even under heavy loads. If you load the car then start the engine, it should rise to normal ride height within about a minute. If the rear suspension is unusually stiff, nitrogen has probably leaked out.

Performance of the 300TDT befits a 3,800-pound car with 123 horsepower and a four-speed automatic transmission, but handling and ride are excellent, and mileage varies from around 21 to 30 miles per gallon. Most wagon owners are fanatical about them.

1980s Diesels

In the early 1980s, 79 percent of Mercedes-Benz of North America new car sales were diesels vs. 21 percent gasoline cars; by 1997, Mercedes-Benz diesel cars had been improved, but thanks to the General Motors diesel debacle, the smaller price difference between gasoline and diesel fuel, and changing markets, their sales share had dropped to just 4 percent. So even though 1990s diesels are more desirable for their technical advances, 1980s models are easier to find.

The W201 Compact Diesels
190D 2.2 1984–85 ★

The new-for-1984 compact four-door sedan

In 1992, the 300SD brought diesel advantages to the W140 S-class models. *MBNA*

(W201 chassis) was a good diesel candidate, but its small, naturally aspirated 2.2-liter, four-cylinder engine made just 73 horsepower, so the car felt slow, especially with an automatic transmission. At least it was quieter, as an engine encapsulation system helped quiet diesel rattle. The model introduced a new multilink rear suspension that offers a good ride and excellent handling. Still, we suggest stepping up to the later 190D 2.5.

190D 2.5 1986–89 ★★

Replacing the 190D 2.2 for 1986, and with 300 cc more displacement, the 190D 2.5 had 93 horsepower, cutting 0–60 miles per hour times to about 15 seconds and extending top speed to 107 miles per hour. Four-speed automatic or five-speed manual transmissions were offered, and ABS brakes were an option. For 1989, the interior was updated, but California emission laws effectively outlawed the car there, and that was its last year in the United States.

190D 2.5 Turbo 1987 ★★★

The fastest and best compact diesel is the turbocharged 190D 2.5 Turbo, but it was sold only for 1987, so today it's rare. The five-cylinder engine, which incidentally did not have a trap oxidizer, made 123 horsepower, so the car was downright peppy. Zero to 60 miles per hour took about

10 seconds; top speed was 120 miles per hour. Normal fuel mileage was 30 miles per gallon, with excellent cruising range. Six louvers in the right front fender draw in air for the intake system.

All 190D 2.5 Turbos have four-speed automatic transmissions, and most were well equipped: options included leather upholstery, a sunroof, a driver's-side air bag, seatbelt tensioners, and power seats. Still, because of California smog laws, these cars were not sold there, and today they are difficult to find.

1987–1995 W124 Midrange Diesels ★★

These cars don't exude rarity or collector interest. They denote utility, luxury, safety, and reasonable cost, all in the same package. One of the best Mercedes-Benz chassis ever was the midsized W124, introduced in 1986. The first U.S. diesel on it was the 300D Turbo, in sedan or wagon guise, and the chassis later became the 300D 2.5 Turbo, then the E300 Diesel.

300D Turbo, 300TD Turbo 1987 ★★

This six-cylinder, 3-liter turbodiesel came to the United States only as a 1987 model. With 148 horsepower, enough for 127 miles per hour, it was then the world's fastest diesel production car. A wagon version, the 300TD Turbo, was available

Technical Specifications			
Model	300D 2.5 Turbo	350SDL Turbo	S350 Turbodiesel
Years	1990–1993	1990–1991	1992–
Engine			
Type	Inline ohc five	Inline ohc six	Inline ohc six
Engine No. prefix	602.962	603.970	603.971
Displacement	2,497 cc (152.4 ci)	3,449 cc (210.5 ci)	3,449 cc (210.5 ci)
Bore x stroke	87.0x84.0 mm	89x92.4 mm	89x92.4 mm
Compression ratio	21.5:1	22:1	22:1
SAE horsepower	121 hp @ 4,600 rpm	134 hp @ 4,000 rpm	148 hp @ 4,000 rpm
Torque	165 lb-ft @ 2,400 rpm	229 lb-ft @ 2,000 rpm	229 lb-ft @ 2,000 rpm
Fuel system	Mechanical fuel injection, turbo (all)		
Fuel required	Diesel (all)		
Chassis			
Type	Unibody; steel (all)		
Chassis No. prefix	124.128	126.135	140.134
Transmission	4-speed auto (all)		
Rear-axle ratio	2.65:1	2.82:1	2.82:1
Rear suspension	Multilink, coil springs	Semi-trailing arms, coil springs	Multilink, coil springs
Front suspension	Shock strut, coil springs	Double wishbones, coil springs	
Wheels	6.5x15 in.	6.5x15 in.	7.5x16 in.
Tires	195/65HR15	205/65HR15	225/60VR16
Brakes	4-wheel disc, vacuum-assisted (all)		
Fuel capacity	18.5 gal	23.8 gal	26.4 gal
Weight	3,390 lb	3,850 lb	4,610 lb
Performance			
0–60 mph	12.4 sec	11.4 sec	12.5 sec
Top speed	121 mph	109 mph	115 mph
Fuel consumption	26–40 mpg	20–30 mpg	20–23+ mpg

for 1987 only. Other than their OM603 diesel engines, these cars are practically identical to the gasoline-powered 300E, which shared the new W124 chassis. The sole U.S.-available transmission was a four-speed automatic.

The reason for the model's short life was the failure of its trap oxidizer, an innovation designed to remove soot and odor from diesel exhaust (see the separate discussion of this device). Fairly or not, these cars earned a bad reputation, so today they can be bought for less; as a bonus, Mercedes-Benz has largely rectified their problem by offering a replacement oxidation catalyst at no charge.

300D 2.5 Turbo 1990–1993 ★★★

Recovering from the trap oxidizer problems that kept turbo-diesels out of America for the 1988 and 1989 model years, Mercedes-Benz put the 190D 2.5 Turbo's OM 602 engine into the mid-range W124 chassis, upgraded it with electronic boost control, and produced the 300D 2.5 Turbo.

The distinguishing slots in the right front fender deliver air to the 5-cylinder engine. Its 121-horsepower sounds humble, but because of strong low-end torque and a transmission that starts in first gear instead of second, this diesel drives and performs like a gasoline-engined car. As a bonus, it's so quiet that you'd hardly know it was a diesel.

Because of tight California emissions laws, these cars were never available in one of the diesel's best markets, so sales were low. Owners, reporting highway mileage in the 35 miles per gallon range, rave about these cars, but they are anything but common.

E300 Diesel 1995–1997 ★★★

When the E300 Diesel arrived as a 1995 model, Mercedes-Benz diesels were once again sold in all 50 U.S. states. This car's naturally aspirated six-cylinder engine was remarkable for its 134 horsepower—more than the 300D 2.5 Turbo's 120—and for its fuel efficiency. The key to its performance was its four-valve-per-cylinder head, the first in a diesel passenger car, and its advanced electronic engine controls.

Thanks to its 23.8-gallon fuel tank, the E300 Diesel can range for more than 700 miles. Since it

The rain-soaked million-mile 1968 220D rests along Highway 1 near Big Sur in California. *FDB*

shares creature comforts with the E320 gas sedan, this diesel will keep you comfortable on long drives, too. Without a turbocharger, this car has good throttle response once up to highway speed. A variable resonance intake manifold spreads 155 lb-ft of torque over a range from about 2,200 to 4,600 rpm.

Unfortunately the E300 Diesel seemed weakly marketed; some Mercedes-Benz new car salesmen knew little about it, and buyers may have perceived the lack of a turbo as a weakness. Even though the car itself was excellent, sales were sluggish.

E300 Turbodiesel 1998– ★★★★

The turbocharger returned for 1998, bringing 176 horsepower and 244 ft-lb of torque to the world's most fuel-efficient luxury sedan. With 30 percent more power than the 1997 E300 Diesel, the updated W210 chassis (with round headlights) hit 60 miles per hour in 8.5 seconds and topped out at 130 miles per hour, making it the world's fastest diesel car at the time. The inline six's fuel efficiency is excellent, too, with EPA ratings of 24 miles per gallon city and 34 miles per gallon highway proving conservative. Electronic traction control (ASR) comes standard, along with Brake Assist (the revolutionary electronic panic braking helper). The Electronic Stability Program (ESP) and xenon headlights are options worth looking for.

A diesel engine is offered in the C-Class only in Europe, not in America, so this E-Class model may be your only choice in a new diesel. The E300 Turbodiesel may also be one of the last of the legendary Mercedes-Benz inline diesel sixes; a 4-liter, 238-horsepower twin-turbo diesel V-8 is expected soon.

S-Class Diesels

Modern top-of-the-line S-Class diesels use the four-door W116 (1978–79), W126 (1980–89), and W140 (1990–1995) chassis fitted with six-cylinder turbocharged engines. Each of these basic chassis is virtually the same as the equivalent S-Class gasoline model. "S" indicates the larger body, and "D" means diesel power. An "L" at the end of the model designation—as in 300SDL—delineates a longer wheelbase, providing 5.5 inches more length for rear passengers, almost decadent. For interior space, luxury, and safety, these are the world's ultimate diesels. That said, they are somewhat less numerous and more expensive than midrange diesel models.

300SD 1979 ★

The 300SD was the world's first turbocharged diesel car. Combining the big W116 chassis of the 1973–1980 450SE gasoline model with the 120-horsepower (SAE), 3-liter, *oel-motor*, it was sold only in the United States. The 300SD did 0–60 miles per hour in 13 seconds and could reach 110 miles per hour. But when the new W126 chassis appeared in 1980, the W116 instantly became yesterday's mashed potatoes.

Frankly, unless you've just *got* to have a 1979 300SD, there's no compelling reason to own one. Most had problems with water pumps, climate control, cruise control, and more. The later W123 midrange turbodiesels were better developed, better performers, almost as roomy, and easier to find. The 1981 and later W126-chassis 300SD were miles better.

300SD, 300SDL, 1981–1987 ★★★

The second-generation 300SD debuted with the W126 for 1981 and ran through 1985; the long-wheelbase 300SDL ran for

1986 and 1987. The 148-horsepower six-cylinder turbodiesel pushed these cars to 60 miles per hour in 13 seconds, then on to 120 miles per hour. A new engine encapsulation system enclosed the powerplant and transmission, and with the OM603 engine's hydraulic lifters, greatly reduced engine noise. All 1987 300SDs and 300SDLs have a trap oxidizer, which can be troublesome (see below).

For such big cars, these were economical, making 20 to 25 miles per gallon in typical driving. Although sharing the 560SE/SEL's body, the latter having downright sinful amounts of rear legroom, the 300SD/SDL did without its limited-slip differential, self-leveling rear suspension, and a few luxury options.

350SD, 350SDL, 1990–91 ★

In the United States, Mercedes-Benz offered no S-Class diesels for 1988–89, but for 1990 it launched the W126-chassis 350SDL sedan. Bored and stroked from 3.0 to 3.5 liters, its aluminum-alloy OM603.970 inline six eschewed the dreaded trap oxidizer and introduced a new electronic engine management system. This and the 500-cc displacement increase produced even more bottom-end torque, making the car feel much more peppy in traffic.

Despite their luxury and improved performance, these expensive cars sold slowly. Unfortunately, many of their OM603.970 engines have since experienced high oil consumption, excessive cylinder bore wear, and even connecting rod failure, usually requiring complete engine overhaul. This is one diesel model that we can't recommend.

1992–95 S-Class (W140) Diesels

For 1992, Mercedes-Benz brought forth the new W140-chassis S-Class. Europeans thought these sedans huge, but Americans, more accustomed to wide-open spaces, were happier. The first W140 diesel, the 1992–93 350SD, became the S350 Turbodiesel when model nomenclature changed in 1994.

350SDL, 1992–1993, S350 Turbodiesel, 1994–95 ★

The W140 sedan is the epitome of luxury and safety. Elaborate systems ensconce occupants in comfort and protect them from the outside world's rudest assaults with high-strength steel, double-pane side windows, and elaborate air filtration systems. Even the diesel version offered an optional 10-speaker Bose sound system, rear vanity mirrors, separate climate controls for driver and passenger, and a heat and air-conditioning outlet for rear passengers.

These were the world's most luxurious and expensive diesel cars, yet we can't recommend them. As in their W126-chassis predecessors, the 3.5-liter engines saw more than their share of serious mechanical failures, often sudden and catastrophic. In 3.0-liter form the OM603 engine was extremely durable, but in the translation to 3.5-liter form, designated OM603.971 in this model, the legendary Mercedes-Benz durability was evidently lost.

The 1996–98 Mercedes-Benz U.S. model lines included no diesel S-Class sedans, but fortunately an excellent alternative is available, the 1999 E300 Turbodiesel. For model year 2000, tighter diesel emission regulations kept all Mercedes-Benz diesel models out of the United States.

Turbocharging

After deciding you want a diesel, your next decision is "turbocharged or not?" Although the normally aspirated four-valve diesels have adequate performance, older models under 3 liters in displacement are uncomfortably slow. If you drive in heavy traffic or on hectic interstates, or if you live at high altitude, a turbodiesel could suit you best. If you're an unhurried small-town dweller and tend to meander along two-lane roads, a normally aspirated diesel may suffice. Turbodiesels are no less reliable than normally aspirated engines and are not significantly more complicated or more expensive to fuel or maintain. Before you decide, drive both.

One key to the 300D's longtime success was the turbocharger, which harnesses exhaust gas energy to pump more air into the engine and thus produce more power. The resulting improvement in performance literally brought the diesel closer to gasoline cars with no drawbacks. Gasoline cars with turbochargers are often susceptible to expensive problems, but because diesel exhaust gas is much cooler than that of gasoline engines, turbochargers on diesels are way more durable. Turbo-diesels not only offer more power than normally aspirated diesels, they are also quieter, lose less power at high altitude, and emit less smoke and soot.

General Motors almost killed diesel sales in the United States when it attempted to adapt a gasoline engine to diesel operation. When that didn't work, all diesels got a bad rap. Mercedes-Benz diesel engines, even though specifically designed as such and having a great track record, were unfortunately tarred by the same broad brush. Today's used diesel buyers can turn that to their advantage when it comes to negotiating price. Today's new diesel buyers can also benefit from Mercedes-Benz advances in computer controlled injection systems, four-valve heads, and more.

An important point for turbodiesel buyers—as these cars age, the turbo system's wastegate, designed to bleed off excess boost pressure, can open too soon, reducing power. Although misinformed mechanics may claim that wastegate opening pressure cannot be adjusted, it can be, and when proper boost (0.6 to 0.8 bar) is restored, performance is dramatically enhanced. KKK-brand turbochargers have externally adjustable boost, but AE-brand turbos do not. An overload switch set at 1.1 bar prevents over-boosting. Most aging turbodiesels can benefit from simply restoring the correct boost level.

Trap Oxidizers

To enable its 1985 turbodiesels to meet tighter California standards for diesel particulate emissions in western states, Mercedes-Benz developed and fitted a new device called a trap oxidizer. This metal canister, in the exhaust pipe upstream of the turbocharger, trapped particles in a ceramic honeycomb. Benefits included less smoke and exhaust odor, at the cost of about 4 percent less power. When performance dropped, you simply ran at full throttle, and hot exhaust gases burned off the crud in the filter.

Unfortunately, the device didn't always work. The ceramic mesh could fracture and enter the turbocharger, damaging its blades. The trap oxidizer could clog and might not burn off the particles. Since the exhaust gas recirculation valve is downstream of the trap oxidizer, its ceramic debris could even enter the cylinders, causing engine bore wear. Fixing this is expensive! When the trap oxidizer clogs, the engine loses power, fuel consumption increases, and overheating may occur.

U.S. models with trap oxidizers include the 1985 300D, 300CD, 300TD, and 300SD California versions (sold in 11 western states) and the 1987 300D Turbo, 300TD Turbo wagon, and 300SDL (California and federal versions).

Mercedes-Benz developed an improved unit for 1986 and 1987 models then installed them on 1985 cars, with free replacement at 30,000-mile intervals, but the remedy was less than totally successful. As time passed, some turbodiesels had multiple replacements of trap oxidizer and turbocharger, and some dealers were reluctant to honor the old warranty. Use of nonapproved fuel additives can also cause trap oxidizer problems. In late 1987, MBAG stopped using the trap oxidizer.

In 1996, Mercedes-Benz offered to replace at no charge all trap oxidizers with a newly developed "oxidation catalyst." Depending on the model, this could include replacing the entire exhaust system, and if an installing dealer found turbocharger wear resulting from a trap oxidizer, he was to replace that unit, too. Obviously, Mercedes-Benz was standing behind its product, but when considering such a car, ask for proof that the necessary work has been done.

Should you buy a turbodiesel with a trap oxidizer or an oxidation catalyst? Theoretically, the problem has finally been solved, but the solution has yet to be time-tested, so the value of such cars has suffered. If you can be sure that the 1997 oxidation catalyst factory fix and resulting warranty are in place, these cars can be bargains, but without that fix, an original trap oxidizer–equipped car may be difficult to sell and should be avoided unless you are prepared to work with a Mercedes-Benz dealer to update the system.

Automatic Transmissions

Unlike gasoline engines, diesels create no vacuum in their intake systems, so they employ a vacuum pump to produce it for the automatic transmission, door locks, and climate control system. Harsh shifting or transmission slippage can often be cured by adjustment of the vacuum modulator according to a factory-specified procedure. The 617 engine has vacuum levers on the valve cover, which can wear and cause rough shifting, but these can be easily repaired. For 1985, Mercedes-Benz added more vacuum components to allow on-the-fly kickdowns to first gear, previously accessible only during initial acceleration (or by manually shifting the transmission).

Many older models use a second-gear start with the shift lever in Drive. Shifting into a lower gear while stopped initiates a first-gear start. For 1997, the four-speed automatic transmission was replaced by an electronically controlled five-speed automatic, granting the E300 Diesel far better performance, fuel efficiency, and drivability.

Climate Control Systems

For model year 1977, the W123 five-cylinder diesels (300D, 300TD) were upgraded from manual to automatic climate control, as was the 1979 240D; for 1981, the system was improved, lasting through the final model year, 1985. When these systems function properly, they are excellent performers, but failures can be difficult and expensive to diagnose and repair. The system may blow hot air when you want cold, or vice versa. Failure often involves the electronics in the dash-mounted switch unit, the servo valve controlling coolant flow, or the vacuum system that operates air flaps. Dirty coolant can jam the servo valve, causing the battery to run down as it tries to operate it. The original plastic servo may crack, causing a coolant leak, but installing a replacement aluminum-bodied servo is inexpensive and simple. Vacuum lines can also be damaged by overflowing or leaking battery acid. If the central door locking works slowly or not at all, a vacuum leak needs finding and fixing. Vacuum-related problems can be found in gasoline-engined models, too.

Air-conditioning compressors fail. The W123 midrange and early W126 S-Class cars used Delco-Remy R-4 compressors, while 1986–on models had the more efficient but far more costly ($1,200+) Nippondenso unit. Post-1985 cars have a recirculation switch, allowing you to recirculate cool air during hot or dusty conditions, and the S-Class has a rear seat air outlet, too. Unlike most American systems, these incorporate a delay so that occupants are not assaulted by cold air, so allow a few seconds for the system to react. Before you buy, check the owners manual, and operate the entire climate control system. If it doesn't work right, have it checked by an expert; fixing it can be expensive. If major work is required on a model with an R12 system, consider converting to R134a refrigerant, a relatively painless process.

Chassis and Engine Prefix Numbers, U.S. Diesel Models

The myriad variety of diesel models baffles buyers (and writers). This summary allows you to know which U.S. model you are looking at, but many European models and other permutations exist. For more details, we recommend the book *Mercedes-Benz Production Models, 1946–1995* by W. Robert Nitske.

This list includes only U.S. models; certain models sold only in Europe or elsewhere are not included.

What to Look For

Apart from the usual used car inspection points, diesels require little special examination. Of course, rust is the biggest enemy of the 1950s through 1970s bodies. On the W114 and 115 chassis, look for it around the headlights, in the rocker panels, in the suspension mounts, and in the spare wheel well in the trunk. These cars are not rare, so if any rust needs fixing, move on and find a better car.

To determine the condition of the engine's piston rings and valves, have a knowledgeable diesel mechanic perform a compression test or a leakdown test. Most pre-1986 diesels need new valve seals (inexpensive) around 100,000 miles. Worn valve seals are evidenced by an excessive amount of oil inside the air cleaner or oil leaking out of the PCV hoses on the cam cover. Have the mechanic check the vacuum pump to see that it develops adequate vacuum. Leaks in a diesel's vacuum system can cause hard shifting and make the engine shut off slowly.

Diesel engine noise varies between models, but 1990s engines are much quieter than those of the 1970s and earlier. Rattling or "nailing" can sound awful during cold starts but should decrease as the engine warms up. Diesel engines vibrate less as they warm up, but a car with more than 100,000 miles may need new engine and transmission mounts. Excessive black exhaust smoke and soot can mean that the injection pump may be misadjusted, or the timing chain may be worn and need replacement. Have a mechanic check the chain for wear when he does the leakdown test.

Good starting is important. If a diesel starts slowly in warm weather, it will be even more reluctant in cold weather. Battery and glow plug condition are critical to good cold weather starting, and a block heater is a necessity in cold climates or at high altitudes.

Diesel fuel leaks are easier to see and smell than gasoline leaks. If you smell diesel fuel inside the car, service station fuel spillage has probably been tracked onto the carpets; replacing them will help.

Summary

Mercedes-Benz diesels are the world's best, combining practicality, reliability, and fuel efficiency with luxury and safety. If you understand their strengths as well as weaknesses and want one, save up and buy the newest possible model, avoiding those with trap oxidizers. Since Mercedes-Benz diesel and gasoline models share almost everything but engines, see the chapters on equivalent gasoline models to learn more about the rest of the car.

While diesels are hardly collector's items and rarely perform as well as the equivalent gasoline model, they can be bargains and do provide excellent long-term transportation value. Enter the market with your eyes open, and you may well join the band of enthusiastic Mercedes-Benz diesel fans.

Model Year & Designation	Chassis Prefix	Engine Prefix	Description
Compact			
1984–85 190D 2.2	201.122	601.921	4-cyl diesel, 72 hp
1986–89 190D 2.5	201.126	602.911	5-cyl diesel, 93 hp
1987 190D 2.5 Turbo	201.128	602.961	5-cyl turbodiesel, 123 hp
Midrange/E-Class			
1968–76 220D	115.110	615.912	4-cyl diesel, 65 hp
1973–76 240D	115.117	616.916	4-cyl diesel, 62 hp
1974–76 300D	115.114	617.910	5-cyl diesel, 77 hp
1976–85 240D	123.123	616.912	4-cyl diesel, 62-67 hp
1976–85 300D	123.130	617.912	5-cyl diesel, 77-83 hp
1982–85 300D	123.133	617.952	5-cyl turbodiesel, 118-123 hp
1978–86 300TD (wagon)	123.190	617.912	5-cyl diesel, 77-83 hp
1980–86 300TD (wagon)	123.193	617.952	5-cyl turbodiesel, 118-123 hp
1978–81 300CD (coupe)	123.150	617.912	5-cyl diesel, 77-83 hp
1981–85 300CD (coupe)	123.153	617.952	5-cyl turbodiesel, 118-123 hp
1987 300D Turbo	124.133	603.960	6-cyl turbodiesel, 143 hp
1987 300TD Turbo (wagon)	124.193	603.960	6-cyl turbodiesel, 143 hp
1990–93 300D 2.5 Turbo	124.128	602.962	5-cyl turbodiesel, 121 hp
1993–95 E300 Diesel	124.131	606.910	6-cyl diesel, 134 hp
1996–97 E300 Diesel	210.020	606.912	6-cyl diesel, 134 hp
1998– E300 Turbodiesel	210.025	606.962	6-cyl turbodiesel, 174 hp
S-Class			
1978 300SD Turbodiesel	116.120	617.950	5-cyl turbodiesel, 120 hp
1980–87 300SD Turbodiesel	126.120	617.951	5-cyl turbodiesel, 118-143 hp
1986–87 300SDL Turbo	126.125	603.961	6-cyl turbodiesel, 143-148 hp
1990–91 350SD Turbo*	126.134	603.970	6-cyl turbodiesel, 134 hp
1990–91 350SDL Turbo*	126.135	603.970	6-cyl turbodiesel, 134 hp
1992–95 300SD/S350 Turbo*	140.134	603.971	6-cyl turbodiesel, 148 hp
*Not sold in California.			

Chapter 19

The Latest Models 1998–

For 1998, Daimler-Benz not only introduced its first V-6 but also a big brother V-8, putting them into entirely new models, one of them built in Alabama. Here we'll review the M-Class and the sports models; for the sedans, see Chapter 17.

The M-Class, 1998–

Traditionally conservative Daimler-Benz has rarely shocked anyone, so building a sport-utility vehicle in the U.S. and selling it for $33,950 came as a surprise of the first order. The resulting M-Class set new standards in an over-populated, highly competitive market, decisively winning the 1997 North American Truck of the Year Award.

The ML320, a V-6 four-door SUV, was introduced in September 1997 as a 1998 model, instantly establishing a long waiting list. This is one sport-ute without that breed's traditional clunkiness. "It feels just like a Mercedes," is the most frequent comment of first-time drivers. Smooth, responsive, comfortable, and roomy join up with safe, fuel-efficient, innovative, and distinctive. Add value, too, with prices below those of the bloated and ancient competition.

ML320 1998–on ★★★

Applying creative thought and experience to the demands of the sport-utility market, Mercedes-Benz created the ML320, a 215-horsepower, V-6 powered four-wheel-drive vehicle combining the best assets of sedans, minivans, and off-road vehicles, yet avoiding most of their liabilities. To keep the price reasonable in a ferociously competitive market, Mercedes-Benz assembles the M-Class in America, although its engine and transmission are made in Germany. Quality is not an issue; Mercedes-Benz trained the cream of the crop of eager employees and blended the best of U.S., Japanese, and German production techniques.

The ML320's twin-spark aluminum V-6, five-speed electronically controlled automatic transmission (no manual gearbox was offered) and the 4ETS four-wheel-drive system is shared with the 1998 E-Class sedans and wagons. The innovative electronically controlled torque-shifting system replaces heavy, noisy, and expensive four-wheel-drive geartrains but bears no resemblance to the earlier 4Matic system. Instead of locking its differentials, the M-Class uses its brakes to direct torque away from a spinning

The first M-Class, the V-6-powered 1998 ML320 (left), has gray bumpers and rocker panels, five-spoke, 16-inch wheels. The 1999 ML430 (right), with V-8 power, has body-color bumpers and trim, seven-spoke, 17-inch wheels. *MBNA*

Technical Specifications		
Model	ML320	ML430
Years	1998–	1999–
Engine		
Type	Sohc V-6	Sohc V-8
Engine No. prefix	112.942	113.942
Displacement	3,199 cc/195.2 ci	4,266 cc/260.3 ci
Bore x stroke	89.9x84 mm/3.54x3.30 in. (all)	
Compression ratio	10.0:1	10.0:1
Horsepower	215 @ 5,500 rpm	268 @ 5,500 rpm
Torque	233 lb-ft @ 3,000 rpm	300 lb-ft @ 3,000–4,400 rpm
Intake system	3-valve, fuel-injected (all)	
Chassis		
Type		
Chassis no. prefix	163.154	163.172
Transmission	5-speed automatic, high/low-range transfer case (all)	
Axle ratio	3.69:1	3.46:1
Front suspension	Double wishbone, torsion bars (all)	
Rear suspension	Double wishbone, coil springs (all)	
Wheels	8x16	8.5x17
Tires	255/65R16	275/55R17
Brakes	ABS	ABS, Brake Assist
Fuel capacity	19.0 gal	19.0
Weight	4,390 lb	4,550
Performance		
0-60 mph	9.0 sec	8.0 sec
Top speed	112 mph (gov.)	112 mph
Fuel consumption	17 city/21 hwy	15 city/18 hwy

wheel to another with traction. Even if just one wheel has traction, the M-Class can move; don't try that in any other SUV.

With a frame that combines the best of the traditional box-section chassis and unit construction, the M-Class body is completely new. The first four-wheel independent suspension on a sport-utility vehicle provides a comfortable ride, good handling, and more responsive steering.

Although moderately sized outside, the M-Class is surprisingly roomy inside, accommodating three across in its second row of seats. Big doors make entry and exit easy. Although the step-up height is relatively low, the driver's seat offers a commanding view over other traffic. Side air bags are standard. Reading the owners manual will make it easier for you to fold the second row seats. Cargo space is bigger than the Ford Explorer and the Jeep Grand Cherokee.

But for option packages, the first ML320s are quite similar. Their standard gray cloth seats look a bit drab and require manual adjustment, but the most popular option package included leather upholstery, a sunroof, wood trim, power seats, and more. Optional folding third row seats can be retrofitted to early ML320s, and other accessories—a trailer hitch,

brush guards, bike and ski racks, fender flares, and more—can be dealer installed. A GPS navigation system is an expensive ($2,500) factory option. Meanwhile, the aftermarket offers an array of other accessories.

The ML320 gets far better fuel mileage than its competitors. Early examples had problems with their new remote locking system, but this and a few other glitches got factory fixes. Previous Mercedes-Benz owners complained a bit about fit and finish and found the controls in unusual (to them) places, but the M-Class rightfully earned rave reviews worldwide. It's still too early to definitively judge the entire vehicle's true reliability and longevity, but you can bet that Mercedes-Benz will allow nothing to sully the reputation of this critical product. Initial demand far outstripped supply, so even if you buy one and don't like it, a line of buyers will form at the end of your driveway.

ML430, 1999–on ★★★

If Americans welcomed the 1998 ML320 with open arms, the additional power and torque of the V-8-powered 1999 ML430 led to blatant public seduction. Performance of the 4.3-liter, 268-horsepower

M-Class (ML320 here) combines ladder-type chassis with unit-body construction and offers the first four-wheel independent suspension of any sport-utility vehicle; spare tire is mounted underneath at rear, behind fuel tank. *MBNA*

ML430 makes it even more attractive, with a 0 to 60 of 8 seconds and a 24-percent boost in torque over the ML320. Inside, leather upholstery is standard, along with the BabySmart child seat sensor. The excellent Electronic Stability Program (ESP), which automatically prevents skids, is standard on this model, too.

The easiest way to tell an ML430 from an ML320 is by the V-8 model's body-colored bumpers, rocker panels, and side moldings. Wheels are 17-inch diameter, up from 16 on the ML320, with 275/55 tires, and Brake Assist is standard equipment (as it is on 1999 and later ML320s). A thin, multi-panel sunroof is an option. ML430s are better equipped than ML320s, but at "under $44,000" they offer slightly less of a bargain. Because demand is high, expect low depreciation and consequently high prices for used examples.

M-Class Driving Impressions

Whatever your experience with SUVs or Mercedes-Benz cars, it's important to approach an M-Class vehicle with an open mind. It's not like other SUVs, and it's not like other Mercedes.

While the roomy M-Class interior may seem familiar to the Mercedes-Benz driver, the headlight switch is on a stalk, not the dash, and the climate control system is manual, not automatic. After all, this is a $34,000 Mercedes-Benz, not a $100,000 Mercedes-Benz. That doesn't excuse the difficulty of folding the second row of seats, though.

On the road, the V-6 has good power, and its ride, steering, and handling are much more car-like

than most SUVs. Emergency handling maneuvers feel stable, and the M-Class can even handle an autocross course. We recommend the ESP option, mostly because it can save you in an emergency highway maneuver. Fuel efficiency is surprisingly good.

Off-road, the M-Class can be amazing because its electronic all-wheel-drive system allows it to proceed even with traction at only one wheel. As with any off-road vehicle, the key is to look and think ahead, move slowly, and let the systems work for you. Before descending steep trails, engage low-range by pushing a button on the dash. Stay off the brakes on steep downhill slopes, and you'll be amazed at how well the engine compression slows the car. The 37-foot turning circle, tighter than those of the Explorer and Grand Cherokee, is handy on city streets or country trails.

What to Look For

Because these models are so new, your best indication of mechanical condition remains a good service record. Mercedes-Benz cured the few initial glitches (remote locking systems, rear sway bar attachments) via service bulletins to its dealers. Your best friend here is the four-year/50,000-mile warranty.

Summary

The all-new ML320 was an instant hit, surprising even Mercedes-Benz. Customer demand for this vehicle and the ML430 V-8 version ensure that your investment is protected. The vehicle's overall competence and the reputation of Mercedes-Benz will remain long after the new car smell disappears.

SLK & CLK

As it introduced the ML320 sport-utility vehicle in late 1997, Mercedes-Benz was in the midst of making its products both more desirable and more attainable. Mercedes-Benz served enthusiasts well with the 1998 SLK sports car and the similarly priced CLK coupe.

SLK230, 1998–on ★★

The SLK was the first real Mercedes-Benz sports car since the demise of the 300SL in 1963. Light and agile, with plenty of power, this two-seater was a natural competitor for the Porsche Boxster and the BMW Z3. A power folding hardtop made the SLK supremely practical to drive (and park) anywhere and eliminated soft top replacement. Safety features

For 1998, Mercedes-Benz produced its first V-6, the 3.2-liter M112, which was modular with the 4.3-liter M113 V-8. Both engines are aluminum and share the same bore and stroke. *DBAG*

include side air bags and an integrated roll-over bar behind each seat. The SLK230's 185-horsepower supercharged (and intercooled) inline four provided good performance with a broad torque band and excellent fuel efficiency.

Europeans could buy the SLK with less-powerful unsupercharged 2.0- or 2.3-liter, four-cylinder engines but with a five-speed manual transmission. U.S. buyers got the top of the line blown 2.3-liter four but for the first year, 1998, could have only a five-speed automatic transmission. Even though the electronically controlled automatic was DBAG's best ever, the one essential ingredient of a true sports car, a good manual transmission, was missing at first.

A manual five-speed transmission option finally appeared in the 1999 model. Zero to 60 miles per hour acceleration time, about 7.2 seconds, is about the same for either transmission. Fuel mileage is excellent—over 20 miles per gallon in town and over 30 on the highway. All SLK230s were fitted with ASR traction control, and, of course, ABS brakes.

In value, the well-equipped 1998 SLK230's $39,700 list price beat the stripped Porsche Boxster all hollow; price the Porsche hardtop and sporting suspension options, and you'll see why. The well-equipped SLK230 originally had only three options: heated seats, metallic paint, and a choice of two mobile or portable phone/CD changer combinations. The larger, mid-engined Porsche may have been more sporting, but most people found the SLK

prettier than the Boxster or the all-too-retro Z3. Even with its appeal limited by an automatic transmission, the 1998 SLK230 sold like hotcakes.

If you're over 6 feet tall, sit in an SLK before you buy it—you'd be amazed how many people don't do that when buying a new car—to assure yourself of sufficient legroom and headroom. When doing this, be sure you know how to adjust the seats. The only other complaint about the SLK is that despite its ASR traction control, it can be dodgy on snow and ice, but that's really a matter of suitable snow tires. Although the SLK's steel top retracts into the upper portion of the trunk, there's ample space below it for a medium-sized suitcase; using soft baggage helps. To save trunk space, the SLK was the first Mercedes-Benz with a collapsible spare tire.

All SLK230s have ASR traction control, but the throttle attenuation can be switched off. Besides its five-speed manual transmission option, the 1999 model was also the first U.S.-bound SLK to offer an AMG-developed Sport package, upgrading handling and trim but not power. The option included 17-inch wheels, up from the standard 16-inch alloys, with 225/45ZR17 front and 245/40ZR17 rear rubber.

CLK320, 1998–on ★★★

By the mid-1990s, car makers everywhere were building excellent midsized coupes, and now that Mercedes-Benz was feeding all markets, it developed a moderately priced coupe, the CLK, based on the C-Class chassis and using E-Class hardware. Power came from a new 218-horsepower, 3.2-liter engine, the first Daimler-Benz V-6. Shared with C, E, and M-Class models, the three-valve-per-cylinder engine was modular with the new 4.3-liter V-8 introduced for 1998. In Europe the CLK could be had with 2.0- or 2.3-liter inline fours, and with a five-speed manual transmission, but the first U.S. version used the 3.2-liter V-6 and the driver-adaptive five-speed automatic. At $39,850, the 1998 CLK230 cost $23,000 less than the previous E320 Coupe.

Although it may appear unassuming, even practical, a CLK320 is a high-performance car. You can drive a CLK daily and drop the kids off at school yet still exploit its high-speed stability, nimbleness, and good handling. The coupe's utility is enhanced by such handy features as a huge trunk (plus folding rear seatbacks) and front seats that automatically slide forward for better rear seat access. Both the BabySmart child seat recognition system and the Brake Assist emergency braking system are standard equipment, as is an electronic key system.

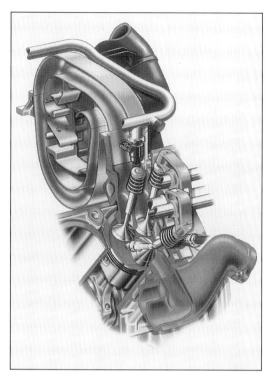

Both the V-6 and the V-8 employ dual-length intake manifold, single overhead roller cams, twin-plug ignition, and three valves per cylinder to provide the best combination of power, emissions, and fuel efficiency. *DBAG*

The smooth V-6's low-rpm torque makes this engine more fun than the earlier inline sixes, which need to rev to perform well. The CLK320's lightness helps it reach 60 miles per hour in 6.9 seconds, and its balance (the engine is aluminum) makes it feel much more nimble than either the C-Class or E-Class models. High-speed stability is especially impressive. The CLK's much lower price than the previous 300E and E320 Coupes and Cabriolets made it much more popular.

CLK430, 1999–on ★★★★

Mercedes-Benz introduced a more sporting CLK for 1999, the V-8-powered CLK430, considerably improving performance while retaining the CLK's good weight distribution. The CLK430's aggressive-looking AMG-developed trim package may seem unusual to traditional Mercedes-Benz owners, but its 275-horsepower engine offers performance to match—0 to 60 miles per hour in 6 seconds.

All CLK430s enjoy the five-speed, driver-adaptive automatic transmission, ESP, 17-inch wheels, low-profile tires, leather upholstery, burl-walnut trim, and a Bose sound system. Again, it's too soon to judge this model thoroughly, but it promises much for lovers of high performance. Its moderately priced combination of performance, luxury, safety, and utility bode well for long-term value.

CLK320 Cabriolet, 1999–on ★★★

On the heels of the 1998 CLK320 Coupe came a four-seat convertible version, the 1999 CLK320 Cabriolet. Mechanically it is virtually the same as the CLK320. Like the coupe version, in Europe the Cabriolet could be fitted with the 2.0-liter inline four or the 2.3-liter supercharged four from the SLK230.

Its power top has a long-lasting glass rear window, thus it has a real defroster there. As in the E320 Cabriolet, the rear headrests provide instant automatic roll-over protection. Trunk space is down from that of the coupe because the folding top requires space. Price is almost $10,000 beyond the equivalent coupe, but production volume is lower, so this car has more collector potential.

Distinguished by its graceful yet practical folding steel hardtop, the SLK230 is an eminently practical sports car, the first supercharged Mercedes-Benz production car since the 1930s. *MBNA*

Technical Specifications

Model	SLK230	
Years	1998–	
Engine		
Type	Inline 4	
Engine No. prefix	111.973	
Displacement	2,295 cc/140 ci	
Bore x stroke	90.9x88.4/3.58x3.48 in.	
Compression ratio	8.8:1	
Horsepower	185 @ 5,300 rpm	
Torque	200 lb-ft @ 2,500–4,800 rpm	
Intake system	4-valve, fuel inj., supercharged	
Chassis		
Type		
Chassis no. prefix	170.447	
Transmission	5-speed automatic (all) (5-speed manual option, 1999-on)	
Axle ratio	3.27:1	
Front suspension	Double wishbone, coil springs (all)	
Rear suspension	Multilink, coil springs (all)	
Wheels	7x16 front, 8x16 rear	
Tires	205/55 front, 225/50 rear	
Brakes	ABS	
Fuel capacity	14.0 gal	
Weight	3,036 lb	
Performance		
0–60 mph	7.2 sec	
Top speed	140 mph	
Fuel consumption	22 city/30 hwy	

Model	CLK430	CLK320
Years	1999–	1998–
Engine		
Type	Sohc V-8	Sohc V-6
Engine no. prefix	113.943	112.940
Displacement	4,226 cc/260.3 ci	3,199 cc/195.2 ci
Bore x stroke	89.9x84/3.54x3.30 in	89.9x84/3.54x3.30 in.
Compression ratio	10.0:1	10.0:1
Horsepower	275 @ 5,750 rpm	215 @ 5,500 rpm
Torque	295 lb-ft @ 3,000–4,400 rpm	229 lb-ft @ 3,000–4,600
Intake system	3-valve, fuel-injected	3-valve, fuel-inj
Chassis		
Type		
Chassis # prefix	208.370	208.365
Transmission	5-speed automatic	
Axle ratio	2.87:1	3.07:1
Front suspension	Double wishbone, coil springs	
Rear suspension	Multilink, coil springs	
Wheels	17x7 front, 17x8 rear	7x16 front and rear
Tires	225/45 front, 245/40 rear	205/55
Brakes	ABS, Brake Assist	ABS, Brake Assist
Fuel capacity	16.4 gal	16.4 gal
Weight	3,426 lb	3,240 lb
Performance		
0–60 mph	6.1 sec	6.9 sec
Top speed	130 mph (gov.)	130 mph (gov.)
Fuel consumption	18 city/25 hwy	20 city/29 hwy

Note: Optional sport packages alter the above specifications.

The V-6 powered CLK320 (top) appears sedate in comparison to the CLK430 (bottom), which has sportier lower body panels, wider wheels and tires, and better performance thanks to its V-8. *DBAG*

SLK, CLK Driving Impressions

Simply put, these are the most enjoyable Mercedes-Benz models for the enthusiast-driver, yet they are eminently practical.

As the tech specs tell you, the SLK230's supercharger provides an extraordinarily broad torque range, so all you have to do is squeeze the throttle. The supercharger allows the light four-cylinder engine to produce even more power than some heavier and larger V-6 or V-8 engines. To tell the truth, you'd never detect the difference between the SLK's rack-and-pinion steering and the traditional recirculating ball unit in the CLK.

Because the SLK is so undemanding, you may find yourself driving faster than you think. Even on this short wheelbase, high-speed stability is excellent, and the wide tires provide plenty of grip on dry pavement. Resist the temptation to install wider tires, which may cause heavier steering, tramlining, and aquaplaning (use the savings to pay for professional high-performance driving instruction). The SLK's small size provides a natural advantage on a tight autocross course.

The CLK is a sleeper. Its combination of V-6 or V-8 power and a relatively light chassis surprises most drivers with strong acceleration. The coupes are especially well-balanced, and their excellent stability actually seems to improve as speed increases. The folding rear seatback and automatically sliding front seats are great touches. Like other 1998 V-6 and V-8 models, the CLK has the Flexible Service System (FSS), which automatically determines the optimum oil change interval based on actual use and oil condition.

Like all the driver-adaptive five-speed automatics, the CLK's transmission senses your driving style based on how quickly you move the throttle. Going uphill or downhill, shifts are delayed accordingly for better climbing and engine braking. For better traction, the winter mode starts in second gear. This is the first Mercedes-Benz automatic to tempt even the die-hard shift-it-yourselfers.

What to Look For

Although we have yet to hear of a problem, the most complex mechanism on the SLK is its folding hardtop, so make sure it operates and fits properly. The SLK230's supercharger seems durable, too, and even if it were to fail, replacement would be simple.

As usual with new models, long-term durability has yet to be proven, but based on early reports and the usually strong Mercedes-Benz reputation for reliability, prospects seem excellent. If you're buying a used example, complete service records are vital.

Summary

More sporting models are always welcome from Mercedes-Benz, which is supremely competent at combining high performance with safety and utility. The SLK and CLK are just the start of a successful line, and you can expect them to hold their value well. Meanwhile, enjoy their driving experience!

Electronic Stability Program

Besides ABS (anti-lock brakes), the most significant new Mercedes-Benz electronic abbreviation is ESP. The Electronic Stability Program detects and prevents skids and slides in low-traction conditions or during emergency evasive maneuvers, and it's an option worth having.

Think of ESP as "sideways ABS." Electronic sensors compare the car's movements with the position of its controls, individual wheel speeds, g-forces, and vehicle yaw. When predetermined parameters are exceeded, indicating understeer (front-end plowing) or oversteer (rear-end fishtailing), the system applies the car's individual wheel brakes. The resulting braking forces quickly yet smoothly swing the car back onto the driver's intended course. The uncanny effect, easily demonstrated on wet or icy pavement, is most valuable in preventing loss of control during emergency lane changes and quick swerves. Limited only by the traction of the tires, it's like having a giant hand holding your car on course.

Appearing first on some 1995 S-Class models, the $1,200–1,500 ESP option soon spread to the E-Class, CLK, and other models. For driving on loose gravel or with snow chains, it can be switched off. Combined with the subtle 4ETS all-wheel-drive system and ABS brakes, ESP gives you a real edge on snow and ice. Still, it's important to remember that these electronic aids rely on the traction of the tires. Exceed that, and you're into the wall. In our experience, winter driving speeds are often limited by braking ability, since ABS is not quite as effective as the other traction-assistance devices.

Brake Assist

In 1997, Daimler-Benz introduced the world's first emergency braking assistance program, Brake Assist. Since most drivers fail to squeeze the brakes hard enough in an emergency, this system does it for them and thus stops the car shorter. Based on how quickly the brake

Like the 300CE Cabriolet and the E320 Cabriolet, the CLK Cabriolet employs automatically rising rear head-rests as roll-over protection. This European CLK230 Kompressor and the CLK200 use four-cylinder engines; the CLK320 has the 218-horsepower V-6. *DBAG*

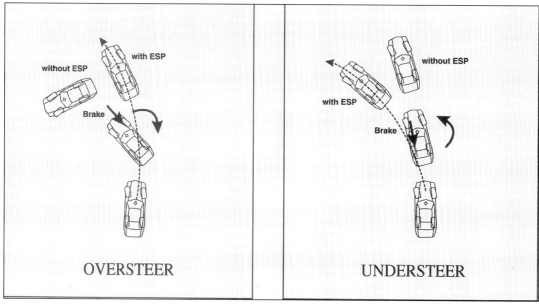

The Electronic Stability Program (ESP) will save you from skids and spins. Dotted line indicates driver's intended path; curved arrows show how ESP "rotates" car using individual front or rear wheel braking to prevent oversteer and understeer. ESP, which works on acceleration, coasting, and while braking, first appeared in 1996. *MBNA*

pedal is depressed, a computer actuates a valve on the vacuum booster to apply the brakes harder. If you really know how to threshold-brake properly, you'll notice no difference, but 99 out of 100 drivers are less skilled and will definitely benefit, to the tune of 15 to 45 percent shorter stopping distances. Brake Assist is another electronic option definitely worth having.

Xenon Headlights

Although European Mercedes-Benz models have had much better than average headlights for years, U.S. models have long been limited by U.S. government lighting regulations. Until the W210 (1996 and later) E-Class brought the new ovoid headlights, most lights on U.S. models were barely adequate for high-speed, open-country running.

The 1996 models brought a better option, xenon gas-discharge headlights. Although the xenon bulbs operate only on low-beam, they stay lit when the conventional quartz-halogen high-beams are on. The xenon units have a bluish "daylight" tint, consume less power than conventional lights, level themselves automatically, and have tougher lenses. Once you've tried them, you'll love the way they turn night into day. If you drive much at night, especially on interstate highways, you'll find them essential. Unfortunately it's impractical to retrofit them to earlier models.

Five-Speed Automatic Transmission

All 1998 models sold in the United States came with a new five-speed, electronically-adaptive automatic transmission, the best ever from Daimler-Benz. Using input from sensors that determine driving style (fast or slow throttle opening, for instance) and conditions (uphill or downhill), the computer adjusts shift points accordingly. A console-mounted "S/W" switch allows you to adapt for Summer or Winter conditions (S starts in first gear, W in second). Electronic links to the engine management system allow amazingly smooth shifts up or down. This transmission is especially impressive when combined with the broad torque curves of the recent V-6 and V-8 engines. When the throttle is punched, quick acceleration results almost no matter which gear is engaged or what rpm the engine is turning. Thanks to electronics, this 722.6 transmission works far better than earlier four- and five-speed automatics.

Side Air Bags

Mercedes-Benz was one of the first manufacturers to install side air bags, and its door-mounted systems are generally thought to be more effective than seat-mounted systems. Side air bags first showed up on the new-for-1996 W210 E-Class sedans and the SL. For 1997, they were on the S-Class and the SLK, and by the 1998 model year, they were fitted to all models, including the M-Class.

Chapter 20

The Rarest Models

Although they aren't titled that way, the next two categories are distinguished by the rarity and cost of their subjects. This chapter could be divided into two sections: Impossible to Buy and Somewhat Available.

Museum Material

You'll probably never get a chance to buy these cars, but who knows? We wouldn't want you to overlook one. More details are available elsewhere, so we won't go into detail here about these extremely rare cars. We just want to be sure you'll recognize the bargain of a lifetime when you see it.

Silver Arrows ★★★★★

Mercedes-Benz Grand Prix racing cars are among the world's most renowned and valuable automotive artifacts. The best-known early cars are the 1908 and 1914 versions, but other successes came in the 1930s with the W125 and W154, and in the 1950s with the W196. Most of these rare cars are safely ensconced in museums. Still, it's

Early Mercedes and Benz racing cars were widely raced in the United States. In 1915, Ralph De Palma won the Indianapolis 500 in this Mercedes. *Indianapolis Motor Speedway*

conceivable that one or two might remain hidden away.

Although rumors persist of examples surviving in Eastern Europe, practically every Mercedes-Benz Grand Prix car made since 1934 is accounted for. Only a few are in private hands. Arguably the best to drive was the postwar W196, the car that carried Juan Manuel Fangio to a world championship. The 2.5-liter straight-eight is renowned for its desmodromic valves and mechanical fuel injection, making it easier for you and your mechanic to maintain than the more complicated prewar supercharged cars!

300SLR ★★★★★

Derived from the postwar 2.5-liter W196 Grand Prix car, the W196S 300SLR was a tube-framed 3.0-liter racer contesting the sports car world championship but used only for 1955. Its 203-horsepower inline eight boasted desmodromic valve gear and was matched to a five-speed transmission, with inboard drum brakes all around. Its legendary successes in the Mille Miglia (Stirling Moss and Denis Jenkinson) and elsewhere were tempered by its tragic crash at Le Mans in 1955. Ten chassis numbers were issued, but only nine cars were built, including two Coupes. All are accounted for.

300SLS ★★★★★

Ah, the mystery of the two disappearing 300SLS race cars. If they survive, somewhere in the world are two factory-built, lightweight race versions of the 300SL Roadster, specially built for Paul O'Shea to use in SCCA races in 1957. The team, backed by George Tilp, entered everything in sight, and while they didn't win everywhere, they swept the championship. Cagey SCCA rules makers legislated this factory race car out of contention for 1958, and the two cars, chassis numbers 8467198106/2 and 8442620070/1, were reportedly sold in the United States for $5,000–$6,000 each. They promptly disappeared, and no one has admitted seeing them since. If you find one, it will be one of the most desirable Mercedes-Benz cars ever.

C111 ★★★★★

Developed in the 1960s as a showcase for the Wankel rotary engine, the C111 appeared in 1969. Its four-rotor motor made up to 350 horsepower. Only six Gullwing-doored Coupes were built, the first with a primitive "mule" body of aluminum, the rest with sleeker fiberglass bodies. The first, even with a steel platform chassis, weighed under 3,000 pounds and had a top speed beyond 185 miles per hour.

This early super-car came close to production but was destined instead to be a concept vehicle and a record-setter. In 1976 and 1978, rebodied C111-IIs set world speed records using a souped-up, five-cylinder, turbodiesel engine. In 1979, a C111-IV with a 500-horsepower, twin-turbo gasoline V-8 set a new world closed-course record of 250.918 miles per hour at Nardo, Italy.

All C111s were retained by DBAG, so your chances of buying one are presently low. Still,

This early Benz racer is being raced on the sand at Daytona Beach, Florida. *MBNA*

Juan Manuel Fangio at the wheel of a W196 Grand Prix car. *DBAG*

The W125 swept the 1937 Grand Prix season; at least one is in private hands. *DBAG*

The W196 was built in both open-wheel and fendered versions. *DBAG*

Mercedes-Benz still enters some of its prize racing cars in historic events; here Stirling Moss exercises a 300SLR at Monterey in 1986. *FDB*

A great road car would be this Wankel-powered C111, posed here next to the factory's fiberglass-bodied 300SL. *DBAG*

How about a custom-bodied European Mercedes-Benz ambulance? It would make a great camper. *FDB*

maybe if you could find something that DBAG *really* wanted . . .

Rally Cars ★★★★

Daimler-Benz often used rallying to demonstrate the durability and strength of its cars. To do so, it stuck quite closely to production cars. Before World War II, rally versions of most small-engined models existed, especially the 170s. After the war and through the early 1960s, sedans were frequently entered.

The most frequently recognized rally car is the 450SLC 5.0, which in modified form was moderately successful during the 1979 European rally season. No production models, these Coupes were fitted with a roll cage as well as being extensively strengthened and lightened. First entered in that year's Rally of Portugal and driven by Bjorn Waldegaard and Hannu Mikkola, a competition 450SLC 5.0 won the 1979 Bandama Rally.

Other successful rally cars included the 1961–1962 300SE sedans of Eugen Böhringer and several 280E sedans that placed well in the 1978 London to Sydney Marathon.

C112 ★★★★★

At the 1991 Frankfurt show, amid a boom in super-car design, Mercedes-Benz unveiled the C112, a midengined Coupe with Gullwing doors, powered by the production 408-horsepower V-12. Despite such advanced features as movable spoilers, active body control, and electronic brake balancing, the car appeared ready for production, but pragmatism ruled, and the C112 joined the C111 as an example of what might have been.

Sauber-Mercedes Race Cars ★★★★★

Rather than jump back into racing in the late 1980s, Mercedes-Benz eased back in, sponsoring

an independent team run by Peter Sauber. Combining his management skills with MBAG support, Sauber did well, so the team evolved into a factory effort. Sauber built quite a few racers, and while it's unlikely that you'll see one for sale, it is conceivable.

Sauber's first Mercedes-Benz powered car was the C8, remembered for a 150 mile per hour backflip on the Mulsanne Straight at Le Mans in 1985. It used a stock-block 5.6-liter V-8 fed by twin turbos to make 650 horsepower in race trim. Kouros, a Yves St. Laurent perfume, was the sponsor, at least on the surface.

The team's first win was at the Nürburgring 1,000-kilometer in 1986. For 1987, Sauber built the C9, which became such a great success that in 1988, the cars were painted silver and finally bore the name "Sauber Mercedes." In 1989, the team won Le Mans and the World Sportscar Championship. The C9's weak link was the Hewland transmission, which had trouble surviving heavy power on rough tracks. The C11, built for 1990, was the last thundering V-8. Its 720-horsepower, 5.0-liter M119 engine worked through a new Mercedes-Benz five-speed manual transmission. For reasons of racing politics, the team declined to enter Le Mans in 1990, and Jaguar won, but the C11 handily repeated as world champion.

For 1991, FISA mandated 3.5-liter, normally aspirated engines, requiring new cars—and earplugs. Mercedes-Benz and Sauber created the new C291 with a radical flat-12 engine and a six-speed gearbox set as low as possible between two ground effects ducts. The C291 had teething troubles, mostly involving bad engine castings, so a planned active suspension program took second priority to finishing races. The C11s were used for Le Mans; the C291s ran everywhere else but won only the final event. MBAG then ended its sports car racing program, and development of another new car, the C292, halted.

CLK-GTR

To compete in the 1997 World FIA GT Championship, Daimler-Benz and AMG jointly developed the CLK-GTR, a V-12-powered racing coupe, in just four months. Its normally-aspirated, 6.9-liter engine developed over 600 horsepower, and after a few teething problems the CLK-GTR won the Championship from Porsche's 911 GT1 and the BMW-McLaren. Only three race versions

The super-car that never was. A production 408-horsepower V-12 was to drive the C112 to 190-mile per hour speeds, aided by ABC (Active Body Control) and slowed by EBV (Electronic Brake Balance). *MBAG*

Even the fin-backs were good racers; here Böhringer throws a 300SE sedan around the Nürburgring in 1964. *DBAG*

were built for 1997, but to homologate them, a number of street versions had to be assembled for sale to the public. Their price tag approached $1 million, and as this is written their U.S. emissions legality was open to question.

Sedan Racers ★★★★

While the World Sportscar Championship was becoming a poor investment, the German Touring Car Championship drew record crowds, so Mercedes-Benz shifted to racing cars resembling production models. The 190E 2.5-16 was run by three factory-supported teams. Judging by the racing's

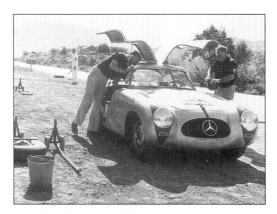

In the early stages of the 1952 Carrera Panamericana, a buzzard broke the windshield of this early 300SL racer. As a result, vertical "buzzard bars" were added, but why not restore it with a broken windshield? *DBAG*

In Europe, a 190E 2.5-16 Evolution production model was introduced in 1990, and 500 were sold to the public as homologation specials for the race cars. Distinguished by a huge rear wing and ovoid fender flares, the 235-horsepower Evo II got to 60 in 7.1 seconds and could hit 155 miles per hour. Even this street version can't be licensed in the United States.

Speaking of sedan racers, an American team led by Rick Hurst, a Mercedes-Benz dealer, entered a 190E 2.3–16 in IMSA's International Sedan series. The team, including driver Bob Strange, was experienced in SCCA Showroom Stock racing, so the car was successful, at least until the rules writers favored other brands. The car still exists.

When the European touring car series died in 1996, a surplus of old race cars hit the market, but by then the factory cars had been developed to a level approaching that of Formula 1, so in original form they are not exactly suitable for amateur use in club events.

Limousines, Station Wagons, Ambulances, and Hearses ★★★

In Germany, Mercedes-Benz is not only the favorite taxi but also the favorite limousine, ambulance, even hearse. In the United States such commercial cars are rare.

ferocity, they must have used up a fair number of cars, so surplus examples must exist. The stock-block engines developed ungodly power (up to 375 horsepower from a normally aspirated 2.5-liter four), so you'd need a race mechanic to keep one running. Emissions laws would never allow the cars to be street-licensed, but what fun on a track.

This 190E 2.3-16 racer was entered by Rick Hurst and driven by Bob Strange in IMSA's International Sedan class. *Rick Hurst Racing*

The 720-horsepower V-8-powered C11, racing here at Montreal in 1990, went on to take the World Sportscar Championship that year. *FDB*

The four-wheel-drive Geländewagen can be had with diesel or gasoline engines; new and used ones are available in the United States. *DBAG*

Tour with your family and friends in a restored 1950s Mercedes-Benz sightseeing bus. *DBAG*

Special-purpose cars were built by outside coachbuilders based on chassis supplied by Daimler-Benz. During the 1950s, the most popular coachbuilder was Binz (not a typo), who built wagons on round-body 190 and 220 chassis. Another was Miesen, in Bonn. Fin-back station wagons were built by the Belgian firm of D'Ieteren and first offered in 1965 by Daimler-Benz in Europe as the "Universal." Gasoline and diesel power were equally popular, but most vehicles were on the low-end chassis with small engines. Only a few 220 and almost no 300 models were built as ambulances or hearses.

During the 1970s several hundred long-chassis 240D limousines were built and sold, reportedly in Canada. These have a wheelbase 24.8 inches longer than the normal car, plus 15-inch wheels. Most 1980s stretch limousines you'll find were built not by Mercedes-Benz, but by German and American body shops of varying talent. Quality is inconsistent. We've seen stretched cars obviously bent at the joint.

Geländewagen ★★★

This off-road, all-wheel-drive Mercedes-Benz is an amazing dual-purpose vehicle. A 280GE won the 6,000-mile 1983 Paris-Dakar Rally. It's a German concept of a better Range Rover. What began as a utilitarian vehicle (we can't call it a car) is softening. In 1990, a more luxurious version was developed, and the latest version is now being sold in the United States.

A Geländewagen could be custom-tailored—short or long wheelbase, diesel or gasoline engines, various roofs and seating arrangements, and any number of serious accessories for storming the shrubbery.

Most of those in the United States were imported through special importers and modified to meet U.S. safety and emissions regulations. Most U.S. Mercedes-Benz dealers don't know much about them, so you must rely on others for service, which works well. Parts are available promptly, and a good Mercedes-Benz mechanic can handle service and most repairs.

By 1995, the G-Wagen's U.S. price hit $120,000, but when the $35,000 ML320 appeared in 1997, sales hardly slowed. Some preferred the G-Wagen's distinctive combination of luxury and brawn. The U.S. distributor of the Geländewagen is Europa International in Santa Fe, New Mexico.

A Geländewagen isn't a collector car in the normal sense, but it breaks every other rule, so we've got to give it respect with a mention here.

With a Unimog, you can pretty much go wherever you like. *FDB*

Buses and Trucks ★★

Daimler-Benz passenger cars are just the tip of the iceberg; buses and trucks make up much of the company's worldwide business. DBAG has tried to crack the U.S. bus and truck market, but the nature of the business has been a formidable barrier.

The most commonly seen buses in this country were the upright diesel-powered "airport bus" O319D types of the 1950s and 1960s. Frequently used hard, few survive.

In the early 1980s, after Daimler-Benz purchased U.S. truck-builder Freightliner, Mercedes-Benz trucks began to appear on U.S. streets and highways. Most were diesel-powered "straight" trucks with van bodies, used for city delivery and short-distance hauling. DBAG established a network of over 200 truck dealers, but in 1992, the system was severely cut due to slow demand.

A series of Class 7 (semitractor) trucks was introduced in the mid-1980s but never became popular. The cab-over-engine LPS 1525 was powered by a 250-horsepower, 10-liter, five-cylinder turbo-diesel with a six-speed transmission and a two-speed overdrive. Like the straight trucks, this model was assembled in Hampton, Virginia, from components made in German, Brazil, and North America.

Unimog ★★

No other company makes anything like the Unimog. A cross between an all-wheel-drive truck and a tractor, it was developed after World War II as a multi-purpose tractor. In the United States these expensive, versatile vehicles are found mostly in cold climes serving ski areas and municipalities. The ability to switch between a variety of implements (snowblowers and plows in the winter, mowers and backhoes in the summer) makes the Unimog more efficient than dedicated vehicles.

The diesel-powered Unimog appeared in 1948. The first ones officially imported into the United States came over in 1959, followed by the 90-horsepower U900 in the late 1960s. In 1963, a bigger version, the five-ton, 120-horsepower turbodiesel U1200, appeared. A modified version of the 168-horsepower U1700 won the 1982 Paris-Dakar Rally. Eight-speed manual transmissions with high and low range offer up to 24 gear ratios forward and reverse. A Unimog can climb a 70 percent grade and go anywhere you can stand. Early models are too slow for interstate use; current models hit 60 miles per hour, but you wouldn't want to do that all day.

After using Case and MBNA as importers, DBAG switched to Schmitt Engineering and Equipment in New Berlin, Wisconsin. Unimogs were sold to many armies, but cost limited civilian sales. Used examples are available at modest prices.

You might not think of a Unimog as a collector car, but we've seen several restored examples, so interest exists. Remember, when the going gets tough, the tough get Unimogs!

Like the 190E 2.5-16 before it, the C-Class was a highly successful competitor in European Touring Car races, at least until the FIA pulled the plug in 1996. Under their familiar skin, these cars are as sophisticated as a Grand Prix car. *MBAG*

Practicality and economy were not huge factors in the design of the street version of the CLK-GTR, which serves mainly as a homologation special to qualify the car for GT racing. *DBAG*

Appendices

Model Numbers

Mercedes-Benz model numbers are confusing, at least at first sight. To work your way through the maze, you need remember only a few simple truths.

The first three numbers (190, 300, 560, and so on) usually indicate engine displacement (1.9 liters, 3.0 liters . . .). If a second number is present (190D 2.2, 280SE 3.5, 300SEL 6.3), it indicates displacement in liters, as when an existing model grew a bigger engine. For example, the 190D came out in Europe with a 2.0-liter engine, but in the United States it had the 2.2-liter motor, so it was the 190D 2.2.

Capital letters, single or in combination, indicate body style and/or engine type:

C: Coupe, as in 280C, 300CD

D: Diesel; typical examples are the 190D, 300TD (turbodiesel)

E: Gasoline fuel injection, from Einspritzer

G: Gelandewagen; off-road, all-wheel-drive vehicle

SD or SDL: Sedan, S-Class, normal or long wheelbase, diesel power

SE or SEL: As above, except gasoline power

SL: Two-seater Convertible, from Sports Light (often loosely applied, as SLs tend to be anything but)

SLC: Four-seater sports Coupe (a stretched SL with fixed steel top)

T: Station wagon, from Touring, as in 280TE (2.8-liter gasoline wagon), 300TDT (3.0-liter turbodiesel wagon), 300TE 4Matic (3.0-liter gasoline wagon with all-wheel drive)

Lower-case letters usually indicate updates within a model series, so they're fairly redundant if you know the year: a, b, c, d: 300, 300b, 300c, 300d; or 190D, 190Db, and so on.

Older Cabriolets are the A (two-seater), B (four-seater, two side windows on each side), and C (four-seater, one side window). The Cabriolet D is a four-seater with four doors, and the Cabriolet F is a long-wheelbase four-seater with four doors.

In a fit of corporate evolution, Mercedes-Benz dazed the automotive world in 1993 by announcing that henceforth, rather than being numbered and lettered, its models would be lettered then numbered. The 1994 compact sedans were thus the C220 and the C280. The Executive midrange cars are the E320, E420, E500, and so forth. The top-rung S-Class encompasses the S320, S420, S500, and S600. Body variations were added to numerical designations: E320 Cabriolet, S500 Coupe, S600 Coupe et al, and the SL models were redubbed SL320, SL500, and SL600. The letters ML in the designation for the M-Class sport-utility bear no real significance.

Clubs

Car clubs provide historical, technical, and restoration information. Their publications contain useful articles plus advertisements for products and services. Experts can answer your questions. National clubs and local branches hold tech sessions, tours, and car shows.

Mercedes-Benz Club of America
(30,000 members)
1907 Lelaray St.
Colorado Springs, CO 80909
800-637-2360
www.mcba.org

190SL Group
(500 members)
16 Theodore Dr.
East Brunswick, NJ 08816

The Gull Wing Group
(500 members)
776 Cessna St.
Chico, CA 95928
530-345-6701

Finding the Part Number

You can still walk into a dealership and buy most mechanical parts for a postwar collectible Mercedes-Benz. Still, when you go in, you'd better have the chassis number and engine number, and it doesn't hurt to have the part number, too.

Number	Location
Chassis	Since 1969, on windshield post (U.S. models); prior to that, usually on driver's doorpost
Engine	On left rear upper corner of engine
Transmission	Stamped into main transmission housing
Axle	Stamped into rear-axle housing; on front spindle
Steering	Stamped into steering box
Paint	Three-digit code number on front radiator support, followed by a "G" or "H"
Upholstery	From mid-1985, same as paint code without "G" or "H," before then, on vehicle data card or warranty ID plate
Key	On one vehicle data card; older cars may have number stamped on locks

Part numbers are in the Parts Picture Catalog for your model.

Chassis and Engine Numbers

An entire book could be written about Mercedes-Benz chassis and engine numbers. Prewar chassis numbers usually matched the original engine numbers. Since 1946, DBAG has used two basic systems, the most drastic change occurring in 1981 in response to U.S. regulations.

Chassis Numbers

The first part of the chassis number describes the model. Throughout a given model run, regardless of model year or production date, cars were assigned individual five- or six-digit consecutive "serial numbers" at the end of their chassis numbers, identifying individual cars. Until the 1984 model year, each model had its own serial number series.

Cars from 1946 to 1950 bore 11-digit engine and chassis numbers. For 1951 and 1952, the last two numbers of the production year were added, for a total of 13 digits. For 1953 through 1959, code letters were added for clutch and transmission types, and the production year digits were reversed.

From 1960 to 1980, 14 digits were used. The production year digits were eliminated, and the codes were changed from letters to numbers. Generally, pre-1981 chassis numbers used 0 or 1 as the fourth digit; 0 indicated fitment of a gasoline engine, 1 indicated a diesel.

For model year 1981, a 17-digit system was started, with VIN on a plate on the left (driver's) side windshield post and on the left front door pillar. The VIN indicates whether a car is to U.S. or other specification, its original passenger-restraint system, its city of manufacture, its model year, and its place in the production run.

Although 1983 and earlier models each had their own individual serial number progression, starting with the 1984 model year, the two main cities of manufacture, Bremen and Stuttgart, each got its own chassis number series (F and A, respectively). Thus it's possible to find two post-1983 cars of the same model with identical last six-digit chassis numbers—but they should have different assembly plant codes! Check the 11th digit from the left.

Of course, model year and production (i.e., calendar) year can differ. Since the 1940s, Mercedes-Benz has traditionally shifted to production of the next model year's cars in early September. Thus a car of one model year may have been built during the last four months of the previous calendar year. Some U.S. states titled cars in the year they were sold, so a leftover car's title date may not agree with the model year, according to the chassis number. In any case, the chassis number governs.

Registration Years

Year	Code
1980	A
1981	B
1982	C
1983	D
1984	E
1985	F
1986	G
1987	H
1988	J
1989	K
1990	L
1991	M
1992	N
1993	P
1994	R
1995	S
1996	T
1997	V
1998	W
1999	X
2000	Y

Engine Numbers

Postwar engine numbers typically used 9 as the fourth digit, the first digit of the engine type number. Note that gasoline engine numbers begin with the digit 1, and diesels begin with a 6.

This list of chassis and engine type prefixes, arranged by model and year, allows you to check the car you're looking at to be certain, for instance, that a 560SEL is not really a reincarnated 380SEL. Asterisks indicate sunroof models.

Model	Years	Chassis Prefix	Engine Prefix	Description
170V	1947–50	136.010	136.920	sedan, gasoline
170Va, Vb	1950–53	136.060	136.923	sedan, gasoline
170Va, Vb*	1950–53	136.072	136.923	sedan, gasoline
170S	1949–52	136.040	136.922	sedan, gasoline
170S*	1949–52	136.049	136.922	sedan, gasoline
170S Cabriolet A	1949–51	136.042	136.922	convertible, gasoline
170S Cabriolet B	1949–51	136.043	136.922	convertible, gasoline
170Sb	1952–53	191.010	136.922	sedan, gasoline
170Sb*	1952–53	191.018	136.922	sedan, gasoline
170Sb Cabriolet A	1952–53	191.011	136.922	convertible, gasoline
170Sb Cabriolet B	1952–53	191.012	136.922	convertible, gasoline
170S-V	1953–55	136.081	136.926	sedan, gasoline
170S-V*	1953–55	136.082	136.926	sedan, gasoline
170D	1949–50	136.110	636.915	sedan, diesel
170Da, Db	1950–53	136.160	636.916	sedan, diesel
170Da, Db*	1950–53	136.172	636.918	sedan, diesel
170Ds	1952–53	191.110	636.918	sedan, diesel
170Ds*	1952–53	191.113	636.918	sedan, diesel
170S-D	1953–55	136.181	636.981	sedan, diesel
170S-D*	1953–55	136.182	636.981	sedan, diesel
220	1951–53	187.011	180.920	sedan, gasoline
220*	1951–53	187.014	180.920	sedan, gasoline
220 Cabriolet A	1951–55	187.012	180.920	convertible, gasoline
220 Cabriolet B	1951–54	187.013	180.920	convertible, gasoline
220 Coupe	1954–55	187.014	180.920	coupe, gasoline
300, 300b	1951–55	187.011	186.920	sedan, gasoline
300, 300b*	1951–55	186.015	186.920	sedan, gasoline
300, 300b Cabriolet D	1951–55	186.014	186.920	convertible, gasoline
300c manual trans	1955–57	186.016A	186.920	sedan, gasoline
300c manual trans*	—	186.017A	186.920	sedan, gasoline
300c manual trans, Cab. D	—	186.033A	186.920	convertible, gasoline
300c auto trans	—	186.016	186.921	sedan, gasoline
300c auto trans*	—	186.017	186.921	sedan, gasoline
300c auto trans, Cab. D	—	186.033	186.921	convertible, gasoline
300d auto trans	1958–62	189.010	189.980	sedan, gasoline
300d auto trans*	1958–62	189.011	189.980	sedan, gasoline
300d auto trans Cab. D	1958–62	189.033	189.980	convertible, gasoline
300d manual trans	1958–62	189.010	189.981	sedan, gasoline
300d manual trans*	1958–62	189.011	189.981	sedan, gasoline
300d manual trans Cab. D	1958–62	189.033	189.981	convertible, gasoline
300S Cabriolet	1951–55	188.010	188.981	convertible, gasoline
300S Coupe	1951–55	188.011	188.920	coupe, gasoline
300S Roadster	1951–55	188.012	188.920	roadster, gasoline
300Sc Cabriolet	1955–58	188.013	199.980	convertible, gasoline
300Sc Coupe	1955–58	188.014	199.980	coupe, gasoline
300Sc Roadster	1955–58	188.015	199.980	roadster, gasoline
180	1953–57	120.010	136.925	sedan, gasoline
180*	—	120.011	136.925	sedan, gasoline
180A, 180b	1957–61	120.010	121.923	sedan, gasoline
180A, 180b*	—	120.010	121.923	sedan, gasoline
180c	1961–62	120.010	121.927	sedan, gasoline
180c*	—	120.011	121.927	sedan, gasoline
180D, 180Db	1953–61	120.110	636.930	sedan, diesel
180D, 180Db*	1953–61	120.111	636.930	sedan, diesel
180Dc	1961–62	120.110	621.914	sedan, diesel
180Dc*	1961–62	120.111	621.914	sedan, diesel
300SL	1954–57	198.040	198.980	coupe, gasoline
300SL (light alloy)	1955–56	198.043	198.980	coupe, gasoline
300SL Roadster	1957–63	198.042	198.980	roadster, gasoline
300SL engine, light alloy, crankcase	post-3/62	N/A	198.928	N/A
190, 190b	1956–61	121.010	121.920	sedan, gasoline
190, 190b*	1956–61	121.011	121.920	sedan, gasoline

Model	Years	Chassis Prefix	Engine Prefix	Description
190c	1961–65	110.010	121.924	sedan, gasoline
190D, 190Db	1958–61	121.110	621.910	sedan, diesel
190D, 190Db*	1958–61	121.111	621.910	sedan, diesel
190Dc	1961–65	110.110	621.912	sedan, diesel
220a	1954–56	180.010	180.921	sedan, gasoline
220a*	—	180.011	180.932	sedan, gasoline
219	1956–59	105.010	180.920	sedan, gasoline
219*	1956–59	105.011	180.920	sedan, gasoline
220S	1956–59	180.010	180.924	sedan, gasoline
220S*	1956–59	180.011	180.924	sedan, gasoline
220S Convertible	1956–59	180.030	180.924	convertible, gasoline
220S Coupe	1957–59	180.037	180.924	coupe, gasoline
220SE	1958–59	128.010	127.980	sedan, gasoline
220SE*	1958–59	128.011	127.980	sedan, gasoline
220SE Convertible	1958–60	128.030	127.984	convertible, gasoline
220SE Coupe	1958–60	128.037	127.984	coupe, gasoline
220 (220b)	1959–65	111.010	180.940	sedan, gasoline
220S (220Sb)	1959–65	111.012	180.941	sedan, gasoline
220SE (220SEb)	1959–65	111.014	127.982	sedan, gasoline
220SE (220SEb) Coupe	1960–65	111.021	127.984	coupe, gasoline
220SED (220Seb) Conv.	1960–65	111.023	127.984	convertible, gasoline
230SL	1963–67	113.042	127.981	roadster, gasoline
250SL	1966–68	113.043	129.982	roadster, gasoline
280SL	1967–71	113.044	130.983	roadster, gasoline
600	1963–81	100.012	100.980	sedan, gasoline
600 Pullman, 4-dr	—	100.014	100.980	limousine, gasoline
600 Pullman, 6-dr	—	100.016	100.980	limousine, gasoline
600 Landaulet	—	100.615	100.980	convertible, gasoline
200	1965–68	110.010	121.940	sedan, gasoline
200D	1965–68	110.110	621.918	sedan, diesel
230	1965–66	110.011	180.945	sedan, gasoline
230 w/INAT carbs	7/66–68	110.011	180.949	sedan, gasoline
230S	1965–68	111.010	180.947	sedan, gasoline
250S	1965–69	108.012	129.920	sedan, gasoline
250SE	1965–68	108.014	129.980	sedan, gasoline
250SE Coupe	1965–67	111.021	129.980	coupe, gasoline
250SE Convertible	1965–67	111.023	129.980	convertible, gasoline
300SE	1961–65	112.014	189.984	sedan, gasoline
300SE Long	1963–65	112.015	189.984	sedan, gasoline
300SE, 160 hp	1962–63	112.023	189.985	convertible, gasoline
300SE, 170 hp	1964–67	112.021	189.987	coupe, gasoline
300SE, 170 hp	1964–67	112.023	189.987	convertible, gasoline
300SEb	1965–67	108.015	189.989	sedan, gasoline
300SEL	1965–67	109.015	189.981	sedan, gasoline
300SEL	1967–70	109.016	189.981	sedan, gasoline
300SEL	1971	109.016	130.981	sedan, gasoline
280S	1967–72	108.016	130.920	sedan, gasoline
280SE & SEL	1967–72	108.018	130.980	sedan, gasoline
280SE	1967–71	111.024	130.980	coupe, gasoline
280SE 3.5	1969–71	111.026	116.980	coupe, gasoline
280SE 3.5	1969–71	111.027	116.980	convertible, gasoline
280SE/SEL 3.5	1970–72	108.018	116.980	sedan, gasoline
300SEL 6.3	1968–72	109.018	100.981	sedan, gasoline
300SEL 3.5	1969–72	109.056	116.981	sedan, gasoline
200/8	1967–76	115.015	115.923	sedan, gasoline
200D/8	1967–76	115.115	615.912	sedan, diesel
230/8	1967–76	114.015	180.954	sedan, gasoline
250	1967–72	114.010	114.920	sedan, gasoline
250	—	114.011	130.923	sedan, gasoline
250C	1968–72	114.023	114.920	coupe, gasoline
250C	—	114.023	130.923	coupe, gasoline
280C (single cam)	1969–73	114.073	130.921	coupe, gasoline

Model	Years	Chassis Prefix	Engine Prefix	Description
280C (twin cam)	1974–76	114.073	110.921	coupe, gasoline
280 (single cam)	1970–73	114.060	130.921	sedan, gasoline
280 (twin cam)	1974–76	114.060	110.921	sedan, gasoline
*With sunroof				

The above includes some European models. Unless stated otherwise, the following are U.S. models, by model year.

Model	Chassis Prefix	Engine Prefix	Description
1971 (U.S. and other models)			
220D	115.110	615.912	sedan, diesel
220	115.010	115.920	sedan, gasoline
230 (6)	114.015	180.954	sedan, gasoline
250	114.010	114.920	sedan, gasoline
250	114.011	130.923	sedan, gasoline
250C	114.023	130.923	coupe, gasoline
280S	108.016	130.920	sedan, gasoline
280SE	108.018	130.980	sedan, gasoline
280SE	111.024	130.980	coupe, gasoline
280SE	111.025	130.980	convertible, gasoline
280SEL	108.019	130.980	sedan, gasoline
280SE 3.5	111.026	116.980	coupe, gasoline
280SE 3.5	111.027	116.980	convertible, gasoline
280SE 4.5	108.068	117.984	sedan, gasoline
300SEL 6.3	109.018	100.981	sedan, gasoline
600	100.012	100.980	limousine, gasoline
600 Pullman, 4-dr	100.014	100.980	limousine, gasoline
600 Pullman, 6-dr	100.016	100.980	limousine, gasoline
600 Landaulet	100.615	100.980	landaulet, gasoline
280SL	113.044	130.983	roadster, gasoline
350SL	107.044	117.982	roadster, gasoline

1972 (U.S. and other models)

Model	Chassis Prefix	Engine Prefix	Description
220D	115.110	615.912	sedan, diesel
220	115.010	115.920	sedan, gasoline
230 (6)	114.015	180.954	sedan, gasoline
250	114.010	114.920	sedan, gasoline
250	114.011	130.923	sedan, gasoline
250C	114.023	130.923	coupe, gasoline
280	114.060	110.921	sedan, gasoline
280C	114.073	110.921	coupe, gasoline
280SE 4.5	108.067	117.984	sedan, gasoline
280SEL 4.5	108.068	117.984	sedan, gasoline
300SEL 3.5	109.056	116.981	sedan, gasoline
300SEL 4.5	109.057	117.981	sedan, gasoline
300SEL 6.3	109.018	100.981	sedan, gasoline
450SE	116.032	117.983	sedan, gasoline
450SEL	116.033	117.983	sedan, gasoline
450SL	107.044	117.982	roadster, gasoline
450SLC	107.024	117.982	coupe, gasoline
600	100.012	100.980	limousine, gasoline
600 Pullman, 4-dr	100.014	100.980	limousine, gasoline
600 Pullman, 6-dr	100.016	100.980	limousine, gasoline

1973 (U.S. models only from here onward)

Model	Chassis Prefix	Engine Prefix	Description
220D	115.110	615.912	sedan, diesel
240D	115.117	616.916	sedan, diesel
220	115.010	115.920	sedan, gasoline
230 (4)	115.017	115.951	sedan, gasoline
280	114.060	110.921	sedan, gasoline
280C	114.073	110.921	coupe, gasoline

450SE	116.032	117.983	sedan, gasoline
450SEL	116.033	117.983	sedan, gasoline
450SL	107.044	117.982	roadster, gasoline
450SLC	107.024	117.982	coupe, gasoline

1974

240D	115.117	616.916	sedan, diesel
230 (4)	115.017	115.951	sedan, gasoline
280	114.060	110.921	sedan, gasoline
280C	114.073	110.921	coupe, gasoline
450SE	116.032	117.983	sedan, gasoline
450SEL	116.033	117.983	sedan, gasoline
450SL	107.044	117.982	roadster, gasoline
450SLC	107.024	117.982	coupe, gasoline

1975

240D	115.117	616.916	sedan, diesel
300D	115.114	617.910	sedan, diesel
230 (4)	115.017	115.951	sedan, gasoline
280	114.060	110.921	sedan, gasoline
280C	114.073	110.921	coupe, gasoline
280S	116.020	110.922	sedan, gasoline
450SE	116.032	117.983	sedan, gasoline
450SEL	116.033	117.983	sedan, gasoline
450SL	107.044	117.982	roadster, gasoline
450SLC	107.024	117.982	coupe, gasoline

1976

240D	115.117	616.916	sedan, diesel
300D	115.114	617.910	sedan, diesel
230 (4)	115.017	115.951	sedan, gasoline
280	114.060	110.921	sedan, gasoline
280C	114.073	110.921	coupe, gasoline
280S	116.020	110.922	sedan, gasoline
450SE	116.032	117.986	sedan, gasoline
450SEL	116.033	117.986	sedan, gasoline
450SL	107.044	117.985	roadster, gasoline
450SLC	107.024	117.985	coupe, gasoline

1977

240D	123.123	616.912	sedan, diesel
300D	123.130	617.912	sedan, diesel
230	123.023	115.954	sedan, gasoline
280E	123.033	110.984	sedan, gasoline
280SE	116.024	110.985	sedan, gasoline
450SEL	116.023	117.985	sedan, gasoline
450SEL 6.9	116.036	100.985	sedan, gasoline
450SL	107.044	117.985	roadster, gasoline
450SLC	107.024	117.985	coupe, gasoline

1978

240D	123.123	616.912	sedan, diesel
300D	123.130	617.912	sedan, diesel
300CD	123.150	617.912	coupe, diesel
230	123.023	115.954	sedan, gasoline
280E	123.033	110.984	sedan, gasoline
280CE	116.053	110.984	coupe, gasoline
280SE	116.024	110.985	sedan, gasoline
300SD	116.120	617.950	sedan, turbodiesel
450SEL	116.033	117.985	sedan, gasoline
450SEL 6.9	116.036	100.985	sedan, gasoline
450SL	107.044	117.985	roadster, gasoline
450SLC	107.024	117.985	coupe, gasoline

1979

240D	123.123	616.912	sedan, diesel
300D	123.130	617.912	sedan, diesel
300CD	123.150	617.912	coupe, diesel
300TD	123.190	617.912	wagon, diesel
230	123.023	115.954	sedan, gasoline
280E	123.033	110.984	sedan, gasoline
280CE	123.053	110.984	coupe, gasoline
280SE	116.024	110.985	sedan, gasoline
300SD	116.120	617.950	sedan, turbodiesel
450SEL	116.033	117.985	sedan, gasoline
450SEL 6.9	116.036	100.985	sedan, gasoline
450SL	107.044	117.985	roadster, gasoline
450SLC	107.024	117.985	coupe, gasoline

1980

240D	123.123	616.912	sedan, diesel
300D	123.130	617.912	sedan, diesel
300CD	123.150	617.912	coupe, diesel
300TD	123.190	617.912	wagon, diesel
280E	123.033	110.984	sedan, gasoline
280CE	123.053	110.984	coupe, gasoline
280SE	116.024	110.984	sedan, gasoline
300SD	116.120	617.950	sedan, turbodiesel
450SEL	116.033	117.985	sedan, gasoline
450SL	107.044	117.985	roadster, gasoline
450SLC	107.024	117.985	coupe, gasoline

1981

240D	123.123	616.912	sedan, diesel
300D	123.130	617.912	sedan, diesel
300CD	123.150	617.912	coupe, diesel
300TD	123.193	617.952	wagon, turbodiesel
280E	123.033	110.984	sedan, gasoline
280CE	123.053	110.984	coupe, gasoline
300SD	126.120	617.951	sedan, diesel
380SEL	126.033	115.961	sedan, gasoline
380SL	107.045	116.960	roadster, gasoline
380SLC	107.025	116.960	coupe, gasoline

1982–1983

240D	123.123	616.912	sedan, diesel
300D	123.133	617.952	sedan, turbodiesel
300CD	123.153	617.952	coupe, turbodiesel
300TD	123.193	617.952	wagon, turbodiesel
300SD	126.120	617.951	sedan, turbodiesel
380SEL	126.032	116.963	sedan, gasoline
380SEC	126.043	116.963	coupe, gasoline
380SL	107.045	116.962	roadster, gasoline

1984

190E 2.3	201.024	102.961	sedan, gasoline
190D 2.2	201.122	601.921	sedan, diesel
300D	123.133	617.952	sedan, turbodiesel
300CD	123.153	617.952	coupe, turbodiesel
300TD	123.193	617.952	wagon, turbodiesel
300SD	126.120	617.951	sedan, turbodiesel
380SE	126.032	116.963	sedan, gasoline
500SEL	126.037	117.963	sedan, gasoline
500SEC	126.044	117.963	coupe, gasoline
380SL	107.045	116.962	roadster, gasoline

1985

190E 2.3	201.024	102.985	sedan, gasoline
190D 2.2	201.122	601.921	sedan, diesel
300D	123.133	617.952	sedan, turbodiesel
300CD	123.153	617.952	coupe, turbodiesel
300TD	123.193	617.952	wagon, turbodiesel
300SD	126.120	617.951	sedan, turbodiesel
380SE	126.032	116.963	sedan, gasoline
500SEL	126.037	117.963	sedan, gasoline
500SEC	126.044	117.963	coupe, gasoline
380SL	107.045	116.962	roadster, gasoline

1986

190E 2.3	201.024	102.985	sedan, gasoline
190D 2.3-16	201.034	102.983	sedan, gasoline
190D 2.5	201.126	602.911	sedan, diesel
300E	124.030	103.983	sedan, gasoline
300SDL	126.125	603.961	sedan, diesel
420SEL	126.035	116.965	sedan, gasoline
560SEL	126.039	117.968	sedan, gasoline
560SEC	126.045	117.968	coupe, gasoline
560SL	107.048	117.967	roadster, gasoline

1987

190E 2.3	201.028	102.985	sedan, gasoline
190E 2.6	201.029	103.942	sedan, gasoline
190E 2.3-16	201.034	102.983	sedan, gasoline
190D 2.5	201.126	602.911	sedan, diesel
190D 2.5 Turbo	201.128	602.961	sedan, turbodiesel
260E	124.026	103.940	sedan, gasoline
300E	124.030	103.983	sedan, gasoline
300D	124.133	603.960	sedan, turbodiesel
300TD	124.193	603.960	wagon, turbodiesel
300SDL	126.125	603.961	sedan, turbodiesel
420SEL	126.035	116.965	sedan, gasoline
560SEL	126.039	117.968	sedan, gasoline
560SEC	126.045	117.968	coupe, gasoline
560SL	107.048	116.967	roadster, gasoline

1988

190E 2.3	201.028	102.985	sedan, gasoline
190E 2.6	201.029	103.942	sedan, gasoline
190D 2.5	201.126	602.911	sedan, diesel
260E	124.026	103.940	sedan, gasoline
300E	124.030	103.983	sedan, gasoline
300CE	124.050	103.983	coupe, gasoline
300TE	124.090	103.983	wagon, gasoline
300SE	126.024	103.981	sedan, gasoline
300SEL	126.025	103.981	sedan, gasoline
420SEL	126.035	116.965	sedan, gasoline
560SEL	126.039	117.968	sedan, gasoline
560SEC	126.045	117.966	coupe, gasoline
560SL	107.048	116.967	roadster, gasoline

1989

190E 2.6	201.029	103.942	sedan, gasoline
190D 2.5	201.126	602.911	sedan, diesel
260E	124.026	103.940	sedan, gasoline
300E	124.030	103.983	sedan, gasoline
300CE	124.050	103.983	coupe, gasoline
300TE	124.090	103.983	wagon, gasoline
300SE	126.024	103.981	sedan, gasoline
300SEL	126.025	103.981	sedan, gasoline

420SEL	126.035	116.965	sedan, gasoline
560SEL	126.039	117.968	sedan, gasoline
560SEC	126.045	117.968	coupe, gasoline
560SL	107.048	116.967	roadster, gasoline

1990

190E 2.6	201.029	103.942	sedan, gasoline
300D 2.5 Turbo	124.128	602.962	sedan, turbodiesel
300E 2.6	124.026	103.940	sedan, gasoline
300E	124.030	103.983	sedan, gasoline
300CE	124.051	104.980	coupe, gasoline
300TE	124.090	103.983	wagon, gasoline
300E 4Matic	124.230	103.985	sedan, gasoline
300TE 4Matic	124.290	103.985	wagon, gasoline
350SDL Turbo	126.135	603.970	sedan, turbodiesel
300SE	126.024	103.981	sedan, gasoline
300SEL	126.025	103.981	sedan, gasoline
420SEL	126.035	116.965	sedan, gasoline
560SEL	126.039	117.968	sedan, gasoline
560SEC	126.045	117.968	coupe, gasoline
300SL	129.061	104.981	roadster, gasoline
500SL	129.066	119.960	roadster, gasoline

1991

190E 2.3	201.028	102.985	sedan, gasoline
190E 2.6	201.029	103.942	sedan, gasoline
300D 2.5 Turbo	124.128	602.962	sedan, turbodiesel
300E 2.6	124.026	103.940	sedan, gasoline
300E	124.030	103.983	sedan, gasoline
300CE	124.051	104.980	coupe, gasoline
300TE	124.090	103.983	wagon, gasoline
300E 4Matic	124.230	103.985	sedan, gasoline
300TE 4Matic	124.290	103.985	wagon, gasoline
350SD Turbo	126.134	603.970	sedan, turbo-diesel
350SDL Turbo	126.135	603.970	sedan, turbo-diesel
300SE	126.024	103.981	sedan, gasoline
300SEL	126.025	103.981	sedan, gasoline
420SEL	126.035	116.965	sedan, gasoline
560SEL	126.039	117.968	sedan, gasoline
560SEC	126.045	117.968	coupe, gasoline
300SL	129.061	104.981	roadster, gasoline
500SL	129.066	119.960	roadster, gasoline

1992

190E 2.3	201.028	102.985	sedan, gasoline
190E 2.6	201.029	103.942	sedan, gasoline
300D 2.5 Turbo	124.128	602.962	sedan, turbodiesel
300E 2.6	124.026	103.940	sedan, gasoline
300E	124.030	103.983	sedan, gasoline
400E	124.034	119.975	sedan, gasoline
500E	124.036	119.974	sedan, gasoline
300CE	124.051	104.980	coupe, gasoline
300TE	124.090	103.983	wagon, gasoline
300E 4Matic	124.230	103.985	sedan, gasoline
300TE 4Matic	124.290	103.985	wagon, gasoline
300SD Turbo	140.134	603.971	sedan, turbodiesel
300SE	140.032	104.990	sedan, gasoline
400SE	140.042	119.971	sedan, gasoline
500SEL	140.051	119.970	sedan, gasoline
600SEL	140.057	120.980	sedan, gasoline
300SL	129.061	104.981	roadster, gasoline
500SL	129.066	119.960	roadster, gasoline

1993

190E 2.3	201.028	102.985	sedan, gasoline
190E 2.6	201.029	103.942	sedan, gasoline
300D 2.5 Turbo	124.128	602.962	sedan, turbodiesel
300E 2.8	124.028	104.992	sedan, gasoline
300E	124.032	104.992	sedan, gasoline
300CE	124.052	104.992	coupe, gasoline
300CE Cabriolet	124.066	104.992	convertible, gasoline
300TE	124.092	104.992	wagon, gasoline
300E 4Matic	124.230	103.985	sedan, gasoline
300TE 4Matic	124.290	103.985	wagon, gasoline
400E	124.034	119.975	sedan, gasoline
500E	124.036	119.974	sedan, gasoline
300SD	140.134	603.971	sedan, turbodiesel
300SE	140.032	104.990	sedan, gasoline
400SEL	140.043	119.971	sedan, gasoline
500SEL	140.051	119.970	sedan, gasoline
600SEL	140.057	120.980	sedan, gasoline
500SEC	140.070	119.970	coupe, gasoline
600SEC	140.076	120.980	coupe, gasoline
300SL	129.061	104.981	roadster, gasoline
500SL	129.067	119.960	roadster, gasoline
600SL	129.076	120.981	roadster, gasoline

1994

C220	202.022	111.961	sedan, gasoline
C280	202.028	104.941	sedan, gasoline
E300 Diesel (1995)	124.131	606.910	sedan, diesel
E320	124.032	104.992	sedan, gasoline
E320 Coupe	124.052	104.992	coupe, gasoline
E320 Cabriolet	124.066	104.992	convertible, gasoline
E320 Station Wagon	124.092	104.992	wagon, gasoline
E420	124.034	119.975	sedan, gasoline
E500	124.036	119.974	sedan, gasoline
S350 Turbo Diesel	140.134	603.971	sedan, turbodiesel
S320	140.032	104.990	sedan, gasoline
S420	140.043	119.971	sedan, gasoline
S500	140.051	119.970	sedan, gasoline
S600	140.057	120.980	sedan, gasoline
S500 Coupe	140.070	119.970	coupe, gasoline
S600 Coupe	140.076	120.980	coupe, gasoline
SL320	129.061	104.981	roadster, gasoline
SL500	129.067	119.960	roadster, gasoline
SL600	129.076	120.981	roadster, gasoline

1995

C220 Sedan	202.022	111.961	inline 4, gasoline
C280 Sedan	202.028	104.941	inline 6, gasoline
E300 Diesel	124.131	606.910	inline 6, diesel
E320 Sedan	124.032	104.992	inline 6, gasoline
E320 Wagon	124.092	104.992	inline 6, gasoline
E320 Coupe	124.052	104.992	inline 6, gasoline
E320 Cabriolet	124.066	104.992	inline 6, gasoline
E420 Sedan	124.034	119.975	V-8, gasoline
S350 Turbodiesel	140.134	603.971	inline 6, diesel
S320 Sedan	140.032	104.994	inline 6, gasoline
S420 Sedan	140.043	119.981	V-8, gasoline
S500 Sedan	140.051	119.980	V-8, gasoline
S600 Sedan	140.057	120.982	V-12, gasoline
S500 Coupe	140.070	119.980	V-8, gasoline
S600 Coupe	140.076	120.982	V-12, gasoline
SL320	129.063	104.991	inline 6, gasoline
SL500	129.067	119.982	V-8, gasoline
SL600	129.076	120.983	V-12, gasoline

1996

C220 Sedan	202.022	111.961	inline 4, gasoline
C280 Sedan	202.028	104.941	inline 6, gasoline
C36 AMG	202.028	104.941	inline 6, gasoline
E300 Diesel	210.020	606.912	inline 6, diesel
E320 Sedan	210.055	104.995	inline 6, gasoline
S320 Sedan	140.032	104.994	inline 6, gasoline
S420 Sedan	140.043	119.981	V-8, gasoline
S500 Sedan	140.051	119.980	V-8, gasoline
S600 Sedan	140.057	120.982	V-12, gasoline
S500 Coupe	140.070	119.980	V-8, gasoline
S600 Coupe	140.076	120.982	V-12, gasoline
SL320	129.063	104.991	inline 6, gasoline
SL500	129.067	119.982	V-8, gasoline
SL600	129.076	120.983	V-12, gasoline

1997

C230 Sedan	202.023	111.974	inline 4, gasoline
C280 Sedan	202.028	104.941	inline 6, gasoline
C36 AMG	202.028	104.941	inline 6, gasoline
E300 Diesel	210.020	606.912	inline 6, diesel
E320 Sedan	210.055	104.995	inline 6, gasoline
E420 Sedan	210.072	119.985	V-8, gasoline
S320* Sedan	140.032	104.994	inline 6, gasoline
S320 Sedan	140.033	104.994	inline 6, gasoline
S420 Sedan	140.043	119.981	V-8, gasoline
S500 Sedan	140.051	119.980	V-8, gasoline
S600 Sedan	140.057	120.982	V-12, gasoline
S500 Coupe	140.070	119.980	V-8, gasoline
S600 Coupe	140.076	120.982	V-12, gasoline
SL320	129.063	104.991	inline 6, gasoline
SL500	129.067	119.982	V-8, gasoline
SL600	129.076	120.983	V-12, gasoline

1998

C230 Sedan	202.023	111.974	inline 4, gasoline
C280 Sedan	202.029	112.920	V-6, gasoline
C43 AMG	202.033	113.944	V-8, gasoline
E300 Turbodiesel	210.025	606.962	inline 6 turbodiesel
E320 Sedan	210.065	112.941	V-6, gasoline
E320 Sedan (AWD)	210.082	112.941	V-6, gas, all-wheel drive
E320 Wagon	210.265	112.941	V-6, gasoline
E320 Wagon (AWD)	210.282	112.941	V-6, gas, all-wheel drive
E430 Sedan	210.070	113.940	V-8, gasoline
S320 Sedan*	140.032	104.994	inline 6, gasoline
S320 Sedan	140.033	104.994	inline 6, gasoline
S420 Sedan	140.043	119.981	V-8, gasoline
S500 Sedan	140.051	119.980	V-8, gasoline
S600 Sedan	140.057	120.982	V-12, gasoline
CL500 Coupe	140.070	119.980	V-8, gasoline
CL600 Coupe	140.076	120.982	V-12, gasoline
SL500	129.067	119.982	V-8, gasoline
SL600	129.076	120.983	V-12, gasoline
SLK230	170.447	111.973	inline 4, supercharged
CLK320	208.365	112.940	V-6, gasoline
ML320	163.154	112.942	V-6, gasoline

*Standard wheelbase; other 1997, 1998 S-Class sedans are long wheelbase.

Index